Esser Co. Keuffel &

The Compass:

Volume 3: 1893-1894

Esser Co. Keuffel &

The Compass:
Volume 3: 1893-1894

ISBN/EAN: 9783337817824

Printed in Europe, USA, Canada, Australia, Japan

Cover: Foto ©ninafisch / pixelio.de

More available books at **www.hansebooks.com**

THE COMPASS.

A MONTHLY JOURNAL

For Engineers, Surveyors, Architects, Draughtsmen, and Students.

Volume 3.—1893-1894.

Edited by

WILLIAM COX.

NEW YORK.
KEUFFEL & ESSER CO.,
127 FULTON ST.

INDEX.

ABBREVIATIONS and Signs used in Surveying, etc.	177
Accuracy of Observations with the Solar Transit.	145
Adie's Line and Curve Ranger.	2
Adjusting an Engineer's Level.	35, 58
Adjustment of Stadia Hairs.	166
Altitude, Apparent or Observed and True.	134
Aluminium Drawing Instruments.	102
Angle, The trisection of an.	44
Artificial Horizon, a Gyroscope.	93
BOOKS, New.	15, 25, 61, 106, 178
Both's Section-Liner and Scale-Divider.	171
CIRCUMFERENCE and Diameter Scale, A.	73
Columbian Exposition, The.	57
Compass and Clinometer, A.	18
Compass, The Prismatic.	17
" The Solar.	39
Concave Lenses, Refraction in.	114
Convex " " "	66, 103
Corrections for Parallax and Refraction in Solar Work.	134
Cross-Section Paper, Logarithmic.	90
Curves, Railroad.	86
DECLINATION Settings, Preparation of.	123
Diameter and Circumference Scale, A.	73
Dip of the Horizon.	134
Directions for using the Solar Attachment to ascertain the Latitude.	130
Directions for determining the Meridian with the Solar Attachment.	122
Direct Measurement of Distances.	152
Double Prisms.	7
Drawing Instruments.	77, 100, 136
" " Aluminium.	102
"Duplex" Slide Rule, The.	74

EIDOGRAPH, Vernier used with.................................... 10
Engineers's Level, Adjusting an..............................35, 58
Engineer's Transit, Scales and Verniers of the.................... 97
Equation of Time... 51
Errors in working with Planimeters............................... 6
FOCUS of Lenses.....................................104, 116, 149
Formulæ for
    Aneroid Barometers......................................139, 140
    Both's Section-Liner.. 171
    Eidograph... 11
    Lenses........................104, 105, 116, 117, 118, 150, 173
    Partition of Land... 119
    Pile Driving.. 62
    Planimeters 5
    Railroad Curves... 88
    Solar Work...70, 82, 85
    Stadia Measurements.................................163, 164, 166
    Telemeter Target......................................126, 155
Fundamental Equation of Lenses, The 150
GLOSSARY and Definitions of Terms employed in Surveying,
    Astronomy, etc 16, 31, 47, 63, 79, 94, 110, 127
Graphometer, The... 34
Gyroscope Artificial Horizon, A................................... 93
HELIOGRAPH, The.—A Suggestion.................................... 120
    "   Captain Kilbourne's Screen................................. 138
IMAGES produced by Lenses.. 149
Improved Reflector for Telescopes................................ 68
Indirect Measurement of Distances................................ 152
LAND, The Partition of 118
Latest Determination of the Sun's Distance....................... 154
Latitude, To ascertain the, with the Solar Transit............... 130
Lenses, Different kinds of....................................... 65
    "   Focus of......................................104, 116, 149
    "   Formulæ for...............104, 105, 116, 117, 118, 150, 173
Light, its Reflection and Refraction..1, 17, 33, 65, 103, 114, 149, 172
Line and Curve Ranger, Adie's.................................... 2
Logarithmic Cross-Section Paper.................................. 90
MAGNETIC Variations, "Unexplained"............................... 94
Magnifying Power of Lenses 173
Mean Solar Time.. 51

Measurement of Heights with the Aneroid Barometer	139
Meridian Altitude of the Sun	107
Meridian, The, Directions for determining with the Solar Attachment	122
Methods of Measuring Distances	152
Metric Weights and Measures, Non-use of, a hindrance to Foreign Trade	125
NEW Books	15, 25, 61, 106, 178
New Pivot Joint for Dividers and Compasses	15
New Telemeter Target, A	125, 131, 155
Non-use of Metric Weights and Measures, a hindrance to Foreign Trade	125
North Magnetic Pole, The	26
OBJECT Prisms	4
Observation for Time with the Solar Attachment	131
Optical Centre of Lenses, The	105, 116
PAPER, Water Marks in	158
Parallax and Refraction in Solar Work, Correction for	134
Partition of Land	118
Pattern Maker's Shrinkage Rules	113
Polar Planimeter, Vernier used with	11
Planimeters, Errors in working with	6
" for Engine Indicator Diagrams	7
" Precision	5
Practical Methods for finding the focal length of a convex lens	151, 172
Preparing Declination Settings, for observations with the Solar Transit	123
Prismatic Compass, The	17
Prisms, Double	1
" Object	4
Professor J. B. Johnson on The Solar Transit	145
Proportional Dividers, "Universal," Vernier used with	11
Protractors	28, 36
RAILROAD Curves	86
Range Finders or Telemeters	33
Readers, To our	161
Reflecting Telemeters	33
Reflection and Refraction of Light	1, 17, 33, 65, 103, 114, 149, 172
Reflector for Telescopes, An improved	68
Refraction and Parallax in Solar Work, Correction for	134
Refraction and Reflection of Light	1, 17, 33, 65, 103, 114, 149, 172
Retrograde Vernier, A	27

SCALES and Verniers of the Engineer's Transit	97
Shrinkage Rules for Pattern Makers	113
Sidereal Time	51
Signs and Abbreviations used in Surveying, etc	177
Slide Rule, The "Duplex," Trigonometrical Computations with	74
Solar Attachment, Accuracy of Observations with the	145
" " Directions for using the	122, 130
" Compass, The	39
" Ephemeris	96, 112, 128, 143, 144, 160, 176, 192
" Transit, The	22, 40, 49, 68, 81, 107, 121, 129
Spherical Co-ordinates, Systems of	40
Spiders' Webs as Scientific Instruments	148
Stadia Hairs, Adjustment of	166
" Measurements	152, 162, 179
" Table for Inclined Sights	184 to 191
Standards of Length and Weight of the United States	12
Sun's Parallax, The	85, 135, 155
Surveys, Topographic	59

TABLES:

Equation of Time	84
Errors in Azimuth for 1 min. error in Declination or Latitude	147
Errors in Planimeter Measurements	6
Estimating Heights by the Aneroid	141, 142
For finding Angles and Spaces with Both's Section-Liner and Scale-Divider	171, 172
Latitude Coefficients	110
Magnifying Power of Lenses	175
Mean Refraction Corrections	85
Real Distances corresponding to Stadia Readings	168
Stadia, for Inclined Sights	184 to 191
Stadia Readings corresponding to Real Distances	169
Sun's Parallax in Altitude	85
Telemeters or Range Finders	33
Telemeter Target, A new	125, 131, 155
Time, Civil and Astronomical	52
" Equation of	51
" Sidereal, True or Apparent Solar and Mean Solar	51
To our Readers	161
Topographic Surveys	59
T-Squares with Protractor Scale and Vernier	29, 36
Trigonometrical computations with the "Duplex" Slide Rule	74

Trisection of an Angle, The.................................. 44
True or Apparent Solar Time.................................. 51
"UNEXPLAINED" Magnetic Variations....................... 94
United States Geological Survey, The........................ 20
"Universal" Proportional Dividers, Vernier used with the........ 11
VERNIERS.................................9, 27, 36, 53, 97
WATER-MARKS in Paper................................... 158
Work, A Definition of....................................... 72

COMPLETE COPIES of the first, second and third Volumes of "THE COMPASS" can be had, bound in cloth, for $1.75 each, postage prepaid.

"COPYRIGHT, 1892, BY WILLIAM COX, NEW YORK."

A Monthly Journal for Engineers, Surveyors, Architects, Draughtsmen and Students.

Vol. III. AUGUST 1, 1893. No. 1.

LIGHT: ITS REFLECTION AND REFRACTION. IX.

Fig. 1.

ANOTHER POPULAR instrument which embodies the principles of the prism, as set forth in our issue of June, Vol. II, is the DOUBLE PRISM, shown in Fig. 1, and in plan in Fig. 2. This neat and handy instrument consists of two similar prisms O and U, whose angles are $22\frac{1}{2}°$, $45°$ and $112\frac{1}{2}°$, placed one above the other in a brass mounting, to the handle of which a plumb line can be attached. The prisms are so placed that their longer sides coincide, the reflecting surfaces crossing each other at E.

When being used, the instrument is held up in front of the observer at S, and as he looks straight ahead through E, he will see in the upper prism the image of an object at P_2, and in the lower prism the image of an object at P_1. By moving his position until these two images coincide vertically, he will then place himself in the apex of the right angle $P_1 SP_2$, whilst if only one prism is used, an object seen at SE prolonged, over the instrument, would make with the object P_1 or P_2 an angle of 45 degrees.

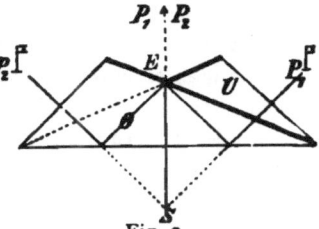

Fig. 2.

It will be noticed in the figure that there is in each prism a *double reflection* of the rays proceeding from the objects P_1 and P_2, the direction of which may be traced from the object at P_1 or P_2, through the prism to the long side, then reflected to E and again reflected to the observer at S.

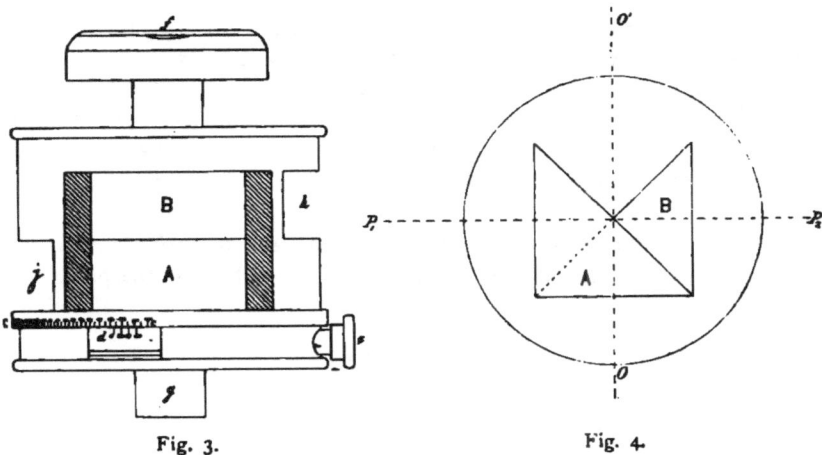

Fig. 3.   Fig. 4.

A more useful adaptation of these same principles is to be found in the improved Adie's LINE AND CURVE RANGER shown in elevation in Fig. 3 and partly in plan in Fig. 4. It consists of two equal-sided rectangular prisms, placed one above the other, the upper one being attached to the under side of the top of the surrounding brass case, while the lower prism is revoluble, being turned round by the small milled head e, which, when the instrument is not in use and is packed in its leather case, is screwed into a small tapped hole in the top of the brass case. A portion of the lower part of the case c, c, is graduated on its exterior surface to single degrees from 0° to 180°, reading by a vernier, attached to the lower prism and revolving with it, to 4 minutes.

The instrument can be screwed on to a staff at g, while its being held plumb may be ascertained by means of a small circular level at f. Windows are provided in the sides of the case at h and j to allow of the rays of light proceeding from distant objects striking the sides of the prisms, the faces *A* and *B* of the same being open to the observer in front. Fig. 3 is about two-thirds the natural size of the instrument.

The uses of this improved Line and Curve Ranger are, as its name implies, various. 1st. *To set out a straight line right and left of the observer.* Set zero of the vernier to 180°, thus making the front faces of the prisms flush with each other, as shown in Fig. 4, then hold the instrument upright in the hand, or supported by a staff. An observer at *O* looking straight into the prisms in the direction $O\ O^1$ will see in the lower prism the reflected image of a pole or other object at P_1 on his left, and in the upper prism a similar image of an object at P_2 on his right. When these two images appear superimposed or coincide vertically, then the straight line $P_1\ P_2$ passes through the centre of the instrument.

2nd. *To measure the angular distance of two objects.* Hold the instrument up so that the image of the right hand object may be seen in the upper prism, then turn the lower prism by means of the milled head *e* until the image of the left hand object is brought to coincide vertically with the upper image. The reading of the graduated scale will be the angular distance of the two objects. This instrument cannot be conveniently used for angles smaller than 20°.

3rd. *To set out a curve on the ground, the central angle being known.* This instrument is especially suitable for this kind of work, the principles

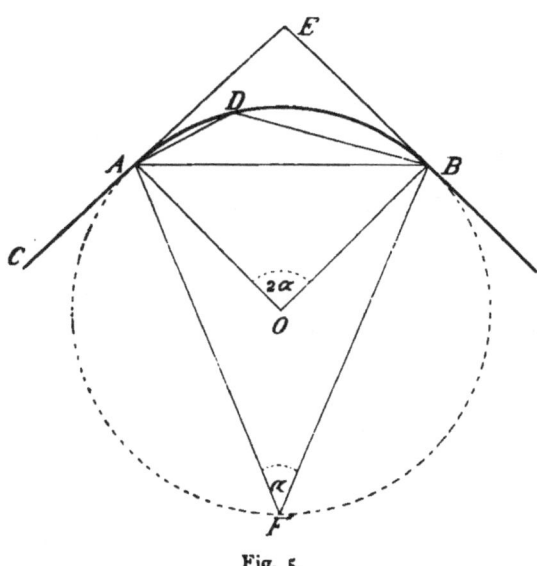

Fig. 5.

being those of Euclid III, 21, viz.: The angles in the same segment of a circle are equal to one another, and Euclid III, 32, If a straight line

$C E$, Fig. 5, touch a circle, and from the point of contact A a straight line $A B$ be drawn cutting the circle, the angles $C A B$ and $B A E$, which this line makes with the line touching the circle, shall be equal to the angles $A D B$ and $A F B$ which are in the alternate segments of the circle. Thus, in the figure, the angle $A O B$ at the centre of the curve being known $= 2 \alpha$, the angle in the segment $A D B = C A B = 180° - \alpha$. Set the vernier of the instrument to the angle thus found, and taking any position, say D, supposed to be in or near to the required curve, hold up the instrument, the observer facing towards the centre of the curve. If the images of a rod at A and another rod at B coincide in the two prisms vertically, then the point D is in the required curve, but if they do not coincide, the observer must shift his position until they are brought into coincidence. In this manner, and by the simple use of the rods at A and B, any number of points in the curve may be found.

4th. *To set out a curve on the ground, the value of the central angle being unknown.* In this case the $P C$ and $P T$, that is the stake mark at the beginning and end of the curve must be known, and a rod be held over each of them, whilst another rod is held at any convenient distance C on the tangent to the curve. The observer places himself at A and adjusts the prisms of the Ranger so that the images of the rods at B and C are brought into coincidence. As the angles $C A B$ and $A D B$ are equal, the instrument is now ''set'' to enable any number of points in the curve being found as just described.

Other uses of this handy instrument will suggest themselves. Curves may also be set out in the manner described by means of the Graphometer or the Box Sextant; (described in Vol. II,) the vertical coincidence of the two rods in the prisms of the curve ranger facilitates this class of work however, as the images are steadier: any movement in the one, caused by tremor of the hand, being simultaneously produced in the other, thus preserving the coincidence during the observation.

Fig. 6.

Figure 6 represents a patent OBJECT-PRISM for attaching before the object glass of a telescope in the same manner as an ordinary sunshade. It is a rectangular prism mounted in metal, and when in position brings into the range of the telescope objects situated in any plane at true right angles to its line of sight. Levels provided with this Object-Prism may be used for laying out perpendiculars, while Transits to which it is attached may be used in mining for vertical *up* or *down* sightings, thus superseding by its simplicity and effectiveness the old practice of attaching an extra telescope to the transit axis for this purpose. The principle on which it operates is that laid down in Vol. II, page 167.

PRECISION PLANIMETERS. I.

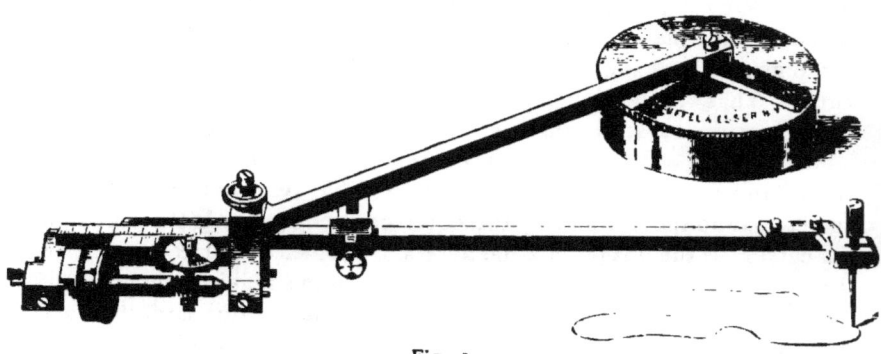

Fig. 1.

WHEN WE DESCRIBED in a former volume some different varieties of the ordinary Polar Planimeter, we stated that the accuracy of the measurements made with these instruments depends upon the care exercised in passing the tracer round the outline of the figure whose area is required, and also upon the construction and adjustment of their various parts. There is another factor, however, which very materially affects the accuracy of the results, and that is the surface of the paper upon which the planimeter is used. The instrument is necessarily a delicately constructed one, and the measuring records being produced by the independent rolling and slipping of the wheel, as well as by its combined rolling and slipping, it will be evident that any unevenness of the surface over which it travels must seriously affect the regularity of its progress, increasing in some cases the record and diminishing it in others.

Professor Franz Lorber, of Leoben, Austria, who has devoted a great deal of time to the examination of different kinds of planimeters, making many thousands of careful and thorough tests of them, came to the conclusion that the error in reading is represented by an equation, which may be reduced to the form of

$$d F_n = Kf + \mu \sqrt{Ff},$$

where $d F_n$ = the error in the result expressed in terms of the area measured,
F = the actual area measured,
f = the value given to one turn of the measuring wheel, according to the setting of the tracer arm,

K and μ are Constants, varying with different kinds of instruments, being for the Polar Planimeters shown in Fig. 1, and which we have already described, $K = 0.00126$, and $\mu = 0.00022$.

Professor Lorber has prepared tables of the results of a number of his tests, from which we extract the following, applying to the instruments under consideration, which will probably interest some of our readers.

Actual Area Measured $= F$	Absolute Error in the Result $= d F_n$	Relative Error in the Result ($f = 100$ $^c/_m{}^2$)	
$^c/_m{}^2$	$^c/_m{}^2$	One in	Per Cent.
200	0.157	1274	0.0785
100	0.148	682	0.148
50	0.141	355	0.282
20	0.135	148	0.675
10	0.133	75	1.33
5	0.131	39	2.62

These tests give the error resulting from one single passage of the tracer point round the area measured, and not the mean of several passages. It will be noticed that the absolute errors, varying from 0.131 to 0.157 $^c/_m{}^2$, differ from one another but slightly, and are not in any degree proportionate to the area measured, while on the other hand the relative error diminishes considerably as the area measured is larger, being almost inversely proportionate to the increase of area.

The following remarks by Prof. Henry S. H. Shaw, Assoc. M. Inst. C. E., taken from the Proceedings of the Institution of Civil Engineers, may also well be quoted in this connection. He says, "In all calculating machines, accuracy of the result must be the question of first importance. Assuming the theory relied on in the various instruments for the mathematical operation to be correct, the accuracy depends primarily upon the mechanical arrangements, though in the case of planimeters it also depends upon the skill and care of the manipulator, and involves the question of a personal error. This latter point need not be considered, partly because this occurs more or less in all results obtained by observers, but also because it is less than might be at first anticipated, from the fact that in tracing the pointer around the curve there is no reason why the error due to moving it on one side should exceed that due to moving it on the other side, that is, why equal errors of opposite effect upon the final reading should not be made."

A correspondent from Wayne, Ill., sent to a recent number of *Engineering News* the following, trusting it might be of some benefit to his fellow-engineers, and as it bears very directly upon this portion of our subject, we here reproduce it.

"Various articles on the use of the polar planimeter have appeared in your journal from time to time, but they were in the nature of descriptions and mathematical demonstrations of its workings, together with various formulas, and not comparisons of actual results in every-day practice. Engineers are seldom met with in railway construction that have ever used the planimeter for the computations of their estimates, or know anything about its advantages for such work. In the calculation of areas of complicated cross-section and overhaul for monthly estimates, where time is always a desideratum, it is to be highly recommended, and its accuracy is shown by the following comparison taken from actual practice on heavy railway construction in earth and rock, where the work was done by steam shovels, and numerous cuttings were necessary to finish each cut.

The instrument used was made by Keuffel & Esser Co., and the arm was graduated its entire length to $\frac{1}{2}$ m/m.[1] For detailed description, formulas, etc., see Mr. Wm. Cox's Manual, published by Keuffel & Esser Co., New York. The Comparison of results is given below:

Comparison of Results by Original Cross-sections, Final Estimate and Polar Planimeter.

Excavation.	By Original Cross-section. cu. yds.	By Final Estimate. cu. yds.	By Polar Planimeter. cu. yds.	Difference. %
Dalrymple cut....	61.164	61.196	60.871	— 0.52
Heine "	52 801	52.801[2]	51 763	— 1.96
Herrick "	44.211	45 521	45.683	+ 0.35
Smith "	43.947	43.223	43.088	— 0.31
Baker "	116.647	113.510	114.502	+ 0.86

(1). The same as Fig. 1 of this article.   (2). A coincidence.

For overhaul in two cases, calculated by analytic and graphic methods: 1,419,187 cu. yds. hauled 100 ft., planimeter made + 0.024% difference; 1,027,839 cu. yds. hauled 100 ft. planimeter made + 0.0316% difference."

Various devices have been adopted whereby the factor of the unequal surface of the paper may be more or less eliminated, but before describing them, we think it may be worth while to first draw attention to a very convenient arrangement applied to some planimeters of the style shown in Fig. 1, whereby the mean height of indicator diagrams may be at once read off.

Two fine steel points are attached, one to the upper side of the tracer or movable arm, and the other to the upper surface of the tube in which this arm slides. To obtain the mean height of the diagram, hold the planimeter upside down and adjust these points so that the distance between them shall coincide exactly with the length of the diagram, then clamp the arm and proceed in the usual way exactly as if the area of the diagram were sought. Instead of giving, however, the area, the setting of the tracer arm is by this means such that the difference of the readings at the beginning and end of the operation, divided by 0.4, is the mean height of the diagram in inches.

Example :—
    Second reading....................4.786
    First reading......................4.322

Then $4.786 - 4.322 \div 0.4 = 1.16$ inches = the mean height.

Supposing the scale of the indicator spring used to have been a No. 60, (that is, equivalent to a pressure of 60 pounds per square inch per inch of height), then the

$$\text{Mean Pressure} = \frac{0.464 \times 60}{0.4} = 69.6 \text{ pounds per square inch.}$$

The advantage of such an arrangement will be evident to the Engineer, who is continually occupied in making indicator tests. A similar method may, however, be used in connection with the Polar Planimeter shown in Fig. 1, by measuring the length of the diagram in half-millimetres and tenths, and subtracting this from a constant to be ascertained for the instrument, the difference being the required setting of the tracer arm.

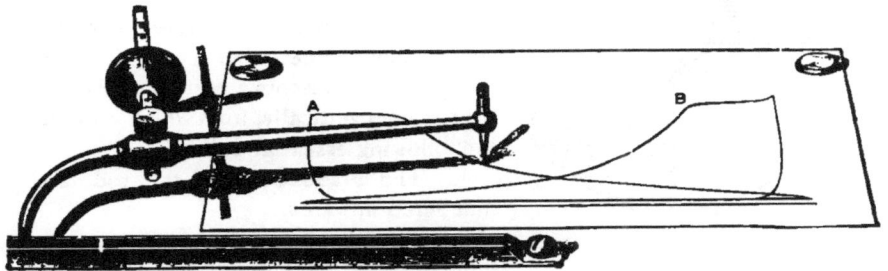

Fig. 2.

Fig. 2 shows another form of planimeter specially designed for measuring indicator diagrams and put on the market by Messrs. Hine and Robertson of this city. The peculiar feature of this instrument is that slipping motion of the wheel does not take place, the only approach to it being the change of direction of the wheel as the tracer follows the outline of the diagram. The wheel is made knife-edge, and moves freely on its spindle, which is graduated, the area circumscribed by the tracer being indicated at the end of the operation by the position of the wheel.

The device is ingenious, and from the tests we have made, may be relied upon for the *special* kind of work for which it is intended. Its capacity is about 9 square inches of actual area circumscribed, the measurements obtained being in square inches and twentieths.

VERNIERS I.

THE NUMBER of instruments in which it is required to read off very fine subdivisions of a graduated scale by means of a vernier is very considerable. These scales may be said to be of two kinds: plain scales of equal parts such as inches, millimetres or any other suitable unit, and circular scales of degrees, minutes and seconds.

The simplest kind of vernier is that applied to a New York leveling rod. The rod is divided into feet, tenths and hundredths, and the vernier is graduated so that 10 of its divisions correspond to 9 divisions or 9 hundredths of a foot on the rod, as shown in Fig. 1; we can thus obtain readings to a thousandth part of a foot, or a tenth of a single division of the rod. In the case of the architect's rod, the main divisions are feet, inches and eighths of an inch, while 8 divisions of the vernier correspond to 7 divisions of the rod or $\frac{7}{8}$ths of an inch, so that the least count is $1/_{64}$th inch. We have already explained the principles of the vernier (Vol. I, p. 28,) so shall not refer to them here more than to explain how to take a reading with the different verniers we are about to describe.

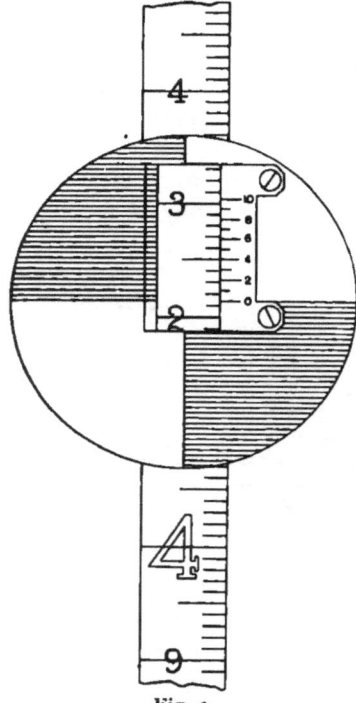

Fig. 1.

Figure 1 represents a portion of a leveling rod held vertically, from which we note the following essential points:—

1. The graduations of the rod are numbered upwards.

2. The divisions of the vernier are numbered in the same direction as those of the rod; they are therefore read *forwards* from the zero point, whence this is generally termed a *direct vernier*.

3. The graduations of the rod are feet, tenths and hundredths.

4. The vernier is so divided that 10 divisions = 9 divisions of the rod, therefore the least count is $\frac{1}{100}$ ft. ÷ 10 = $\frac{1}{1000}$ ft.

These four points require to be noted in the case of every scale and vernier before the method of using it or the value of the "least count" or "smallest reading" can be ascertained.

Having therefore obtained these particulars, we see that Fig. 1 reads, on the rod:—

4 feet $+ \,^{2}/_{10}$th foot $+ \,^{1}/_{100}$th foot

$= 4.21$ ft., and on the vernier $\frac{4}{10}$ths of $\frac{1}{100}$th foot $= \frac{4}{1000}$ths foot, making the real position of the vernier zero correspond to 4.214 feet on the rod.

The principle is identically the same if the scale be one of inches, centimetres, millimetres, or any other real or arbitrary unit, where it is desired to subdivide the smallest division of the scale (of the rod, transit, protractor, etc.,) into any number of equal parts by means of a vernier. The vernier always consists of a short scale divided into this given number n of equal parts, and these are equal to $n - 1$ parts* or smallest divisions of the scale of the instrument. Knowing the value x of the smallest division of the scale of the instrument, the least count or smallest reading obtained by means of the vernier $= x \div n$.

Similar verniers are used in the case of Fine Pantographs, Eidographs, Polar Planimeters, "Universal" Proportional Dividers, etc. In these the unit of measure or the smallest division of the instrumental scale is frequently an arbitrary one, owing to the different sizes in which such instruments are constructed, and to its being in general desirable to maintain throughout the different sizes of one and the same instrument, the same species of graduations.

The question is often asked whether the divisions on such instruments are *inches* or *metric* divisions. They are frequently neither, being as stated, arbitrary ones, and merely serve, by means of the formula employed, to *indicate a given point on the arms, etc., which shall divide their whole length into two parts bearing to each other a given desired ratio, irrespective of the real value or measure of such parts.* Thus, in the EIDOGRAPH shown in Fig. 2, the bar and the arms are each divided into 200

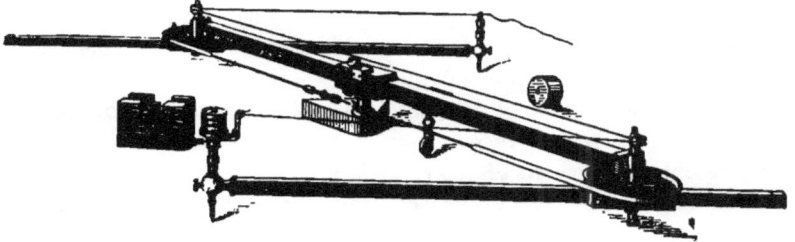

Fig. 2.

equal parts, each one of which is further subdivided into tenths by means of a vernier. In order that the same formula for obtaining settings may answer for the two usual sizes of this instrument, (30 and 36 inches) the unit of these scales of equal parts is an arbitrary one fixed in relation to

---

* In some cases $n + 1$ parts; this will be referred to and explained later.

the size of each instrument. In the smaller one 100 divisions occupy 1.3 ft., and in the larger one 1.56 ft., the value of a single division or unit being 0.013 ft., and 0.0156 ft. respectively. In each case, however, 10 divisions of the vernier are equal to 9 units of the scale of the instrument.

The formula by which we obtain settings for the Eidograph is $\frac{200 \times y}{x + y}$. where x is the greater term, and y the lesser term of the ratio. If it is required to enlarge in the proportion of 3 to 5, we obtain 75 as the setting of the fulcrum and arms, thus dividing the beam and arms into two parts, composed respectively of 75 and 125 units. If these units were of the same magnitude in instruments of different sizes, then clearly either the constant 200 in the formula would have to be correspondingly altered, or else the setting as obtained would not give the correct proportional division of the beam and arms.

In the POLAR PLANIMETER, referred to and shown in another article in this number, the movable or tracer arm is graduated and divided into 260 equal parts, beginning at the left and proceeding towards the tracer point for three-fourths of its length. In this case the divisions are half-millimetres, but this is in reality an arbitrary unit, selected probably because its further subdivision into tenths by means of the vernier, gives a means of obtaining very close and exact settings of the arm, seeing that the vernier unit or smallest reading is equal to rather less than one five-hundredth of an inch. The essential point is that the different positions to which the arm should be set should be exactly known, so that correct area readings may be obtained, whatever may be the scale to which the drawing, plan, etc., is made.

The "UNIVERSAL" PROPORTIONAL DIVIDERS are divided from end to end into 200 equal parts, further subdivided by means of the vernier into 2000 parts. In this case the total length of the instrument is 10 inches, so that the instrumental unit is $\frac{1}{20}$th inch, and the vernier unit $\frac{1}{200}$th inch; this division is also an arbitrary one as a $\frac{1}{30}$th inch for the instrumental unit would answer just as well. The use of the scale is merely to obtain by means of the formula used a point on the instrument to which the fulcrum should be set, which will divide the legs into two parts bearing to each other the desired ratio.

In these different instruments therefore, the vernier serves to decimally subdivide the smallest division of the scale of the instrument, by means of which the location of a desired point on the arm, etc., is determined, in relation to a given point of origin. The setting of such instruments is thus performed mathematically instead of by the old time-honored method of "try and try again." The value of the instrument unit is therefore clearly immaterial.

STANDARDS OF LENGTH AND WEIGHT OF THE UNITED STATES.*

THE CUSTOMARY WEIGHTS and Measures of the United States, that is to say, those commonly in use in this country, are either identical with or are derived from those which were lawful during the colonial period. Of necessity, then, they are almost entirely of English origin.

The Constitution gives Congress power to establish a system of weights and measures and to fix standards of the same....

Congress not having acted upon the subject of weights and measures, the matter was left in the various States to local and legislative control, and consequently the practice was exceedingly irregular. In many States, indeed, units of length and mass and other standards were merely traditional, and had no force based upon legislative action or other higher authority. While such confusion as existed might be tolerated in ordinary private commercial transactions, Congress saw that it was wise to establish at least a standard of weight which might be used in determining the mass of coins. This led to the passage of the act of May 19, 1828, which is the first, and indeed almost the only definite act of Congress upon the subject of weights and measures. This act provides that a certain piece of brass, now known as the Mint Troy Pound, should constitute the standard by means of which the coinage of the United States should be regulated....

The origin and growth of the metric system is familiar to everybody. The superior character of this system, both as to simplicity and scientific precision was recognized at an early day by those who gave attention to the subject of weights and measures in this country, but as it did not seem for a considerable time at least that this system, notwithstanding its great excellence, was likely to receive general international approval, or even locally the approval of the French nation, no very serious movements took place towards its introduction in this country. A little after the middle of the present century, however, it became evident to all intelligent observers that this system was destined to become in time, and at no very distant time, the great international system of weight and measure. It had already come into extensive use among scientific men of all nations and even among English-speaking people, and serious efforts began to be put forth to secure its recognition by legislation in Congress. The result of this agitation of the question was the passage of the very important act of July 28, 1866, in which the use of the metric system of weights and

---

* Extracts from a paper by Prof. T. C. Mendenhall, Superintendent of the United States Coast Survey, read at the 437th meeting of the SOCIETY OF ARTS, held at the Massachusetts Institute of Technology, Boston, November 22, 1892.

measures is authorized and made lawful throughout the United States of America. In the same act a set of tables was adopted as establishing in terms of the weights and measures now in use in the United States the equivalents of the weights and measures expressed therein in terms of the metric system....

The use of the metric system hereafter spread rapidly throughout the world, and it became important that the entire system of standards should be revised in a proper manner, and to this end an international commission was organized at the invitation of the French Government. The result of this was the final establishment of a permanent International Bureau of Weights and Measures near Paris, which is supported by contributions from nearly all the civilized governments of the world and controlled by representatives of these same governments.

After nearly fifteen years of labor, including much original investigation and research relating to the principles which should control standards of weight and measure, and many experiments as to the best methods of constructing and intercomparing such standards, the International Bureau had, in 1890, successfully completed the preparation of a considerable number of copies of the original metre of the Archives and of the original prototype Kilogramme. That metre which agreed most nearly with the metre of the Archives, and that Kilogramme which agreed most nearly with the Kilogramme of the Archives, were selected as the great international prototype units of length and mass. The other copies were distributed by lot to the various contributing nations, and thus the United States came into possession of two copies of the metre bearing respectively the numbers 21 and 27, and two copies of the prototype kilogramme, bearing the numbers 4 and 20....

In reference to these prototypes, action has recently been taken by the Office of Weights and Measures, which, while practically it has little or no bearing upon the value of the customary weights and measures in this country, yet from a theoretical standpoint must be regarded as of great importance. Referring again to the act of July 28, 1866, it will be remembered that in virtue of this legislation the use of the metric system was made lawful throughout the United States of America. No such action has ever been taken by Congress in reference to the customary system of weights and measures, and the authority of the yard and pound to-day rests entirely upon local legislative action. It will thus be seen that by the act of 1866 the metric system in the United States is placed upon a basis entirely different from and indeed quite superior to that of the customary system of weights and measures. Indeed, *it is the only system of weights and measures which has ever been made lawful by act of Congress,* and in this the use of the mint pound according to the act of 1828 is not excepted, for that was made lawful only for purposes of coinage....

As Congress has never in any manner defined a yard or a pound, or adopted any material representation of these units, the best that can be said for them is that the words are to be used in the ordinarily accepted sense. We have on the one hand, therefore, a system of weight and measure which has received the approval of nearly the entire civilized world, the fundamental standards for which have been constructed in accordance with the highest requirements of metrological science and which has been authorized and made lawful for the whole United States by special act of Congress. Further than this, Congress has for many years authorized and sustained the participation on the part of the United States Government in all the operations of the International Bureau of Weights and Measures, in which the metric system was being and is being perfected and perpetuated.

On the other hand we have a system of weights and measures whose only recommendation is that it has been for many years in customary or common use. It is irrational in theory, irksome in practice, and has been condemned by all who are competent to speak upon a subject of this kind. Furthermore, it has never been authorized or made lawful by act of Congress, and as a matter of fact is almost without recognition in the history of Congressional legislation. It has been determined by the Superintendent of Weights and Measures that a proper and wise recognition of these facts justifies, if does not demand, the acceptance of the international prototype metre as the unit of length, and the international prototype kilogramme as the unit of mass—their representative material standards now in the possession of the government being utilized for such comparisons as may be deemed necessary and expedient. This implies that the yard shall hereafter be defined as a certain fraction of a metre, and that a pound shall be defined as a certain fraction of a kilogramme, *and this will be the practice of the office of Weights and Measures henceforth.** While not interfering in the slightest degree with the practical or commercial use of the yard and the pound, there are very important theoretical and scientific advantages in thus referring these units to the great international prototypes, which are already the standards of length and mass for the greater portion of the civilized world. It is hoped, therefore, that this action will meet with the approval of all who are interested in the advancement of the science of metrology and in the increase of precision in both theoretical and applied science.

---

* These definitions, according to the act of 1866, are as follows :

$$1 \text{ yard} = \frac{3600}{3937} \text{ metre.} \qquad 1 \text{ pound} = \frac{1}{2.2046} \text{ kilogramme.}$$

NEW BOOK.

We have received from Mr. Arthur P. Davis, C.E., of Los Angeles, Cal., a copy of his TABLE FOR OBTAINING DIFFERENCES OF ALTITUDE, *for any even minute up to* 15 *Degrees, and for any Distance.* Large 8vo ; Muslin ; 16 pages, $1.50. Also in stiff paper cover, $1.00.

An example will best serve to show the arrangement of this table. Let it be required to find the difference of altitude corresponding to an angle of elevation of 9° 18' at a distance of 3.628 miles. On page 11 we have under 9° 18' the following differences of altitude for distances from 1 to 9 miles.

Miles	1	2	3	4	5	6	7	8	9
9°18'	864.7	1729	2594	3459	4323	5188	6053	6917	7782

Whence for a distance of

3 miles, the difference of elevation is...................... 2594 feet.
6 " 5188 ft., making for 0.6 miles.................... 519 "
2 " 1729 " " " 0.02 " .... 17 "
8 " 6917 " " " 0.008 " .... 7 "

Total for 3 628 miles................... 3137 feet

To this must be added the correction for curvature, refraction and height of instrument, which, according to two special columns, repeated on each page, is 12 feet for a distance of 3.6 miles, thus making a total difference of elevation of $3137 + 12$ feet $= 3149$ feet. The height of the instrument is assumed throughout as $4\frac{1}{2}$ feet. The correction for curvature and refraction is based on miles $^2 \times 0.572$ ft.

The printing of the table is clear and the paper good, so that the labor of making such computations is materially reduced by its use. Although specially worked out for plane-table map work, this table will be of use to the engineer in many other ways.

A NEW PIVOT JOINT FOR DIVIDERS AND COMPASSES.

BY AN OVERSIGHT we omitted to state in our last issue that the device for a new Pivot Joint, invented by Mr. Herman Esser, is secured by letters patent granted to him under dates March 14th and 28th, 1893.

GLOSSARY AND DEFINITIONS OF TERMS EMPLOYED IN SURVEYING, ASTRONOMY, ETC. I.

ABERRATION. Latin, *aberratio*, a wandering away from.* (*Astronomy*.) A small periodical change of position in the stars and other heavenly bodies, due to the combined effect of the motion of light and the motion of the observer. This change is termed *annual* or *diurnal aberration* according as the observer's motion is caused by that of the earth in its orbit, or on its axis, and amounts, when greatest, in the first case to 20".4, and in the latter to 0."3. (Optics.) The convergence to different foci, by a lens or mirror, of rays of light emanating from one and the same point, or the deviation of such says from a single focus. It is called *spherical aberration* when it is due to the spherical form of the lens or mirror, such form giving different foci for central and marginal rays; and *chromatic aberration* when it is due to the different refrangibilities of the colored rays of the spectrum, those of each color having a distinct and different focus. (*Webster*.)

ACHROMATIC. Greek, *a*, negative privative, and *chroma*, color. Free from color, thus an *achromatic lens* is one usually composed of two separate lenses, one concave and the other convex, of different substances, as crown and flint glass, each having different refractive and dispersive powers, their curvatures being so proportioned that the chromatic aberration produced by the one shall be corrected by the other, thus causing light to emerge from the compound lens undecomposed. An *achromatic telescope* or *microscope* is one in which the chromatic aberration is corrected.

ACTINIC. Pertaining to Actinism.

ACTINISM. Gr. *aktos*, gen. *aktinos*, a ray. In optics that power in the sun's rays by which chemical changes are produced, as in photography.

ADIATHERMIC. Gr. *a* neg. priv., *dià*, through, and *therme*, heat. Not pervious to heat. "Glasses of a green color, in combination with a layer of water, or a very clear plate of alum, are called by Melloni *adiathermic*, from their being perfectly opaque for heat, notwithstanding light passes through them freely." (*Nugent*.)

AGONIC. Gr. *a*, neg. priv., and *gonia*, an angle. Not forming an angle; thus, in Surveying the *Agonic Line* is that line on the earth's surface on which the magnetic needle points to the true North, or on which there is no declination of the compass needle.

---

* As a general knowledge of the derivation of scientific terms is both instructive and helpful in enabling the meaning of other terms to be grasped, we give them here, on the authority of Webster.

"COPYRIGHT, 1892, BY WILLIAM COX, NEW YORK."

A Monthly Journal for Engineers, Surveyors, Architects, Draughtsmen and Students.

Vol. III.   SEPTEMBER 1, 1893.   No. 2.

LIGHT: ITS REFLECTION AND REFRACTION. X.

PROBABLY THE MOST useful and popular application of the laws of reflection, as exemplified in prisms, is to be found in the PRISMATIC COMPASS, invented by Captain Henry Kater about 1814. This handy pocket instrument, different forms of which are shown in Figs. 1 and 2, consists mainly of a circular metal case 2 to 4 inches in diameter, with a magnetic needle which revolves upon a point fixed in the centre of the case. Hinged to one end of the case is a sight-vane with a fine metal thread stretched across it longitudinally, while opposite to this and in line with the centre of the needle is a hinged slit sight, below which is a rectangular prism, by means of which the compass bearings may be read while a distant object is being sighted. Such are the main features of the prismatic compass, which is, however, frequently modified considerably in the details of construction. We will examine somewhat more closely the types shown in the figures.

Figure 1, which represents a 2½ inch instrument, is intended to serve two purposes, those of a Compass and a Clinometer. The needle is attached to the under side of a card, divided around its edge into degrees and half degrees, (except in the smallest and larger instruments, in which the divisions are single degrees and quarter degrees respectively). When

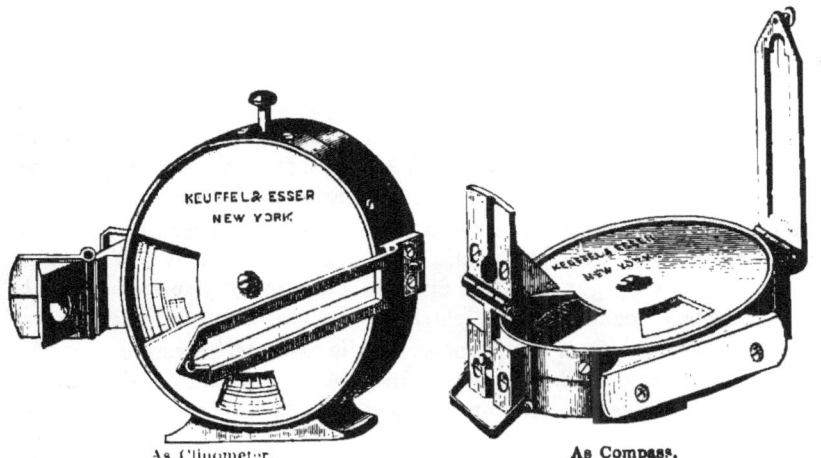

As Clinometer.   As Compass.

Fig. 1.

used as a Compass the small sliding piece to which the sighting slit and the prism are hinged, is raised and the latter turned over the dial, and adjusted for height so that the divisions and figures on the card can be distinctly seen by reflection when looking into the face of the prism. The faces of the prism are made slightly convex, so as to magnify somewhat the fine divisions on the card and make them more distinct, and also to enable subdivisions to be estimated.

The sight-vane being raised as shown in the figure, and the instrument held horizontally in the right hand, the wire may be seen through the sighting slit in conjunction with the divisions of the card seen through the prism, and the magnetic bearing of a distant object noted. Pressure with the finger upon a small stop in the side of the box, under the sight-vane, enables the needle to be gradually brought to rest, thus facilitating the work in hand. The card is usually numbered to give readings from 0° at the north, round by 90° at east, 180° at south, 270° at west to 360° at the north, this latter figure equally denoting the zero. The readings being taken by means of the prism at the eyesight end of the instrument, the numbers on the card begin in reality at the south end of the needle and proceed west, north, east and round again to south.

But this Compass can also be used as a Clinometer, as shown to the left of Fig. 1. When about to be so used, the sight-vane should be turned down over the compass box, thus raising the needle off its pivot. When the instrument is set vertically upon a flat inclined surface, and the knob on the top of the case drawn out, the slope of such surface can be at once read in the lower window on a weighted revolving card disc, either in inches per yard or in degrees, the several divisions of the card being brought into coincidence with a fine line engraved on the glass in the window which protects the card from injury, and keeps the dust out of the compass box.

Another important use to which this Prismatic Compass may be put, is for ascertaining altitudes. If it be required to take the angle of elevation or depression of a distant object, the sight-vane is raised, and the prism turned over the compass box, as shown to the right of Figure 1. Holding the instrument vertically in the left hand in such manner that the object can be seen through the slit, and covered by what is now the horizontal wire of the sight vane, the angle of elevation or depression can be simultaneously read on the weighted disc by means of the prism to half degrees. The height of the prism above the case can be varied, and must always be adjusted before sighting so that the figures and divisions on the compass card or on the clinometer card (whichever one is being used) can be distinctly seen.

A mounting for Jacob Staff which can be screwed into the under side of the case, and a leather sling case as shown in Fig. 2, complete this instrument, which is not only extremely portable, but will be found very useful in preliminary reconnoissances and in filling in details of a survey after the principal points have been noted with the transit.

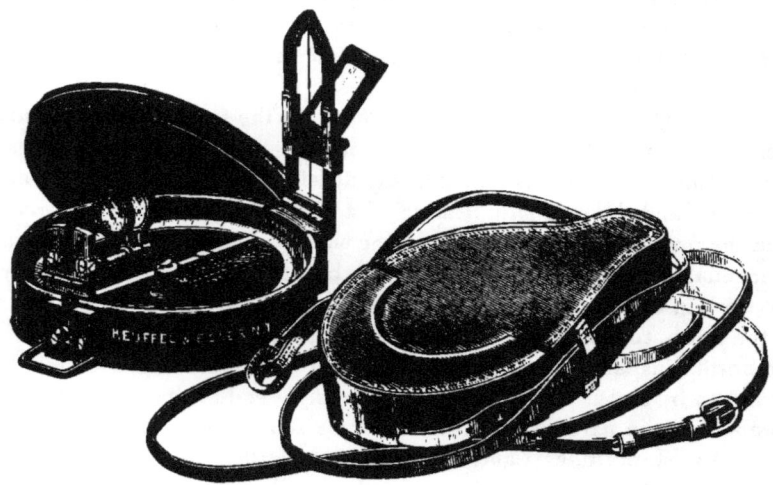

Fig. 2.

The Prismatic Compass, as described, can only be used, however, for taking the bearings of objects nearly in the same horizontal plane. Useful as it is, it lacks, therefore, in its simplest form, one important element. In all surveys the distances and angles between different points, however much they may vary in altitude, require to be projected upon the same horizontal plane in order that a map or plan of the same may be made. What is required therefore, to make the prismatic compass complete for such special work, is an attachment by means of which horizontal angles between objects not in the same plane may be measured. Fig. 2 shows such an instrument, 3 inches diameter, its main parts, as needle, prism, sighting slit and sight-vane being the same as those already described. The compass card is, however, replaced by an aluminum ring graduated to half degrees, (the readings of which can, by the magnifying power of the prism, be easily estimated to 10 minutes), to which the needle is attached, the whole being well balanced. This ring is entirely exposed to view, being covered with glass, while the box has a metal detachable lid to protect the whole. A mirror, hinged to a small brass piece so adjusted to the sight vane that it can slide along it with the face of the mirror directed upwards or downwards, enables objects to be seen through the sight-vane by reflection, although they may be considerably above or below the horizontal plane of the observer. If used for ascertaining the magnetic azimuth of the sun, the two neutral glasses pivoted to the prism slide, require to be placed in front of the sighting slit, and when sighting objects in the direction of the sun, the use of one of these glasses will be found a great relief to the eye.

The use of a tripod with the prismatic compass will often be found advantageous, as with it the instrument can be adjusted with a small pocket level so that the hair in the sight-vane shall be vertical, thus ensuring far greater accuracy in the results, especially if the objects sighted have a considerable elevation. By this means bearings may easily be estimated to within 5 minutes.

THE UNITED STATES GEOLOGICAL SURVEY.

ITS VALUE FROM A PRACTICAL STANDPOINT.[*]

Of the many important lines of scientific investigation carried on by the General Government, that of the geological survey may fairly claim a prominent position, not only on account of the magnitude of the undertaking, but also for the far-reaching influence it will ultimately have in the development of the mineral resources of the country.

Were this its only merit it could afford to rest upon that alone, but a characteristic of scientific investigation of any kind is that its entire meas-

---

[*] Written for *Florida*, by H. L. Baldwin, Topographer.

ure of usefulness can never be estimated immediately, but, only after the lapse of time is the full value apparent, for new uses are constantly arising which may be subserved.

A thorough geological survey carries with it not only a determination of what is under ground, but also the surface, for a stratum, which in one place may be very far underneath, can be satisfactorily studied for its entire extent by its limited surface outcroppings at a distant point.

Therefore, the geologist calls to his aid the civil engineer to construct the typographic maps necessary, and upon the exellence of these, much of the value of the future work depends, for naturally the topographical survey precedes the geological survey.

Aside from their geographical use these maps will serve many other purposes which are perhaps more immediately practical in their nature. I here quote from the published utterances of Mr. Henry Gannet, a scientist of world-wide reputation, speaking through a prominent English magazine:

"Experience has shown that maps designed for the use of the geologist are equally useful in various other ways, such as the location of roads, railways and canals, and for planning towns and extensive manufactories, and drainage and irrigation systems, and for all other works depending upon the nature of the ground.

"The resources and industries of the country are rapidly developing and the uses of maps for other than geological purposes are increasing with each decade. There is accordingly a double incentive to the energetic prosecution of the topographical survey of the country."

Among local uses for these maps will be found the possibility of ascertaining therefrom the high portions of land which are comparatively free from frost. They will also enable the determination of the best position for the proposed canal across Florida, which would otherwise require expensive preliminary surveys.

At present there are three corps of topographic surveyors at work in as many separate locations adjacent to Ocala, each corps being composed of three scientific assistants, with sufficient field and camp helpers to prosecute the work to the best advantage.

The maps under construction will show all the natural features of the country, such as hills, valleys, lakes, etc., as well as the roads, railroads, towns and dwellings. The plan of the work involves first, the determination by astronomical methods, of the latitude and longitude of several widely separated points, and these are connected by very carefully measured base lines which serve to locate definitely the position of the principal land survey lines, and incidentally the determination of their errors sufficiently well to assist in the map making.

Lines of precise levels are next run, determining the absolute elevation of a large number of places above sea level, and which serve as starting points for the close network of levels which will cover the entire area of the map.

Assisted by compass and odometer, all the roads are traversed and levels carried along as an aid to the topographer in the sketching. By a system of contour lines of equal elevation and ten foot vertical interval, all differences of elevation of that amount are determined and represented in such manner that the size and shape as well as the absolute and relative elevation of every hill and hollow in the limits of the map can be seen at a glance.

The maps, which are uniform in size and on a scale of one mile to the inch, are printed in colors and are issued generally within about a year of the completion of the field work. They can be obtained by making a request through a member of Congress, naming the principal city in the area of which a map is desired.

THE SOLAR TRANSIT. I.

THERE IS A GROWING conviction among surveyors that the magnetic compass does not of itself meet present-day requirements in land surveys. A great factor of uncertainty exists where bearings are solely taken by its means, the consequences being very frequently serious, if not indeed disastrous. Resort therefore must be had to some more exact method. A true meridian can, it is true, be obtained by means of the Transit, but the process is laborious and generally involves a great amount of calculation; the growing necessities of the times demand therefore a more expeditious but equally reliable instrument for the determination of true meridians.

The best and simplest instrument that we know of, and that can be used for this purpose is an Engineer's Transit with vertical circle, combined with a Saegmuller patent Solar Attachment, shown in Fig. 2, the instrument thus completed being what is termed a Solar Transit, shown in Fig. 1.

Before proceeding to the consideration

Fig. 1.

of this attachment, it will be necessary to describe briefly the astronomical problems whose solution is generally required by the surveyor. To make them as clear as possible we have specially prepared the figure shown on

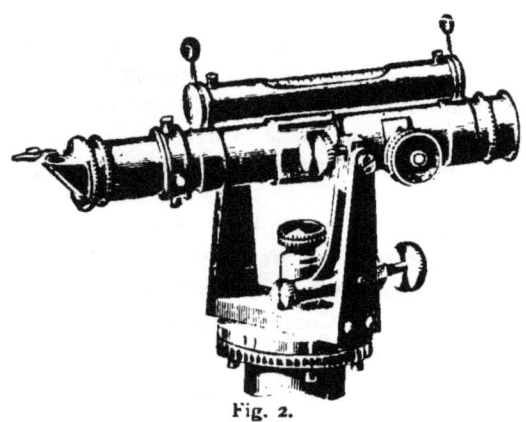

Fig. 2.

Plate I, which embraces the following features, which ought to be carefully noted and remembered.

In the centre of the figure is supposed to be situated the EARTH (exaggerated in size), surrounded on all sides by infinite space. The imaginary and endless limits of this latter form, what is termed the CELESTIAL SPHERE, which is studded upon its inner or concave surface with an almost infinite number of celestial bodies. The centre of the earth is conceived to be likewise the centre of this sphere, and these bodies are *supposed*, as they appear to us to do, to revolve around this assumed centre from east to west, their apparent motions being governed by the diurnal rotation of the earth upon its axis from west to east, as well as by its annual motion in its orbit. Certain planes are supposed to pass through the earth's centre and to reach to the celestial sphere, forming on its inner surface GREAT CIRCLES, several of which are shown in the figure, and which we shall now describe.

The observer being supposed to be situated on the earth's surface at A in latitude 40° N, an imaginary straight line $Z\ A\ O\ N_1$ passing through his position and the centre O of the earth, and produced in both directions to the celestial sphere, is called the VERTICAL or NORMAL LINE, the upper point Z where this line meets the sphere over the observer's head being the ZENITH, and the lower point N_1 beneath his feet being the NADIR. As we have shown in the case of the adjustments of Transits and Levels, so in astronomy, that earth's radius upon which the observer is located must be the basis of all operations by means of which he seeks to determine his relative position, as by means of the plumb line or the spirit level, *absolute* direction can be given to it, on whatever point of the earth's surface he may be situated. This line is therefore, as stated, the normal, and to it all lines and circles are more or less related.

Another imaginary straight line $P O P_1$ which is formed by the supposed extension of the axis of the earth in both directions until it meets the celestial sphere, is called the AXIS OF THE HEAVENS, the points of contact P and P_1 being the NORTH and SOUTH POLES of the heavens, and around this axis the celestial sphere appears to rotate.

A plane $N_a A S_n$, perpendicular in every direction to the normal line, and touching the earth at the observer's position, and intersecting the celestial sphere, forms a circle (in the figure we have only shown the diameter of this circle so as to avoid crowding), called the SENSIBLE HORIZON, while another plane, parallel to this one, but passing through the centre of the earth, likewise intersecting on all sides the celestial sphere, forms a great circle $N E S_1 W$, called the TRUE or CELESTIAL HORIZON or the AZIMUTH CIRCLE, its poles being the Zenith and Nadir.

That great circle $C U H D V$, whose plane is perpendicular in all directions to the axis of the heavens, and passes through the centre of the earth, is called the CELESTIAL EQUATOR or the EQUINOCTIAL. This circle coincides with the plane of the terrestrial equator produced to the sphere.

VERTICAL CIRCLES are imaginary circles formed on the inner surface of the celestial sphere by vertical planes passing through the Zenith, the centre of the earth and the Nadir, and meeting the surface of the sphere; they intersect, therefore, the vertical or normal line and all have this line for their common diameter. That vertical circle $N P Z S_1 N_1$, whose plane passes through the normal and the axis of the heavens, is called the CELESTIAL MERIDIAN, and is astronomically equivalent to the observer's terrestrial meridian, while the vertical circle $Z E N_1 W$, whose plane passes through the normal and is perpendicular to the celestial meridian, is called the PRIME VERTICAL. The points N and S_1 where the meridian intersects the celestial horizon are the NORTH and SOUTH POINTS of the horizon, the line of intersection of the two planes being the MERIDIAN LINE $N O S_1$, and the points E and W of the horizon intersected by the prime vertical are the EAST and WEST POINTS of the horizon, the intersection of the two planes being the EAST and WEST LINE $E O W$.

Vertical Circles, as $Z S B N_1$, whose planes pass through the normal line and a celestial body as S, are called GREAT CIRCLES OF ALTITUDE. All such circles have the normal line for a diameter and their planes are perpendicular to the plane of the horizon.

Great Circles, as $P S D P_1$, whose planes pass through the axis of the heavens, and are consequently perpendicular to the plane of the equator, are called HOUR CIRCLES or CIRCLES OF DECLINATION. The celestial

Plate I.

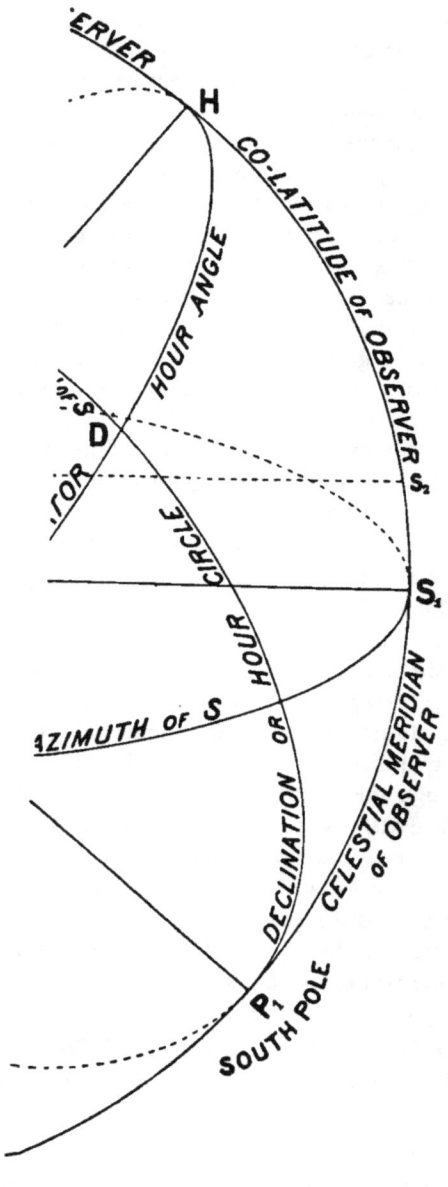

"Copyright 1893, by WM. Cox, New York.

meridian is also a circle of declination, as its plane intersects the axis of the heavens and is perpendicular to the plane of the equator.

We have one more great circle to describe and that is the ECLIPTIC $FUJV$, or the circle of the sphere which the sun *appears* to travel over from west to east by reason of the earth's annual motion in its orbit. This circle is not coincident with the equator, but crosses it twice, its OBLIQUITY, or the angle JVH which it makes with the equator being about 23° 27'. The points of intersection are called the EQUINOCTIAL POINTS or the EQUINOXES, the VERNAL Equinox V being the point where the sun crosses the equator northwards on March 21, and the AUTUMNAL equinox U being the point where the sun crosses the equator southwards on September 21, thus forming the alternation of the seasons in northern and southern regions.

RESUMÉ.

1. The Earth.
2. The Celestial Sphere.
3. A Celestial Body, as a Star or the Sun S.

LINES.

4. The Vertical or Normal Line, $Z A O N$.
5. The Axis of the Heavens, $P O P_1$.
6. The Meridian Line, $N O S_1$.
7. The East and West Line, $E O W$.

GREAT CIRCLES.

8. The True or Celestial Horizon, or the Azimuth Circle, $N E S_1 W$.
9. The Celestial Equator or Equinoctial, $C V D H U$.
10. The Prime Vertical, $Z E N_1 W$.
11. Vertical Circles or Circles of Altitude, $Z S B N_1$.
12. Hour Circles or Circles of Declination, $P S D P_1$.
13. The Ecliptic, $F U J V$.

THE POLES.

14. The Zenith, Z. } of the Horizon.
15. The Nadir, N_1. }
16. The North, P. } of the Equator.
17. The South, P_1. }

BOOKS RECEIVED.

THE MICHIGAN ENGINEERS' ANNUAL, 1893. The annual convention of the members of the Michigan Engineering Society was held at Lansing, January 17, 18 and 19, 1893. Financially and numerically this society is evidently in a prosperous condition, and its thirteenth annual contains a greater number than ever of interesting papers on important topics of the day, foremost among which we find the now ever recurring question of "good roads." The annual closes with a digest of more than two hundred recent legal decisions which will be of special interest to engineers. We wish this Society a better showing still at its next annual meeting.

PROCEEDINGS OF THE 13TH ANNUAL MEETING OF THE INDIANA ENGINEERING SOCIETY, held at South Bend, Ind., January 23, 24 and 25, 1893. Some very interesting papers will be found in this annual, which will well repay perusal. We have read with particular pleasure those on "Stadia Measurement in Land Surveying," by John W. Fawcett, Surveyor and C.E., Delhi, Ind., and "In the Mountains of Utah" by F. Hodgman, the well-known secretary of the Michigan Engineering Society, and author of "A Manual of Land Surveying," who describes in a taking way some of his earlier experiences in a then unknown and wild tract of country.

THE NORTH MAGNETIC POLE.

OF THE SEVERAL projected Arctic expeditions of this year, probably only one has a purely scientific purpose. This is a party of trained observers whom Col. W. H. Gilder will take to determine the present locality of the north magnetic pole. No other polar enterprise gives equal promise of yielding important scientific and practical results. Any researches that will make the compass a more trustworthy guide for the mariner and surveyor must be worth what they will cost. The magnetic needle does not point to the geographical pole, but to a place which is at least 1200 miles south of it, and, in respect of New York, far west of the North Pole; nor does it point steadily in the same direction, for it is subject to daily variations, and also, at present, to a very slow and decreasing variation toward the west. This constant variation long ago gave rise to the theory that the magnetic poles of the earth move along a path of greater or less extent. When Schwatka and Gilder were in King William Land in 1879, their magnetic observations seemed to show that the north magnetic pole had moved more than 2° of longitude west of its position as approximately fixed by James Ross in 1831. The questions that Colonel Gilder's party are to study are of the highest scientific interest, and three years will be required to complete the undertaking. The party are expected not only to fix the present place of the north magnetic pole, but also to set at rest the question, still in dispute among scientific men, whether the position of the earth's magnetic poles is fixed or variable; and if the north magnetic pole is found to move, the long period over which the observations are to extend will enable the party to determine the direction and rate of motion. In a word, a magnetic survey of the area containing the north magnetic pole is to be made; and there can be no doubt that the practical result will be to increase our knowledge of terrestial magnetism and of the laws that govern the movements of the magnetic needle. More than sixty years have elapsed since the position of the north magnetic pole was approximatively fixed. Scientific men are agreed that, in the light of our present knowledge of terrestial magnetism, and with our vastly improved instruments, most important results must follow the taking up again of the researches begun over half a century ago.—*The Mechanical World.*

VERNIERS II.

WE STATED IN our last that in some cases $n + 1$ parts or smallest divisions of the scale of the intstrument are equal to n parts of the vernier.

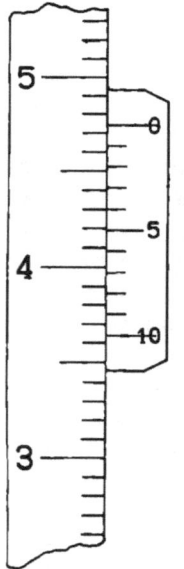

Fig. 1.

Fig. 1 represents such a vernier in which 11 parts or divisions of the instrumental scale are equal to 10 divisions of the vernier. This is called a *retrograde vernier* to distinguish it from the direct one shown in Fig. 1 of our last issue. In this case the reading of the instrumental scale is taken upwards, while the vernier reading is taken *backwards, i. e.* downwards. The value of the least count is obtained precisely as with the direct vernier. If $x =$ the value of the smallest division of the instrumental scale $=$ say $\frac{1}{10}$ inch, and the vernier is composed of 10 divisions, then the value of the least count of the vernier $= \frac{1}{10}$ inch $\div 10 = \frac{1}{100}$ inch.

The figure shows therefore on the main scale $4.7'' +$, whilst the vernier shows $0.04''$, making a total of $4.74''$. Such verniers are but little used, although they are sometimes found on mercurial barometers.

To be able at once to know whether a vernier is retrograde or direct, make zero of the vernier coincide exactly with any division of the instrumental scale, then if the vernier equal parts are seen to be smaller than the equal parts of the scale, the vernier is a direct one and must be read in the same direction as the scale, whereas if the vernier equal parts are larger than those of the scale, it is a retrograde vernier and must be read as just described.

We now come to the second kind of verniers, namely those applied to circular scales of degrees, minutes, etc.

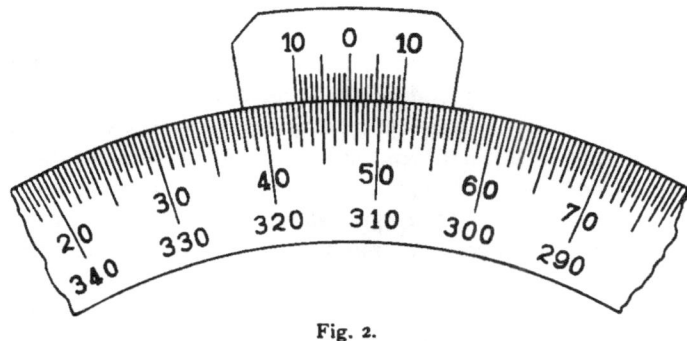

Fig. 2.

Figure 2 represents a scale and vernier very commonly met with, and which is largely applied to Protractors, as shown in Fig. 3, which is a 5½ inch Circular German Silver Protractor with a revoluble arm and vernier.

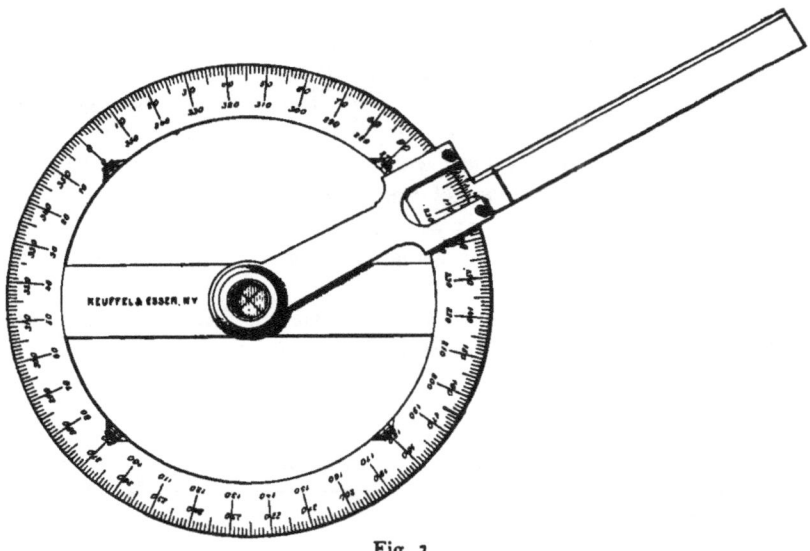

Fig. 3.

In this case the Protractor scale is graduated to half degrees, the value of the least division being therefore 30 minutes. The vernier attached to the arm comprises 20 divisions, the centre one being numbered zero, while the two extreme divisions are each numbered 10. It will be seen that 9 divisions of the protractor scale are eqal to 10 divisions of the vernier, this is therefore a *double direct vernier*. The centre division being numbered zero shows at once that the vernier can be read both ways, to the right and to the left of the zero, according to the direction in which the circular scale is being read ; and as scales of such protractors are usually numbered backwards and forwards, that part of the vernier scale must be used which corresponds to the direction in which the protractor scale is numbered, and consequently being read. As the least division of the circular scale is equal to 30', and as 10 vernier divisions correspond to 9 scale divisions, the least count or smallest reading of the vernier will be 30 ÷ 10 = 3 minutes. The figure shows therefore readings, firstly:— according to the outer series of numbers of the instrumental scale, proceeding from left to right of 47° +, and on the vernier 8 divisions × 3' = 24', thus making a total of 47° 24'; and secondly:—according to the inner series of numbers of the instrumental scale, proceeding from right to left of 312° 30' +, and on the vernier 2 divisions × 3' = 6', thus making a total of 312° 36'. That these readings are correct is at once seen by adding them together, their sum being 360 degrees. These small size protractors have a least count vernier of 3 minutes, but with practice it is easy to set off with them single minutes, by making the coincidence of the vernier lines *bare*, or *full*. Similar protractors are, however, made 8 and 10 inches diameter, and for these the instrumental scale is generally divided to quarter degrees, or equal parts of 15 minutes each; in such cases 15 divisions of the vernier, which is also a double one similar to Fig. 2, are equal to 14 divisions of the protractor, so that the least count of the vernier = 15 min. ÷ 15 = 1 minute. Such instruments are intended for very close work, and being machine divided, their correctness may be relied upon.

Semicircular protractors of the same style are also made, which will be found useful for plotting a traverse with the T-Square.

Fig. 4.

Figure 4 represents a steel T-Square with protractor scale and vernier, for setting off angles and plotting, while Fig. 5 shows the scale and vernier in detail.

Here it will be noted:—

1st. The protractor scale is divided to half-degrees, numbered right and left from the central zero, which corresponds to the position of the blade when perpendicular to the head, thus allowing of angles of elevation and depression to be set off.

2nd. The vernier is divided into 30 equal parts, the central division being numbered 0 *and* 30, whilst the extreme divisions are numbered 15

3rd. These 30 divisions of the vernier correspond to 29 divisions of the protractor scale, giving consequently single minutes as the least count of the vernier.

Such a vernier is called a *double-folded-vernier* or a *crossed* vernier; and serves to read both right and left, although occupying but half the space of the ordinary double vernier shown in Figure 2. It is generally used where the size of the vernier limb does not allow of a longer one being used, as in this case, where the vernier is on the steel blade, which in the case of a 24 inch instrument is but 1¼ inches broad.

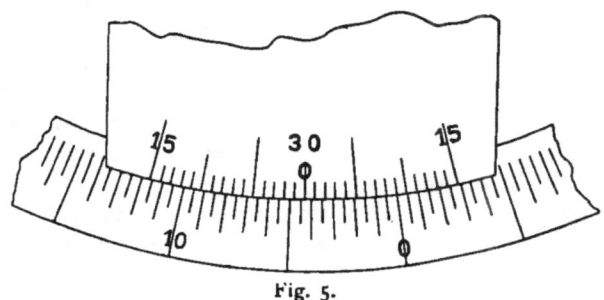

Fig. 5.

The mode of reading such a vernier is to follow the vernier from zero in the direction in which the scale is being taken, to the 15 division. If any lines coincide, then such indicate the vernier reading, but if none between 0 and 15 are found to coincide, then follow the vernier from the opposite 15 towards the 30 line until coinciding lines are found. Thus in Fig. 5, the vernier zero is at 4° + on the left hand of the protractor zero, the reading being consequently supposed to be from right to left. Between the vernier zero and the left hand 15 of the vernier no lines coincide; we therefore turn to the right hand 15 line of the vernier and follow it towards the centre or 30 line, (that is, left-ward). We then find that the vernier line 21 coincides with a graduation of the protractor scale. The total reading is, therefore, 4° on the scale + 21′ on the vernier = 4° 21′.

If, on the other hand, we are reading the instrument from left to right, we have on the protractor scale 85° 30′ + and on the vernier scale 9′, making a total of 85° 39′.

Such double-folded-verniers are frequently met with, and will with the foregoing explanations be easily read. They can nearly always be detected at sight, as the middle division of the vernier will be generally found to be numbered zero or the highest number of the vernier scale, or both as in our figure. We shall have occasion to refer again to this class of verniers when examining other instruments provided with this most useful adjunct.

GLOSSARY AND DEFINITIONS OF TERMS EMPLOYED IN SURVEYING, ASTRONOMY, ETC. II.

ALIDADE. Arabic, *al-hadât*, a sort of rule, from *hadaj*, to guide on the right way. An Alidade is a straight edge or rule provided with sights or a telescope, by means of which the direction of the line of sight may be transferred to the plan or drawing on which it is placed.

ALTAZIMUTH. Lat. *altus*, high, and Arabic *as-samt*. pl. *as-sumût*, a way or path; *samt al ras*, the vertex of the heaven; hence *zenith*, a corruption of *zemt*, or *semt*, and *al-samt*, a point of the horizon, and a circle extending to it from the zenith, commonly called the *azimuth*. An altazimuth is, in general, an instrument by means of which altitude and azimuth may be determined; the term is, however, commonly applied to pocket instruments giving only magnetic bearings, and altitude angles by means of a weighted disc.

ALTIMETER. Lat. *altimeter*, from *altus*, high, and *metrum*, measure. A hand or pocket instrument for determining levels and grades.

ALTITUDE. Lat. *altitudo*, from *altus*, high, and a common termination denoting state, condition or manner. Altitude is the perpendicular elevation of one object above another, or of the horizontal plane passing through an object above a parallel plane passing through another object. In astronomy it denotes the angular elevation of a heavenly body above the horizon, measured upon a vertical circle. It is the *true* altitude when the angular elevation is measured from the true horizon, or that plane which passes through the centre of the earth at right angles to the earth's radius upon which the observer is standing, as shown in Plate I, where the arc SB is the altitude of the celestial body S. It is the *apparent* altitude when the angular elevation is measured from the sensible horizon, that is from that plane parallel to the true horizon which touches the earth at the point of observation. A subtractive correction must always be made for refraction.

AMPLITUDE. Lat. *amplitudo*, from *amplus*, ample. In astronomy amplitude is the angle at the zenith formed by the plane of the prime vertical circle passing through a celestial body situated on the horizon. This angle is measured on the horizon from the east or west points of the prime vertical, *i. e.*, true east and west, (from the former when the body is rising and from the latter when it is setting); it is consequently the complement of the azimuth. In Plate I, if the body be supposed to be on the horizon at B, then the amplitude is measured by the arc WB, the zenith spherical angle being WZB, formed by the planes WOZ and BOZ. The amplitude of a star is often employed at sea for ascertaining the declination of the compass.

ANALLATIC. Gr. *a*, negative privative, and *alasso*, to alter: — unchangeable. An anallatic telescope is one in which by the addition of an extra lens the focus is made constant, so that in stadia measurements the distances are obtained from the centre of the transit, the addition of a constant being consequently unnecessary.

ANEMOMETER. Gr. *anemos*, wind, and *metron*, measure. An instrument for measuring the velocity of a current of air, generally made self-registering, and largely used for testing the ventilation of mines. Anemometers are also made to indicate the force of wind.

ANEROID. Gr. *a*, neg: priv:, *neros*, wet, and *eidos*, form. An aneroid barometer is one in which the column of mercury is replaced by a metallic box with flexible sides, from which the air has been exhausted. The atmospheric pressure acts upon this and the variations of pressure are transmitted to a needle reading into a circular graduated scale.

ANGLE. Lat. *angulus*, a corner. The degree of opening or inclination of two converging straight lines which meet in a point.

APHELION. Gr. *apo*, from, and *helios*, the sun. The point of a planet's or comet's orbit which is the most distant from the sun.

APLANATIC. Gr. *a*, neg: priv:, and *planetikos*, disposed to wander. An aplanatic lens is one in which two glasses of different curvatures are so combined that the aberration of the one neutralizes that of the other, the resulting compound lens being consequently practically free from spherical aberration.

APOGEE. Gr. *apo*, from, and *ge*, the earth. That point of the moon's orbit at which it is at its greatest distance from the earth.

ASCENSION. Lat. *ad*, to, and *scandere*, to mount or climb. The right ascension of a celestial body is an arc of the equinoctial included between a plane passing through the equinoxes and the poles of the earth, and the plane of a declination circle passing through the body. It is reckoned from west to east from the first point of aries, or the vernal equinox, and is expressed in hours and minutes of time, one of the former being equivalent to 15 degrees. In Plate I, the arc VD is the right ascension of the celestial body S.

WE REGRET that we are unable to take up the question of the Telemeter Target in the present number, as circumstances have prevented us from making certain trials which we had in view. We hope to refer to this matter in our next issue.

"COPYRIGHT, 1892, BY WILLIAM COX, NEW YORK."

A Monthly Journal for Engineers, Surveyors, Architects, Draughtsmen and Students.

Vol. III.   OCTOBER 1, 1893.   No. 3.

LIGHT: ITS REFLECTION AND REFRACTION. XI.

BESIDES THE instruments already described there are a number of others in which the principles we have set forth are variously utilized, the reflection of the rays of light being effected in some by means of mirrors, whilst in others prisms are used for the same purpose. These instruments mostly belong to that numerous class generally called TELEMETERS or RANGE FINDERS, by means of which the distance of an object may be ascertained without actual measurement by chain or tape. Stadia and gradienter measurements are examples of the highest work of this kind, but they require that the object shall be accessible, and that a graduated rod be held there to be sighted at. In the case however of, what we may call, the *reflecting* Telemeters (whether by mirrors or prisms) the object sought is to obtain the distance to a remote object, whether accessible or not, by means of the instrument and a short base line at the observer's position, whose length may be easily determined, the distance being obtained after the observation from the instrument directly, or by a very simple calculation.

The general method of procedure is very similar with all these instruments, being mostly based upon the properties of right-angled triangles, by which having the base and the adjacent angle given, the perpendicular is found by simply multiplying the base by the tangent of the angle. It is usual with such instruments to use a base of fixed length, as 100, 50, 30 feet, etc., this base starting from the observer's position and being at right angles to a line drawn through his position and the object whose distance is required. If the base selected is 100 feet, then the tangent of the angle at the other end of the base multiplied by 100 gives the distance in feet of the object. Such is more or less the main principle on which the various reflecting Telemeters depend, the carrying out of it being however considerably varied in the different styles of instruments. That there should be so many different devices for measuring distances, is explained by the fact of a demand having sprung up for suitable pocket instruments of late years (especially in military circles) whereby these distances could be measured without access to the object being a necessity.

The Graphometer, shown in the figure, and which we described in full in Vol. II. of THE COMPASS, as well as the Box Sextant, are clearly

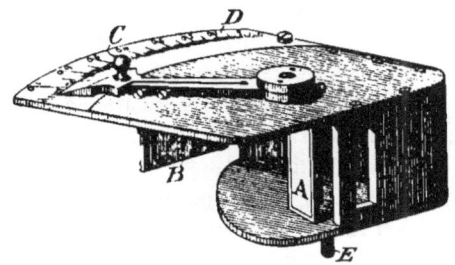

in this sense Telemeters. Let us, however, suppose that in place of the graduated arc shown above, at

45°	be placed	100
56° 18′	"	150
63° 26′	"	200
68° 12′	"	250 and so on to
80° 17′	"	1000

with suitable intermediate graduations, we should then have a Telemeter which would, with a base of 100 feet, at once, when the distant object was brought by reflection into coincidence with the observer's station, give us the distance in feet of an object anywhere from 100 to 1000 feet distant from us. Such would be a simple, portable, convenient and very fairly accurate instrument, and one which would be very useful in preliminary surveys, giving as it would the distance without calculation, or without reference to a table of tangents. The same instrument would also serve to set off the base perpendicular to the line of sight to the distant object, by setting the index to 100, the desired length of base.

Such, with modifications specially pertaining to each distinct instrument are the principles and methods of applying them, which belong to the different reflecting Telemeters or Range finders, such as the *Labbez* Telemeter, the *Weldon* Range Finder, and others, some of which we purpose describing at greater length in future numbers.

ADJUSTING AN ENGINEER'S LEVEL.
By E. F. Officer, C. E., Toltec, Ark.

Referring to the criticism of Mr. E. T. Abbott of Minneapolis, regarding a method of Adjusting an Engineer's Level communicated by me and which you published on page 187 of last July number of The Compass, I will say that the method therein set forth is unquestionably more troublesome and requires a longer time to perform than the ordinary way of reversing the telescope in the wyes. What I claim is, that my method is *more accurate* and *trustworthy*. If an instrument is new and without defects, I do not deny that it can be adjusted as Mr. Abbott does, as this method is theoretically correct.

I will now show cases where this adjustment will not render a level capable of doing accurate work where unequal back and fore sights are taken, while my method will do so.

In adjusting by reversing telescope in the wyes the object secured is the making of the level tube parallel with the supporting wyes. Suppose for simplicity that the telescope rests on the bottom points of the collars, and suppose one of the latter is somewhat worn, bruised or has some foreign substance attached thereto, making its diameter say one-hundredth of an inch smaller or larger than the other one, and that the wyes are one foot apart. It is evident, that, when the bubble is in the centre of the tube and the supporting wyes are on the same level, that the line of sight will be elevated or depressed one inch in a hundred feet, since it has been previously placed in the mathematical axis of the telescope tube. Again, since throughout my method, the telescope remains fastened in the wyes, there is less liability to individual error than there is in lifting it out and reversing, which requires a steady hand to avoid moving the wyes.

Experience has shown me that my adjustment renders it possible to obtain accurate results with any level, while the old method sometimes fails.

In practice I generally use Mr. Abbott's method to get an instrument approximately in adjustment, and then apply my method to get it in accurate condition.

There are other instrumental errors eliminated by my method, but I will not trespass farther on your space to detail them.

VERNIERS III.

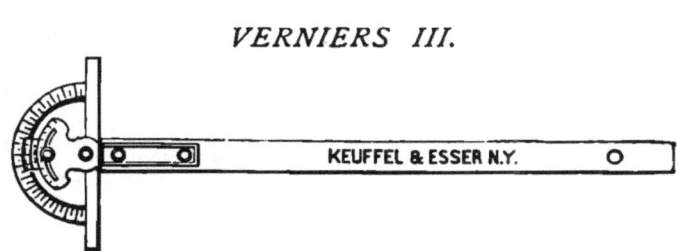

Fig. 1.

THE ABOVE FIGURE represents a T-Square which combines two useful scales and verniers, which we frequently meet with. In this instrument the head is composed of a semicircular protractor numbered in quadrants both ways from the centre, while to the blade is attached a graduated arc of nearly 120 degrees reading both ways from the centre zero. A small tongue is swivelled between the blade and the head, to either of which it can be independently clamped. This tongue has two verniers on it, one reading into the arc of the blade, and the other into the protractor of the head.

The special object of this arrangement is to allow of the T-Square being used and *angles directly plotted:*—

When the drawing board is not rectangular, or if the drawing is not placed squarely upon it;

To plot angles on a drawing when the base line is not perpendicular to the side of the drawing board; or

When a reference line has to be first drawn at a *given angle* with the base line, and angles then plotted in reference to this sloping line.

To do this, loosen the clamps and set zero of the outer vernier to zero or 90 of the protractor scale and clamp the vernier to the protractor; now by means of the inner arc and vernier set the blade to the required angle of slope, or make it coincide with any given base line already on the drawing, and clamp the vernier to the arc. Angles may now be plotted in reference to this slanting base line by means of the protractor scale and vernier which reads to single minutes, the vernier of the inner arc reading to 5 minutes. This instrument, which will often be found very useful in the draughting room, is well made, the head being of German silver and the blade of steel, nickel plated. The details of the scales and verniers, both of which are double folded, are shown in Fig. 2.

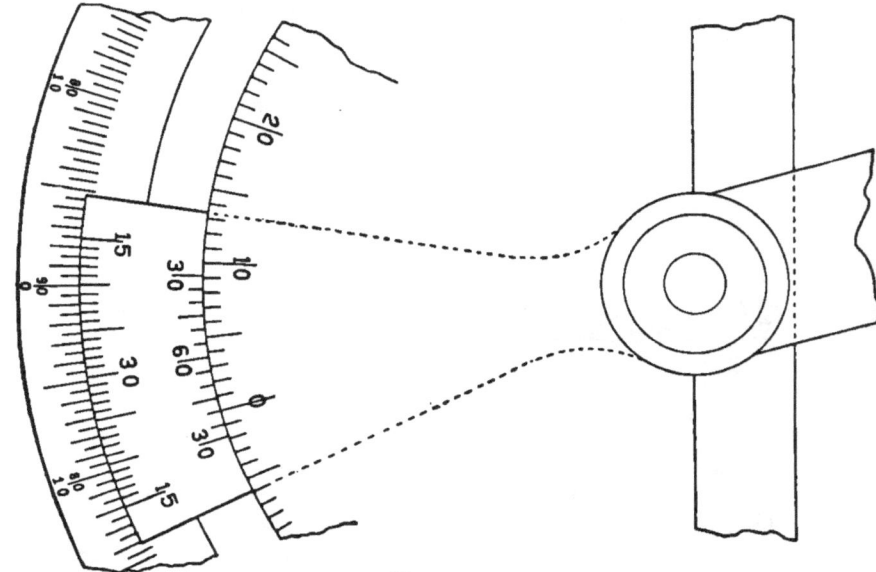

Fig. 2.

The outer or protractor scale and vernier are composed thus:—

1st. The protractor scale is divided to half-degrees, and these are numbered in two rows, the inner one being marked 90 in the centre and progressing backward in both directions to zero at each end, while the outer row is marked zero in the centre and progresses forward to 90 at each end; by this means angles may be at once plotted with reference to a horizontal or perpendicular base line.

2nd. The vernier is divided into 30 equal parts, the central division being numbered 30, whilst the extreme divisions are each numbered 15.

3rd. It will be seen that the 30 divisions of the vernier correspond to 29 divisions of the scale, consequently the vernier reads to single minutes.

4th. The 30 of the vernier being in the centre of the scale, it is at once seen that this is a double-folded vernier, and both scale and vernier are read exactly as described and shown in Fig. 5 of our last number.

The inner arc has the following features:—

1st. The scale is divided to single degrees, and these are numbered zero in the centre and proceed both ways to 50 at each end of the arc.

2nd. The vernier is divided into 12 equal parts, the central division being numbered 60, and the extreme divisions 30 each; this is consequently also a double-folded vernier, necessitated by the desire to make the tongue as compact as possible and to give to the whole a harmonious division of its parts.

3rd. The 12 divisions of this vernier correspond to 11 divisions o the arc scale, hence we have $60 \div 12 = 5$ minutes as the smallest reading of the vernier.

The mode of reading these two scales and verniers is the same as that already explained, thus for the outer scale we have, reading downward, $4° 30' +$ and on the vernier 18' making a total of $4° 48'$. To obtain this vernier reading, we commence at the central division and proceed *downwards* towards the vernier 15, then, if no lines coincide, we commence again with the top 15, and proceed downwards until we find that the third line coincides with a line of the scale, which gives as consequently $15 + 3 = 18$ minutes on the vernier. If we read upwards we have $85° +$ on the scale and 12' on the vernier, making a total of $85° 12'$.

The reading of the inner arc shows that the reference line for which the blade is set, has an upward slope of $3°$ on the scale $+$ 8 divisions $\times 5' = 40'$ on the vernier, making a total of $3° 40'$. As the centre line of the vernier falls upon the upper half of the arc, the vernier must be read upwards.

In this instrument we have an example of two different methods of setting; thus, the lower *vernier* is set to the protractor, while the scale of the upper *arc* is set to the upper vernier. The same difference is frequently met with in other instruments, but it presents no difference in the mode of reading; it is merely an arrangement generally dependent upon details of construction. It is evident in the case before us that the placing of the two verniers upon a small tongue is in every sense the best means that could be devised for effecting the desired object.

These scales and verniers are also very generally met with in certain surveying instruments. Thus, the horizontal circle of the Architect's or Builder's Y Level being usually a 3 inch one, the divisions are single degrees, and the vernier a double-folded one of 12 divisions reading to 5 minutes, as the inner arc scale of Fig. 2. In these instruments the vernier is usually set to the circle.

The vertical circle of Engineer's Transits is generally divided to halfdegrees, while the vernier is also, on account of the limited space disposable, a double-folded one of 30 divisions reading to single minutes, as the outer protractor scale of Fig. 2. In this case the circle is set to the vernier, it being attached to the telescope axis.

Other examples of such double-folded verniers may be frequently met with, but in all the manner of reading them is the same, and the value of their least count is ascertained as already explained.

THE SOLAR COMPASS.

Minneapolis, September 12, 1893.

To the editor of THE COMPASS:

My friend Culley, of Cleveland, suggests Solar Compass work for reducing all bearings to true Meridian, and mentions the one uncertain thing in old meanders as being the bearings, which fact we all know to be true. I suggest a better scheme than that, it seems to me, and one which I adopt. That is, take the angle between some one of the bearings and Polaris, stating the date, hour and time when taken. In these days of good watches the time recorded would not vary but a few minutes from the true time, and if ever necessary to retrace the line it can be done with little trouble and great accuracy. You can get the time wrong fifteen minutes and then be nearer right than any Solar Compass work I ever saw. I will give the boys another gratuitous tip. There is hardly any locality in the United States where you can get a great way from an observatory, and in case you want to retrace one of these surveys, ask the Professor a categorical question, thus:—"At a point $26\frac{1}{2}$ miles South and 14 miles West of the City Hall in Cleveland, at 11.20 P.M. September 1st, 1893. where was the Pole Star with relation to the true meridian?" He will answer you and the whole problem is solved instanter. This may be unprofessional, but it will get there, and I admit that life is too short as far as I am concerned to fool away any time on a Solar Compass, to say nothing of my lack of ability to run one, added to the fact that I never yet saw or checked a meridian established with one that was closer than 5 or 6 minutes of being right. I don't say it cannot be done, but I never saw any person who could do it. With a Transit, a business card and a candle, I can get a meridian in which there is no guile, and do it twice the same way.

Yours truly,
E. T. ABBOTT, C.E.

In Mr. John L. Culley's letter to us, which we published in the April number of THE COMPASS, he recommends the use of the Solar TRANSIT and not the Solar Compass, and we have every reason to believe that this is the instrument he would wish to see adopted. With a good transit and a Saegmuller attachment, the true or astronomical meridian can be obtained in a few minutes, and that with a remarkable degree of accuracy.

THE SOLAR TRANSIT. II.

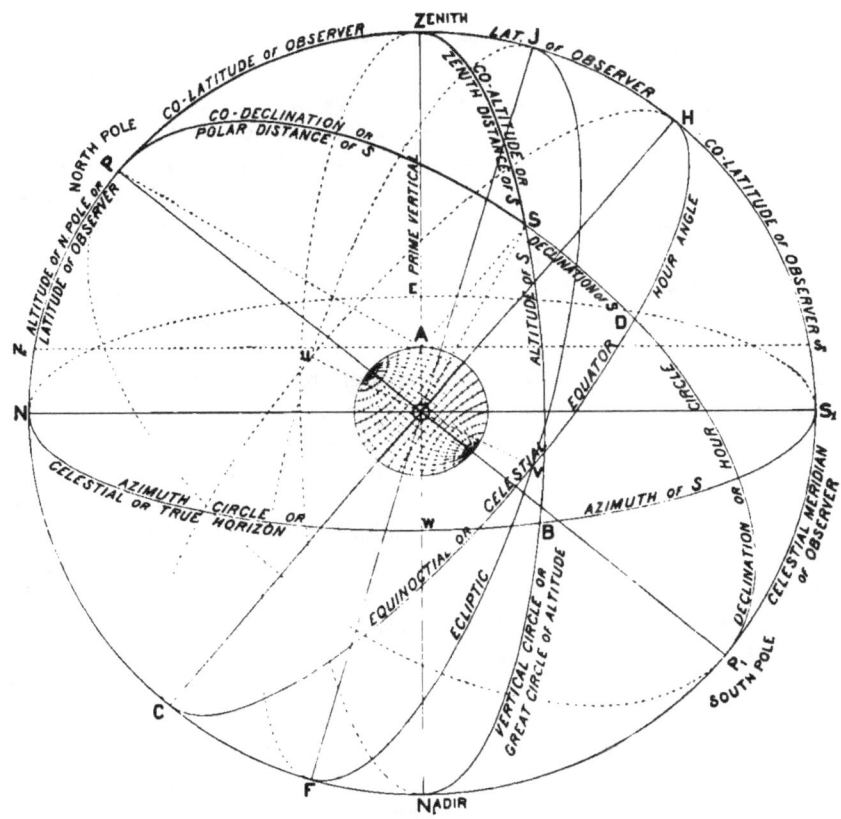

Copyright 1893, by William Cox, New York.

As we can locate the position of any point in a plane by means of rectangular co-ordinates, so the position of a celestial body in the sphere may be determined by means of spherical co-ordinates.

Different systems may be used for this purpose, varying with the PRIMITIVE CIRCLE of reference adopted and the *secondary circles*, (great circles perpendicular to and passing through the poles of the former), these different circles corresponding to the *axes* in analytical geometry. We shall now explain some of those most frequently employed.

First System.

In this system the Primitive Circle selected is the True or Celestial Horizon, with the Zenith and the Nadir for its poles on the celestial meridian, while the Secondary Circles are vertical circles or great circles of altitude, passing through the zenith and the nadir.

The co-ordinates are the ALTITUDE, which is the angular elevation of the body S, measured upwards from the horizon on a circle of altitude = arc SB; and the AZIMUTH, which is the angular distance of the body S measured by the arc of the horizon intercepted between the circle of altitude and a given point of the horizon assumed as the point of origin = arc $S_1 B$. Astronomers generally reckon from the south point of the horizon, proceeding thence to $W. N. E.$ and round to S. Sometimes azimuth is reckoned from the north or south point of the horizon, whichever is nearest; and sometimes from the north point of the horizon in northern latitudes, and from the southern point in southern latitudes, the azimuth being then east or west according as the body is east or west of the meridian.

The angular distance from the zenith to the horizon, measured on a circle of altitude being a quadrant, it naturally follows that the angular distance ZS, from the zenith to the body S, measured on the same circle of altitude, is the complement of the altitude, that is $= 90° - SB$; it is called the co-altitude or ZENITH DISTANCE of the body S.

The azimuth of a body S may also be expressed as being the spherical angle at the zenith formed by the plane of the observer's meridian $S_1 H Z A O$ and the plane of the great circle of altitude $B S Z A O$ passing through the body = angle $B Z S_1$ when reckoned from the south, and angle $B Z N$ if reckoned from the north, each one of these angles being the supplement of the other.

Second System.

The Primitive circle chosen in this case is the Equinoctial or Celestial Equator, with the north and south poles of the heavens as its poles, while Secondary Circles are Hour Circles or Circles of Declination passing through the body and the poles P and P_1.

The co-ordinates are the DECLINATION, which is the angular elevation or depression of the body S, measured north or south from the equinoctial on the circle of declination or hour circle passing through the body, = arc SD; and the HOUR ANGLE, which is the angular distance of the celestial body S measured by the arc of the equinoctial intercepted between the circle of declination and the observer's meridian = arc HD.

The hour angle of a body S may also be expressed as being the spherical angle at the pole formed by the intersection of the plane of the observer's meridian $H Z P O$ and the plane of the great circle or circle of declination $D S P O$ passing through the poles and the body S, = angle $H P D$ or $Z P S$.

The complement of the declination of the body S is its co-declination or POLAR DISTANCE = the arc $P S$, measured on the same circle of declination, = $90° \pm D S$. Declination when north of the equinoctial is positive or $+$, and when south of the equator it is negative or $-$, hence the polar distance of a body whose declination is south = $90° +$ the declination.

Altitude and Declination always require to be corrected for refraction, seeing that as the rays of light coming from celestial bodies pass from a rarer to a denser medium, those bodies appear higher than they really are.

THIRD SYSTEM.

The Primitive Circle is the Equinoctial as in the second system, its poles being the north and south poles of the heavens, while Secondary Circles are also Circles of Declination.

The co-ordinates are the DECLINATION already described, and the RIGHT ASCENSION, which is the angular distance of the body S, measured by the arc of the equinoctial included between the vernal equinox and the point where the declination circle of the body intersects the equinoctial = arc $V D$. It is reckoned from the vernal equinox, from west to east and from $0°$ to $360°$, reduced to its equivalent of hours, minutes and seconds of time, one hour being equal to 15 degrees.

Any point of the equinoctial might serve as the point of origin of right ascension, just as in the case of terrestial longitude (to which it is analogous) the meridians of Greenwich, Paris, Washington etc. are used by the countries in which those cities are situated. Astronomers however always reckon from the vernal equinox, or, as it is sometimes called, the first point of Aries, although the positions of the two are not now coincident, by reason of the precession of the equinoxes.

It remains for us now to mention another co-ordinate, and that is the observer's latitude, which being produced to the sphere is coincident with the arc of the meridian included between the zenith and the equinoctial = arc $Z H$. The complement of the latitude is the arc of the same meridian included between the zenith and the north pole = arc $P Z = 90° - Z H$.

We now summarize these various co-ordinates, which are clearly shown in the figure, allotting to each a certain designatory letter to facilitate the solution of problems in which they occur.

RESUMÉ.

First System.

Primitive Circle.—The Celestial or True Horizon.
Poles.—The Zenith and the Nadir.
Secondary Circles.—Circles of Altitude.

Co-ordinates of Celestial Body S.

Altitude, $h = $ arc SB.
Azimuth, $a = $ arc $S_1 B = $ angle BZS_1.
Zenith Distance or Co-altitude, $\Big\}$ $z = $ arc $ZS = 90° - h$.

Second System.

Primitive Circle.—The Equinoctial.
Poles.—The North and South Poles.
Secondary Circles.—Declination or Hour Circles.

Co-ordinates of S.

Declination, $d = $ arc SD.
Hour Angle, $t = $ arc $DH = $ angle SPZ.
Polar Distance or Co-declination, $\Big\}$ $p = $ arc $PS = 90° \pm d$.

Third System.

Primitive Circle.—The Equinoctial.
Poles.—The North and South Poles.
Secondary Circles.—Declination Circles.

Co-ordinates of S.

Declination, $d = $ arc SD.
Right Ascension, $r = $ arc VD.
Polar Distance or Co-declination, $\Big\}$ $p = $ arc $PS = 90° \pm d$.

We further have

Observer's Latitude, $l = $ arc $ZH = $ arc NP.
Observer's Co-latitude $= $ arc PZ.

THE TRISECTION OF AN ANGLE.

WE HAVE RECEIVED the following communications which we reproduce, feeling that they will interest some of our readers.

CORNING, OHIO.

In the July number of your journal appeared a cut and a demonstration of the trisection of an angle by "common geometry," as is claimed. It is universally agreed to by mathematicians that the phrase "common geometry" means only the straight line and the circle, both drawn and in position, and without motion. Any movement puts the solution outside of common geometry. The trisection of an angle by geometry as thus explained has never been accomplished. By other methods it is very simple. In Lardner's *Algebraic Geometry* you will find a method not only of trisecting an angle, but also of dividing it into any number of equal parts—an *algebraic* method.

Twelve or fifteen years ago while I had charge of the Department of Mathematics and Civil Engineering in the Ohio State University, an ingenious machinist of Cincinnati, a graduate of an Ohio College, sent me his methods of trisecting an angle by "common geometry," as he supposed. He had found *sixteen* different ways, and had invented a machine for each method, so that each machine by the motion of its parts, would perform the trisection. This feat, I think, stands unrivaled in the history of the subject.

Three years ago, an acute mathematician, a professor in another Ohio College, submitted to me his solution of this celebrated problem. Here is another in the July number of THE COMPASS. Suffice it to say that all these *eighteen* ways proceed on *one* principle, and that a method invented by NICOMEDES more than two centuries B. C., and well known for more than 2000 years. Its oft-repeated re-invention does not constitute a new discovery, except to the man who makes it.

THE CONCHOID OF NICOMEDES.

This is the curve by which the trisection is made. Take any two

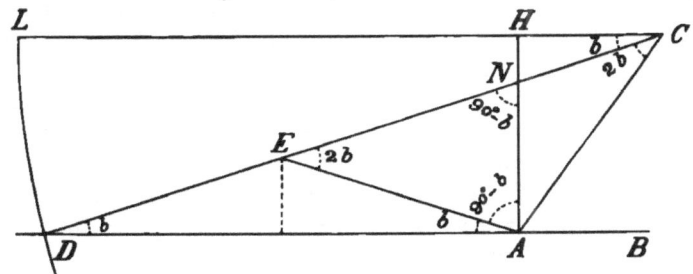

Fig. 1.

parallel lines, LH and DB. Let the line AC cross them. It is required to trisect either of the equal angles LCA or CAB. From A draw the perpendicular AH. Take $LH = 2AC$. Use a ruler longer than LC. Place the ruler in the position LHC, and let it turn about C as a centre, only with this proviso, that the point H must slide along HA, so that the part of the ruler to the left of AH shall always be equal to LH. Then the point L describes the conchoid. And when the ruler comes to the position DC, one-third of the angle at C is cut off. Here is the proof.

E is the middle point of the hyypotenuse ND. A perpendicular dropped from E will strike the middle point of AD: wherefore the lines ED, EN, EA and AC are all equal, and AED and AEC are isosceles triangles. The angles LCD, CDA and EAD are all equal and are marked b. The angles AEC and ACE are also equal to each other, and each one is equal to $2b$. Now it is plain that the line CD cuts off one-third of the angle LCD. And this is the old method of Nicomedes, now nearly 22 centuries old.

I will now show that Mr. Tennison's solution is identical with this. Here is his figure with two additional lines AH and CL, respectively

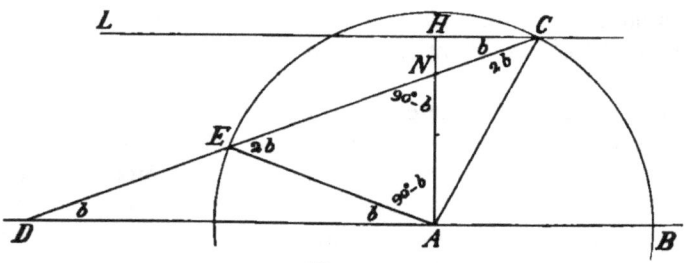

Fig. 2.

perpendicular and parallel to DB. Equal angles are marked with the same letter. Two angles more are also marked, viz., ENA and EAN, each the complement of b. The angle EAN is shown by the figure to be $90° - b$. This angle added to the angle at E ($2b$), and the sum taken from $180°$ will give the remaining angle at N, thus $2b + 90° - b$ from $180°$ leaves $90° - b$. Wherefore $EN = EA = AC = ED$; so E is the middle point of ND, the same as in Fig. 1. Wherefore the circle merely shows the middle point of ND, which is, however, better found at once by mere bisection. AED and AEC are isosceles triangles, for the radii are equal, DE was made equal to the radius, and EN is proved equal to AE. And now as in Fig. 1, you see at once that the line CD cuts off one-third of the angle LCA. Mr. Tennison revolves the line CD about C the same as in Fig. 1. I have shown that $DN = 2AC$

= LH, and the construction is in both cases the same, except that Mr. Tennison omitted the curve between L and D, but used the point D, the only point concerned in the trisection. I think then that I may be allowed to write Q. E. D., and these letters may be freely translated as meaning "this thing was demonstrated a long time ago."

R. W. McFarland,
formerly Professor of Mathematics and C. E.,
Ohio State University.

Raton, New Mex.

I notice in the July number of The Compass a solution of the "trisection of an angle."

Refraining to detract any of the honor belonging to Mr. O. M. Tennison of New Orleans, but in behalf of my research in October 1891, when Assistant in Mathematics and Engineering in the Missouri State School of Mines, I prepared the following, which I intended publishing in "Scientia Baccalaureus," a publication of said school. The publication of Scientia Baccalaureus was, however, suspended about that time, and under pressure of school work, my article was almost forgotton, until I saw the solution by Mr. Tennison in your July issue.

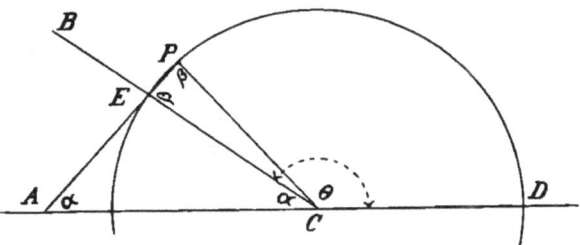

Fig. 3.

In above figure let BCD be any angle required to be trisected. Produce CD indefinitely and with any convenient radius as CD describe a circumference cutting BC at E. Draw $AP =$ Radius CD, passing through E and terminating in the circumference at P, and connect PC. Now APC and PCE are isosceles triangles: hence

$$\text{Angle } \Theta = \alpha + 180° - \beta \dots \dots \dots \dots \dots (1)^*$$
$$\text{and angle } \beta = 180° - 2\alpha \dots \dots \dots \dots \dots (2)$$

Substituting (2) value of β in (1)

$$\text{Angle } \Theta = \text{Angle } 3\alpha.$$

You will see that the equations given above (1) and (2) satisfy every

---

* Note. Angles α are PAC and PCA.

condition from 0° to 360°. Remembering that angle β is that angle included between the outside radius (always terminating in the point P) and the auxilliary radius $P\,C$, it matters not whether P falls to the right or left of E, or below the diameter.

Thus, when $\beta = 180° = 180° - 2\,\alpha$, from (2) then $\alpha = 0$ and also from (1) angle $\Theta = 0$.

If we put $\beta = 90° = 180° - 2\,\alpha$,

$$\text{then } \alpha = 45° \text{ and angle } \Theta = 135°.$$

Also if $\beta = 0 = 180° - 2\,\alpha$,

$$\text{then } \alpha = 90° \text{ and angle } \Theta = 270°, \text{ and so on.}$$

The equations are perfectly general and figures may be constructed to trisect any angle from 0° to 360°.

F. A. JONES, C.E., M.E.

GLOSSARY AND DEFINITIONS OF TERMS EMPLOYED IN SURVEYING, ASTRONOMY, ETC. III.

AZIMUTH. Arabic, *as-samt*, plural *as-summût*, a way or path. The azimuth of a celestial body is the *arc of the horizon* (measured in degrees, minutes, etc.), included between a vertical plane passing through the given body, the zenith and the nadir, and the plane of the observer's meridian; it is also consequently the *angle* formed at the zenith or at the centre of the earth by the intersection of these two planes. The circle in the celestial sphere formed by a plane thus passing through a given point, the zenith and the nadir, is called an azimuth or a vertical circle. The horizontal limb of an engineer's transit, when leveled, gives azimuth angles, hence, to turn a transit telescope on its vertical axis is frequently designated as turning it "in azimuth", just as revolving the telescope on its horizontal axis, is termed revolving it in altitude.

BAROMETER. Gr. *baros*, weight, and *metron*, measure. An instrument graduated so as to indicate the weight or the pressure of the atmosphere, and by induction, the consequent and expected changes of weather, and also the differences of altitude of positions on the earth's surface varying in elevation. They are generally mercurial or aneroid; in the former the atmosphere acts upon a column of mercury, and in the latter upon a vacuous metallic box having flexible sides.

BINOCULAR. Lat. *bini*, two and two, and *oculus*, eye. A binocular Telescope, Field Glass or Microscope is one in which, by a special arrangement, an object may be viewed with both eyes at once.

CALIPER. Lat. *qua libra*, of what pound, of what weight; applied first to the weight, and hence to the diameter of a cylindrical or spherical object. It is sometimes written caliber. Calipers are generally a kind of specially shaped dividers, by which the exact thickness of a metal plate, bar, etc., may be gaged.

CALORIFIC. Lat. *calor*, heat, and *facere*, to make. Solar rays are composed of three different elements, namely the luminous or *light* rays, the calorific or *heat* rays, and the chemical or *actinic* rays.

CATOPTRICS. Gr. *katoptrike* from *kata*, from, and *oran*, to see. That branch of optics which specially treats of light rays reflected from plane or curved surfaces, such as mirrors, prisms, etc.

CENTROLINEAD. Lat. *centrum*, centre, and *linea*, a line. An instrument employed for drawing the vanishing lines in a perspective drawing, when the vanishing point is situated beyond the sheet of the drawing paper.

CHROMATIC. Gr. *chromatikos*, from *chroma*, color. In optics the chromatic dispersion is the dispersion by means of a lens of each several ray of light proceeding from a distant object into rays of different colors, each one being refracted at a different angle and having consequently a different focus. (See ABERRATION and ACHROMATIC.)

CLINOMETER. Gr. *klinein*, to incline, and *metron*, measure. An instrument by means of which slopes or grades are determined, whether in degrees, rate per cent, or inches per yard, etc.

COLLIMATION. Lat. *collimare*, to aim. The line of collimation of a telescope is an imaginary line passing through the optical axis of the objective and the point of intersection of the cross hairs at the common focus of the objective and eye-piece. To make the optical axis of the telescope coincide with the point of intersection of the cross hairs is therefore termed adjusting the telescope for collimation.

COLLIMATOR. Lat. as above. An apparatus specially devised to determine errors of collimation in engineering and astronomical instruments.

COLURE. Gr. *kolouros*, dock-tailed. In astronomy the colures are two great circles whose planes, which are at right angles to each other, pass through and intersect each other at the poles of the equator. One of these circles, called the *equinoctical colure*, intersects the celestial equator at the equinoctical points V and U_1 (Plate I), and the other, called the *solstitial colure*, intersects the equator at the summer and winter solstices, that is, the points H and C.

"COPYRIGHT, 1892, BY WILLIAM COX, NEW YORK."

A Monthly Journal for Engineers, Surveyors, Architects, Draughtsmen and Students.

Vol. III. NOVEMBER 1, 1893. No. 4.

THE SOLAR TRANSIT. III.

IT IS NECESSARY that we should now devote a little space to the question of time, as this is a factor which enters more or less into every astronomical computation.

TIME, as we know it in the daily routine of our ordinary life, consists of consecutive days, each one divided into 24 hours of equal length; it is not, however, thus divided by the apparent motions of either the stars or the sun.

A DAY is that period of time which is occupied by the earth in making one revolution upon its axis. It is measured by the interval of time which elapses between two successive passages of the sun or a star across the observer's meridian, every such interval being divided into 24 *hours* of 60 *minutes* each, each minute being again subdivided into 60 *seconds*.

If the motions of the earth were confined to its continuous and regular rotation upon its axis, then the interval between successive passages or TRANSITS of the sun or a star would be equal, but owing to the annual motion of the earth and its consequent daily varying position in its elliptical orbit (which corresponds to the great circle of the celestial sphere apparently traveled over by the sun, called the *Ecliptic*,) this interval varies in duration. The stars being infinitely distant, this variation is, however, inappreciable, and the interval of time between two successive transits of a star is considered as a fixed quantity; but in the case of the sun, there is a very appreciable and variable variation in the interval between its successive passages across the observer's meridian, in consequence of which the length of a day as fixed by this luminary is not a fixed quantity.

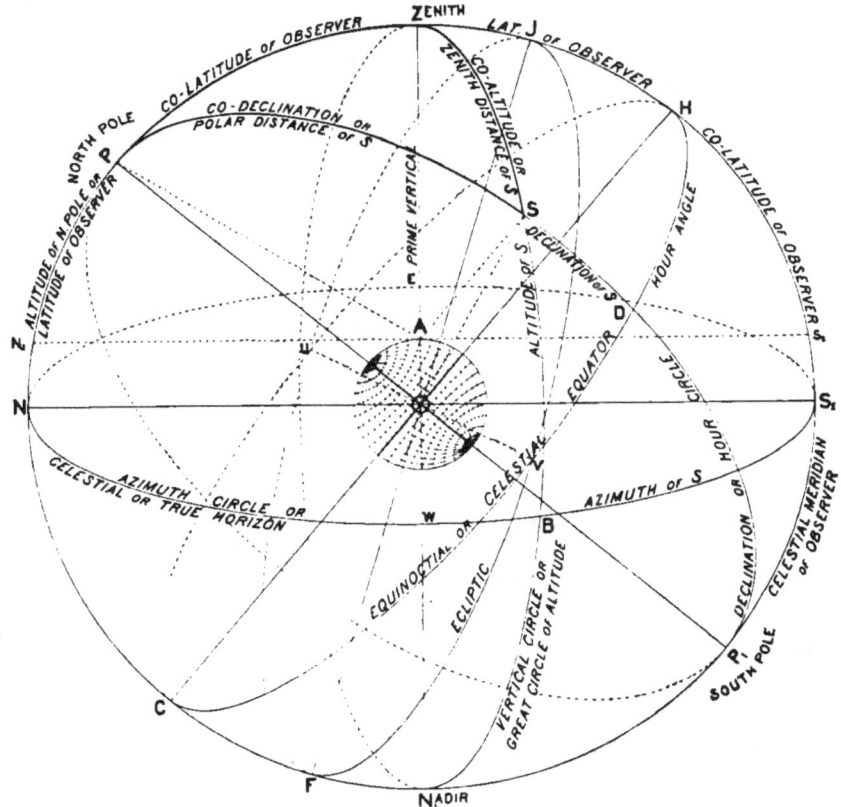

We have, therefore, by reason of the apparent *regular* motion of the stars, a SIDEREAL DAY, and by reason of the apparent *irregular* motion of the sun, a TRUE OR APPARENT SOLAR DAY.

As it would be impossible to regulate mundane affairs and the march of time by a body whose motions are apparently erratic, recourse is had to a fictitious or imaginary sun, whose motions are supposed to be perfectly regular and uniform, which is termed a MEAN SUN; the interval between two successive passages of this supposed luminary across the observer's meridian constituting a MEAN SOLAR DAY, also divided into 24 hours.

As a consequence of these days of various duration, we have also Time with various units of value, thus SIDEREAL TIME, TRUE OR APPARENT SOLAR TIME, and MEAN SOLAR TIME, the absolute value of one hour being different in each case. The difference between Mean Solar Time and Apparent Solar Time is called the EQUATION OF TIME, the difference being sometimes *plus* and sometimes *minus*, but our clocks and watches are regulated to give mean solar time.

The comparative values of mean solar and sidereal time are shown by the following relations according to Bessel.

365.24222 Mean Solar Days = 366.24222 Sidereal Days, whence

$$1 \text{ Mean Solar Day} = \frac{366.24222}{365.24222} \text{ Sidereal Days}$$

$$= 1.00273791 \text{ Sidereal Days};$$

and

$$1 \text{ Sidereal Day} = \frac{365.24222}{366.24222} \text{ Mean Solar Day}$$

$$= 0.99726957 \text{ Mean Solar Day};$$

so that

24 Hours Mean Solar Time = 24^h 3^m $56^s.555$ Sidereal Time

and

24 Hours Sidereal Time = 23^h 56^m $4^s.091$ Mean Solar Time,

whence 1 Mean Solar Day is 3^m $55^s.91$ longer than a Sidereal Day, reckoned in mean solar time, and 3^m $56^s.55$ longer than a Sidereal Day, reckoned in sidereal time, from which we have

1 Mean Solar Hour = 1 Sidereal Hour + $9^s.8565$,

and

1 Sidereal Hour = 1 Mean Solar Hour − $9^s.8296$,

= 59^m $50^s.1704$ Solar Time.

These values are required for the reduction of sidereal to mean time, also for the reduction of sidereal time at Greenwich to sidereal time at any other place whose longitude is known.

As it is, however, impossible to note the passage of a "mean" or imaginary sun across the observer's meridian, we are obliged to make use of the REAL sun, and by observation of that body, ascertain noon of apparent time, which is then reduced to mean time by the addition or subtraction of a small quantity, known as the EQUATION OF TIME. In popular almanacs this difference is frequently denoted as "Sun after the clock," and "Sun before the clock." In astronomical almanacs, such as the "American Nautical Almanac," published regularly several years in advance, by the authority of the Secretary of the Navy, (price 50 cents) the equation of time to be added to or subtracted from both apparent time and mean time are given for every day in the year, with differences for each hour, so that having obtained by observation the exact moment of the sun's transit, the correction for mean time is easily applied. Tables are also appended for the reduction of sidereal into mean solar time and vice versa.

The Hour Angle, t, ($=$ Arc HD) is equivalent to terrestrial longitude, and although set off in degrees, minutes, etc., is required to be known in hours, minutes, etc., of time; the same also with Right Ascension, r, ($=$ Arc VD). As the earth makes a complete revolution upon its axis in 24 hours, we have

$$360 \text{ degrees} = 24 \text{ hours,}$$

whence we have the proportion

$$360° : 24^h :: t \text{ or } r \text{ in degrees}; t \text{ or } r \text{ in time.}$$

Or we may say

$$360° = 24^{\text{hours}}$$
$$15° = 1$$
$$15' = 0 \quad 1^{\text{minute}}$$
$$15'' = 0 \quad 0 \quad 1^{\text{second}}$$

also

$$1° = 0 \quad 4^{\text{minutes}}$$
$$1' = 0 \quad 0 \quad 4^{\text{seconds}}$$
$$1'' = 0 \quad 0 \quad 0 \quad 4^{\text{thirds}}$$

from which conversions from one to the other are very easily made, either arithmetically or by the slide rule.

It now remains for us to refer to CIVIL TIME and ASTRONOMICAL TIME. The former is that which we use in our ordinary intercourse with our fellow beings. The day, which commences at midnight, is divided into two periods of 12 hours each, counted from 0 to 12, but the former is designated as A. M. (*ante-meridiem* or before noon), while the latter is designated as P. M. (*post-meridiem* or after noon).

The astronomical day comprises but one period of 24 hours, counted from 0 to 24; it commences at noon of the civil day of the same date. The twelve hours A. M. of the civil day correspond therefore to the hours 12 to 24 of the preceding astronomical day, and the twelve hours P. M. of the civil day correspond to the hours 0 to 12 of the same astronomical day. We thus have for example,

Civil Time.   *Astronomical Time.*
October 8th, 4 A. M. $=$ October 7th, 16 h.
"   8th, 4 P. M. $=$ "   8th, 4 h.

Both civil time and astronomical time are mean time, the value of an hour in each being the same. The connection of each with a given date requires however to be borne in mind when making astronomical computations.

The following rules for the reduction of civil time to astronomical, and vice versa, are deduced from the foregoing.

1. If civil time is A. M., take one from the date, and add 12 to the hours.
2. If civil time is P. M., the date and hour are the same for astronomical time.
3. If astronomical time is greater than 12 hours, add one to the date, deduct 12 hours, and affix the sign A. M.
4. If astronomical time is less than 12 hours, the civil time is same date and hour, with the sign P. M.

VERNIERS IV.

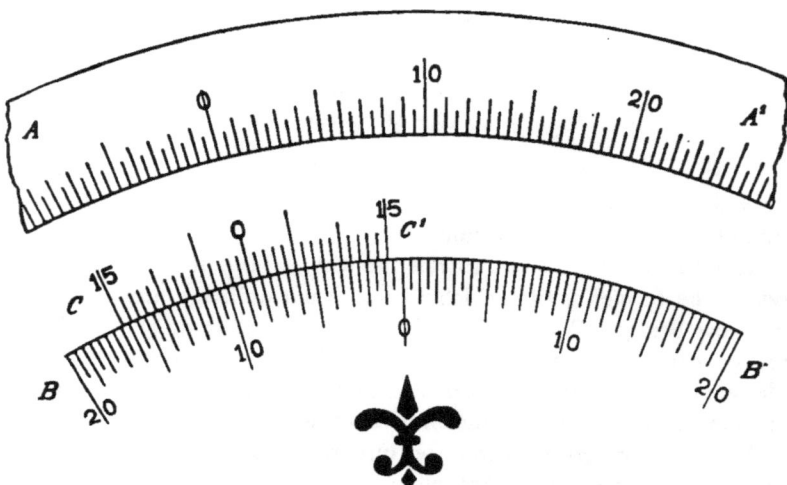

A VERNIER SOMETIMES met with is that shown in above figure which represents the general arrangement of a double vernier, as applied to the latest and most approved form of Transits and Surveyors' Compasses for the purpose of setting off the magnetic declination. In the figure the scale $A A^1$ is a portion of the compass graduated circle, $B B^1$ is a declination arc of 40 degrees, and $C C^1$ is the vernier reading into the same.

As in previous examples we note the following points:—

1st. The declination arc BB^1 is divided to half-degrees, and these are numbered both ways from zero in the centre to 20 at each end.

2nd. The vernier $C C^1$ is divided into 30 equal parts, the central division being numbered zero, while the extreme divisions are each numbered 15; it is therefore a double-folded vernier and serves for right or left-hand angles.

3rd. Thirty divisions of the vernier correspond to 31 divisions of the arc, consequently it is a retrograde vernier, reading to single minutes.

The mode of reading such a vernier is to follow the vernier divisions *backwards*, and if no coinciding lines are met with, turn to the opposite 15 and proceed towards the central zero until coinciding lines are found. In the figure the reading is 8°34'.

It is, however, not usual now to place retrograde verniers on Surveyors' compasses of the most modern type, but to use an ordinary double folded vernier as shown in Fig. 5 of our September issue. We have introduced it here merely so that our readers should be acquainted with it.

The figure therefore, as stated, represents the arrangement of Keuffel & Esser Co.'s improved Transit and Surveying Compasses with declination plate. The compass ring with the graduated circle $A A^1$ is made movable and can be partially revolved on the bottom plate of the compass box by means of a rack and pinion placed beneath the top plate of the transit or the compass plate. The pinion shaft is provided with a small capstan-head with holes to receive an adjusting pin, by which it may be turned and the compass ring proportionately revolved as desired. This mode of adjustment is much more delicate than the ordinary method with a milled thumbnut, and has the further advantage that the rack and pinion being placed under the plate instead of above it, are protected from rain and dirt. The vernier $C C^1$ is on the inner vertical portion of the compass ring, and reads into the small graduated arc $B B^1$ on the bottom plate of the compass box.

It is well known that the magnetic needle does not, except in a few favored localities, point to the true North. In the North-Eastern States it points more or less to the West of true North, while in the Southern and Western States it points to the East of true North, the divergence amounting in the extreme North-East and North-West to about 20 degrees. Were this divergence in any given locality at all times the same, it would present comparatively few difficulties, but the *declination* of the magnetic needle is subject to variations of different kinds and amount, which at times baffle the surveyor. The *changes* in the angle formed by the true meridian and the direction of the magnetic needle are called the *variations* of the declination. These variations are different in kind and degree, but the one which concerns surveyors most is what is termed the *secular variation*, whose wanderings have been, as the result of most extensive observations, reduced to something like system.

When the North end of the magnetic needle points to the West of true North, the declination is called WEST, and when it points to the East of true North, it is called EAST, the sign $+$ (plus) being used in the former case, and the sign $-$ (minus) in the latter.

In order that the surveyor may not have to correct all his bearings for the declination, compasses and transits fitted up with all improvements, are provided with an arrangement by means of which the declination may be set off on the graduated circle, as already described. If the declination is West, then the compass ring must be turned towards the *left* the exact amount of the declination, as read off by the declination arc and the vernier. If it is East, the compass ring must be similarly turned round towards the *right*, or as the hands of a watch revolve. Thus, the reading of the figure is 8°34' West, which is about the declination for New York for the year 1893, so that when the *sights* are directed to read 8°34' W., the zero of the compass graduated circle will be in line with the North end of the needle; the real direction sighted is therefore true North.

We have described and illustrated circular scales and verniers reading from 10 minutes to single minutes. The latter is the fineness of reading most usual, but naturally in some cases closer work is required. We have therefore for such scales and verniers readings to 30, 20 and 10 seconds, the principles in all being the same as those described.

The following list gives full particulars of the different methods of graduating the circle and the vernier, with the corresponding smallest readings of the vernier.

Reading of the Scale.	Divisions of the Scale.		Divisions of the Vernier.	Reading of the Vernier.
Degrees,	5	=	6	10 minutes
"	9	=	10	6 "
"	11	=	12	5 "
30 minutes,	9	=	10	3 "
30 "	29	=	30	1 "
15 "	14	=	15	1 "
20 "	39	=	40	30 seconds.
15 "	44	=	45	20 "
10 "	59	=	60	10 "

THE COLUMBIAN EXPOSITION.

We present to our readers on the opposite page a view of Keuffel & Esser Co.'s Exhibit at the above, in the Liberal Arts Building. All the goods there displayed have been manufactured at their factories at Hoboken, N. J., and well illustrate what native industry is capable of.

To the left in the foreground is a mammoth Engineer's Transit, 8 feet high without tripod. The instrument is perfect in all its details, having a portion of its 54 inch horizontal limb accurately divided to single minutes. This transit, which is of wood, was specially made in such proportions, so that the distinctive features and improvements, which they have devised and applied to their instruments, might be more readily examined and noted.

Tastefully arranged in different parts of their exhibit are seen other transits, levels, rods, "Excelsior" tapes, etc., for field use, as well as drawing tables of various kinds and for all tastes, "Paragon" scales, T-Squares, triangles, straight edges, railroad curves, etc., for the draughting room.

In other sections of the building were also exhibited collections of many of the special instruments of which the firm are the sole importers, such as the "Paragon" drawing instruments, which have obtained such merited success in this country.

It is gratifying to be able to state, that up to the present time, six medals have been awarded them for their own manufactures and the articles which they control, namely,

    Engineering and Surveying Instruments,
    "Paragon" Drawing Instruments,
    German Drawing Instruments,
    K. & E. Pocket Folding Rules,
    Reckoning Machines, and
    Bubbles for Surveying Instruments,

all of which have been more or less described in these pages.

The students of the Engineering School of the University of Georgia will hereafter be taught to handle the Camera and use it as a means of surveying. It is only of recent years that much attention has been given to what may be called inverse perspective; viz: Given the picture or perspective of a landscape taken with a known lens to make from it the plan to a proper horizontal scale. The engineers of the United States army make large use of this method in securing accurate knowledge of the country around their western posts. *(Annual.)*

ADJUSTING AN ENGINEER'S LEVEL.

By E. T. Abbott, C. E., Minneapolis, Minn.

Referring to Mr. Officer's item in the October number of The Compass, regarding Level adjustments, I wish to say that he has wiped out all chance for argument when he says his method of adjustment will eliminate all instrumental errors and is more accurate than can be done by revolving and reversing the telescope in the wyes. That assertion is certainly true, but the instrument ceases to be a "Wye Level", when it cannot be accurately adjusted by the "Wye adjustment."

I am just *heretical* enough to believe that the Dumpy construction is the true and best construction for levels, the only disadvantage being the adjustment, which Mr. Officer has succinctly disposed of.

Jim Debrissey ran the location levels on the Canadian Pacific R. R. from Flat Creek to the Saskatchewan River (450 miles). I had charge of the construction of 110 miles of it, and never found the height of a stake wrong as returned by him; there were a few instances where the elevations of stations were wrongly carried out, but none in the heights of turning points or benches. The levels were run at the rate of from 3 to 8 miles per day with a 12 inch English Dumpy.

I have never seen this feat of leveling even approached for accuracy. He told me that he put the level in careful adjustment when he started and never turned a screw on it again.

I adopted his form of keeping Level notes and have rigidly adhered to it ever since and never permitted an assistant to keep notes any other way. As it may be of some interest I append the form below.

Station	B. S.	F. S.	Int. S.	H. I.	Elev.	
Bench	9.62			109.62	100.00	Water Table
1			4.62			
2			3.80			
3			2.76			
Peg	11.21	0.96		119.87	108.66	
4			8.40			
5			7.78			
Peg		8.87			111.00	
	20.83	9.83			100.00	
	9.83				11.00	
	11.00					

Therefore the difference between the sums of the Back and Fore Sights on turning point is 11.00, also the difference between elevations as carried out is 11.00, showing conclusively that the additions and subtractions by which the Instrument Height and elevations have been determined, are correct.

The elevation of the last peg (111.00) is now carried to the next page and the work goes on as before. The only points necessary to be observed are that the first Sight on each page shall be a *Back Sight*, and the last one on each page a *Fore Sight* on the Peg. The only possible chance of carrying an error along is then that of copying or carrying over the last elevation on each page wrong on the new page, but when a levelman has only one case of error to look out for instead of forty, it is inexcusable carelessness to make it.

I presume all Engineers have wrestled with the erstwhile errors in carrying out the notes, and I can say that this system will eliminate the whole trouble, and you can at once be sure when the levels do not check, that it is not in the notes.

TOPOGRAPHIC SURVEYS.

Mr. Herbert A. Ogden of the U. S. Coast and Geodetic Survey read a paper before the Civil Engineering division of the International Engineering Congress, recently held at Chicago, on "Topographic Surveys". As it contains information which may be of interest to some of our readers, we present to them the following abstract of it, taken from the columns of *Engineering News.*

The paper discussed briefly the methods of foreign topographic surveys and described quite fully the various topographic surveys in the United States. The main topographic survey in this country is the well known Geological Survey established in 1878. The Coast Survey also covers the topography of the territory immediately bordering the sea coast. In speaking of these the author states that the chief essential in securing uniform work is an established criterion to gage the efficiency of the work. Such a criterion was formulated about a year ago by a conference of topographers assembled in Washington, D. C., as follows: All topographic work is to be based upon computed triangulation. The scale hould be 1 : 30,000 except on mountain tops and flat areas with little natural detail, where the scale of 1 : 40,000 is recommended. In considering types for interior work New England was selected as representing the greatest variety of natural and artificial detail. Rules for this type were prepared and were taken as a basis for all other types, receiving such additions or modifications as were found desirable. A general topographic survey should show hills, valleys, plains, waterways, settlements and domiciles. These may be subdivided in ways that will naturally suggest themselves. For the New England States the contour interval was taken at 20 ft. The heights of hills are to be given within 5 ft.

The cost of topographic surveys varies, of course, with the amount of detail. The average cost of the Ordnance Survey of Great Britain on a scale of 1 : 25,000 is $186 per sq. mile. In Germany the cost is $79 and in Austria about $400 per sq. mile on the same scale. In India the costs on scales of 1 in., 2 ins. and 6 ins. to the mile were $11, $26 and $400 per sq. mile, respectively. In the United States the geological survey of Massachusetts, Connecticut and Rhode Island has cost $13, $9.80 and $9. per sq. mile respectively. The topographic work of the Mississippi River Commission cost for hydrographic work $48 per sq. mile, and the topographic work of the Coast Survey and the Survey of the Great Lakes, involving many intricate details, cost on an average $151 per sq. mile. It is probable that the survey of the whole United States on scales of 1 : 30,000 and 1 : 40,000 could be conducted on the rules laid down by the conference before mentioned at an average cost of from $35 to $45 per sq. mile.

Probably the most important advances which have been made in topographic surveying in this country have been improvements in the methods of using the plane table. The first of these was the development of the graphic method of finding a position from three other determined positions known as the three-point problem. Another advance was in substituting contour lines for hachures to indicate differences in level. The method of topographic work on the Coast Survey has now reached a development that requires only experience on the part of the topographers to produce results sufficiently accurate for all the ordinary purposes of a topographic survey.

Mr. F. Stebben, of Cologne, Germany, in a paper presented to the International Engineering Congress, held recently at Chicago, discusses the principles to be observed in laying out cities. Inter alia, he says, "City traffic demands the laying out of radial, ring, diagonal and by-streets, as well as business squares and focal points. A mere rectangular system is unfit for a street plan." We think that such an arrangement is both more pleasing and more convenient; it is certainly less monotonous.

BOOKS RECEIVED.

REPORT OF THE COMMISSIONER OF EDUCATION for the year 1889-90. Volumes I and II.

BENJAMIN FRANKLIN AND THE UNIVERSITY OF PENNSYLVANIA, Edited by Francis Newton Thorpe, Ph. D., Professor of American Constitutional History in the University of Pennsylvania.

ABNORMAL MAN, being essays on Education and Crime and related Subjects, with Digests of Literature and a Bibliography. By Arthur MacDonald, Specialist in the Bureau of Education.

AERONAUTICS. New York: American Engineer and Railroad Journal. Vol. 1, No. 1, October 1893. Price, 10 cts. per Copy, Annual subscription, $1.

An International Conference on Aerial Navigation formed one of the series of congresses recently held in Chicago. The meetings, August 1, 2, 3 and 4, were successful beyond expectation, and the papers, of which some 45 were contributed, were of great interest to those who have any concern in the fascinating subject of aerostation. They covered many of the problems of aeronautics and aviation, and presented the observations and results of experiments of experts who are eminent as scientific men, or experienced engineers, or both.

At the conclusion of the Conference the papers and proceedings were placed at the disposal of Mr. M. N. Forney, the editor of the *American Engineer and Railroad Journal* for publication if he saw fit. As the interest in the subject is increasing so rapidly, it was considered desirable to have the proceedings of the conference made accessible to all; hence the appearance of this new monthly periodical, which will not only preserve a record of the papers and proceedings, but will also give each month the latest accessible notes, news and information about aeronautical engineering, with reports of experiments, investigations, and illustrations of new inventions, etc.

The names of the authors of the papers presented to the conference, are sufficient guarantee that the subject will be discussed by those who are competent to do so, and that it will be taken out of the ranks of "Crankdom".

THE ENGINEERING SOCIETY ANNUAL, Vol. I, 1893, published by the Engineering Society of the University of Georgia.

That the Engineering School of this University is determined to make its influence known and felt, is proved not only by the records of its graduates since entering upon their active life avocations, but also by the present effort put forth by the members of its Engineering Society. The annual contains some fifteen papers on various topics bearing upon the practical work of the Civil Engineer. We wish the Society success, and hope to have the pleasure of perusing many subsequent issues of its annual.

PILES AND PILE-DRIVING. New York. Engineering News Publishing Co. 1893. Price 50 cents.

This is a reprint of some of the more important articles which have appeared in *Engineering News* since December 29, 1888, when, what has since become known as the "Engineering News Formula," as applicable to ordinary pile-driving, was announced. It is as follows:—

"The maximum or ultimate bearing power which is a CERTAINLY UNSAFE load, in the sense that experience shows that piles will rarely bear this load (or any close approach to it), for any length of time without settling, is given by the formula:

$$M = \frac{12\,w\,h}{s+1}$$ in which

$M =$ the maximum or ultimate bearing power by any unit of weight.
$w =$ the weight of hammer in the same unit.
$h =$ the fall of hammer in feet.
$s =$ the set of pile under last blow in inches, and
$1 =$ a constant which is made necessary by the fact that there is an extra initial resistance in getting a pile under way, and is intended to give the nearest feasible equivalent for the effect of that extra resistance in modifying the mean resistance to penetration. With individual piles it may or may not be a little more or less.

"The safe or working load for piles, i. e., the load which it is CERTAINLY SAFE to place upon a pile under all conditions, except as below defined and limited, is shown by experience to be not over one-sixth of the above ultimate load, i. e.:

$$\text{Safe load} = \frac{2\,w\,h}{s+1} = \frac{M}{6}$$

in which the symbols have the same values as in the prior formula."

This formula is then explained and defended in response to criticisms which have been made adverse to its general adoption.

The book also includes a reprint of a valuable pamphlet on "Bearing Piles," by Rudolph Hering, M. Am. Soc. C. E, and a full abstract of a paper by Mr. Foster Crowell before the American Society of Civil Engineers on "Uniform Practice in Pile Driving", with the discussions thereon.

GLOSSARY AND DEFINITIONS OF TERMS EMPLOYED IN SURVEYING, ASTRONOMY, ETC. IV.

COMPLEMENT. Lat. *complementum*, from *complere*, to fill. In mathematics the complement of an angle is the difference between the angle and 90 degrees, as the *supplement* is the difference between the angle and 180 degrees. Thus in Astronomy, the Polar Distance of a star is its Co-Declination, or the Complement of the Declination, and the Zenith Distance of a star is its Co-Altitude or the Complement of the altitude. In Plate I therefore, $PS + SD = 90°$. In Trigonometry the sine or the tangent of an angle is the same as the cosine or the cotangent of the complement of the angle, thus, sine $30° =$ cosine $60°$.

CONCAVE. Lat. *concavus*, from *con*, with, and *cavus*, hollow. A hollowed or rounded-out surface, as in a concave lens. It is the opposite of convex.

CONCENTRIC. Lat. *concentricus*, having a common centre. Several circles having a common centre are said to be concentric. In a transit the different centres or sleeves revolve concentrically with each other, and all of them around their common central spindle, this spindle revolving around a common central axis. (*The axis of a revolving body is a geometrical straight line composed of length without breadth.*)

CONJUGATE. Lat. *conjugatus*, from *con* and *jugare*, to join. In optics when converging rays, or rays which proceed towards one point, are intercepted by a convex lens, they are refracted so as to converge to a point or focus nearer the lens than its principal focus. As the point of convergence of the rays recedes from the lens, the point to which the rays are refracted also recedes from it; and as the point of convergence of the rays approaches the lens, the point to which the rays are refracted also approaches it. The point of convergence of the natural rays, and the point of convergence of the refracted rays are called the *conjugate foci*, because the place of the one varies with that of the other.

CONJUNCTION. Lat. *conjunctis*, the state of being conjoined. In astronomy two celestial bodies are said to be in conjunction when they are seen in nearly the same part of the heavens, or when they have the same longitude or right ascension.

CO-ORDINATES. Lat. *con* and *ordinare*, to regulate. They are two lines by means of which the exact location of a point may be determined with reference to two other known and fixed lines, called the co-ordinate *axes*, whose point of intersection is the *origin* of the co-ordinates. Distances, termed *abscissæ* and *ordinates*, are laid off on the axes respectively, and lines parallel to each of the latter are drawn from the points of these distances, the point of their intersection being the point whose location is required. *Rectangular* co-ordinates have all their lines straight lines, at right angles to each other, and in the same plane. *Spherical* co-ordinates are such by means of which the position of a point on the surface of a sphere may be determined.

CONSTELLATION. Lat. *con*, together, and *stella*, a star. Groups or clusters of stars designated by the names of animals or other terrestrial objects, to which they are supposed to bear some resemblance.

CONTOUR. French, *contour*, a bounding line, the periphery. Contour lines are a series or system of lines on a topographical map by means of which the irregularities of the earth's surface are represented by equidistant (in a vertical sense) level planes, whose boundaries they indicate. They were introduced by the Geographer Philip Bauche, in 1744.

CONVERGE. Lat. *con*, and *vergere*, to turn or incline. Converging lines or rays are those which proceed from different points of an object in such directions that they tend to meet together in one common point.

CONVEX. Lat. *convexus*, from *convehere*, to bring together. A convex surface is a spherical surface as viewed from the outside, as opposed to a concave one, which is a similar surface, but as viewed from the inside. The former is a protusion, the latter a cavity.

CULMINATION. Lat. *culmen*, the top. It is the passage of a celestial body across the observer's meridian. Circumpolar stars culminate twice a day; the sun and stars, whose polar distance is greater than the observer's latitude, culminate but once.

CURVATURE. Lat. *curvatus*, from *curvare*, to bend, to curve. The continuous bending away or departure of a line from the direction of a straight line. In leveling, when the distance gone over is considerable, the *apparent* difference of level between the two points has been obtained, and this has to be corrected for the earth's curvature in order to obtain the *true* difference of level.

DECLINATION. Lat. *declinare*, to lean from, to incline. The declination of a celestial body is its angular elevation or depression, measured north or south from the equinoctial or celestial equator, on the circle of declination or hour circle passing through the body ($= S D$, Plate I). It is also the complement of the polar distance of the body measured on the same declination circle. Declination corresponds to terrestrial latitude.

"COPYRIGHT, 1892, BY WILLIAM COX, NEW YORK."

A Monthly Journal for Engineers, Surveyors, Architects, Draughtsmen and Students.

Vol. III.   DECEMBER 1, 1893.   No. 5.

LIGHT: ITS REFLECTION AND REFRACTION. XII.

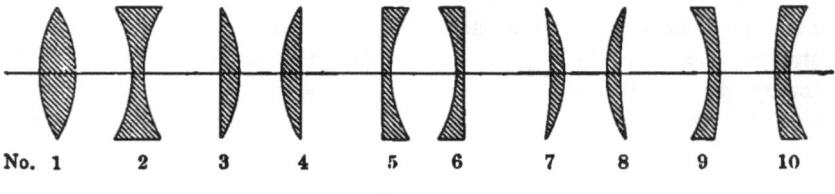

Fig. 1.

HAVING EXAMINED the principles governing the refraction of rays of light by prisms, we now come to the consideration of lenses. A lens is a piece of glass or other medium having two opposite regular surfaces, either both spherical, or one spherical and the other plane.

Sections of the various forms of lenses are shown in above figure, in which the rays of light are supposed to proceed from the left to the right; their designations are as follows:—

1. Double convex, having two convex spherical surfaces, their centres being on opposite sides of the lens.

2. Double concave, having two concave spherical surfaces whose centres are on opposite sides of the lens.

3 and 4. Plano-convex and convexo-plane, (according to the side which receives the rays of light), having one side a plane and the other a convex spherical surface.

5 and 6. Plano-concave and concavo-plane, having one side a plane and the other a concave spherical surface. The first term of the designation indicates the direction from which the light proceeds.

7 and 8. Concave meniscus and convex meniscus, having one side concave and the other convex. (Greek, *meniskos*, diminutive of *mene* the moon, hence a new moon, a crescent.) The radius of the concave side is longer than that of the convex.

9 and 10. Concavo-convex and convexo-concave, having one side concave and the other convex, the radius of the convex side being longer than that of the concave.

When a lens is thicker in the middle than at the edges, as Nos. 1, 3, 4, 7 and 8, it is essentially a convex lens, but when it is thicker at the edges than in the middle, as Nos. 2, 5, 6, 9 and 10, it is essentially a concave lens. When rays forming a pencil of light pass through the former, they tend to converge; whereas when they pass through the latter, their tendency is towards divergence, because refraction always bends the rays towards the thickest part of the glass.

The law of refraction which we have already discussed in its application to the plane surfaces of prisms, (Vol. II, page 148) applies equally to the spherical surfaces of lenses, that point of the curved surface which a ray touches being virtually a plane, perpendicular to the radius of the arc which meets the surface at the point of contact of the ray.

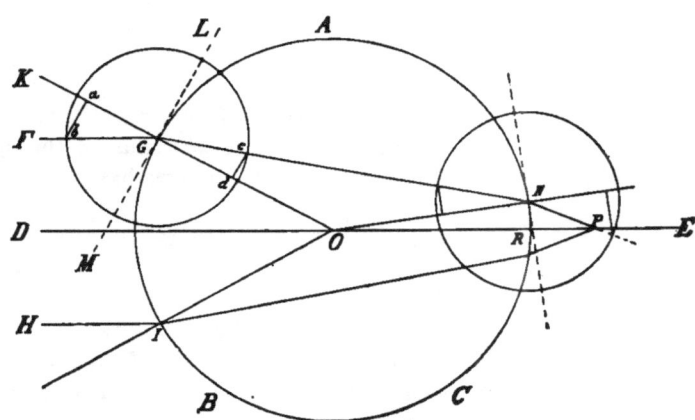

Fig. 2.

Let in above figure $A\ B\ C$ be a glass sphere whose axis is $D\ O\ E$, and let $F\ G$ and $H\ I$ be parallel rays of light falling upon the sphere at G and I, these rays being also parallel to the axis $D\ O\ E$. Let $O\ G\ K$ be a radius produced, intersecting the surface of the sphere in G, the point of contact of the ray FG, and let $L\ M$ be a plane perpendicular to OG, representing the plane of the surface of the sphere in the point G, whence KG is the normal. Supposing the index of refraction of the glass to be 1.6, we now draw $a\ b$ to be by any convenient scale equal to 1.6 or 16 parts, parallel to $L\ M$; then with G as centre and $G\ b$ as radius, describe the circle $K\ b\ c$. We next, with the same scale, lay off $c\ d$ equal to 1.0 or 10 parts, also parallel to $L\ M$, then join $G\ c$ and produce it to N on the opposite surface of the sphere. Angle $F\ G\ K$ is, therefore, the angle of incidence of the ray FG, and $O\ G\ N$ the angle of refraction, the ratio of the sine $a\ b$ of the former being to the sine $c\ d$ of the latter as 1.6 to 1.0, consequently $G\ c\ N$ is the direction of the ray of light $F\ G$ as it penetrates and traverses the sphere.

We now proceed in the same manner with the emerging ray, the ratio of the sine of the angle of incidence being to the sine of the angle of refraction (or the angle of emergence) as 1.0 is to 1.6, consequently the path of the ray on emerging from the sphere is a still greater converging one, as regards the parallel ray $H\ I$, finally meeting the axis of the sphere at the point P.

If the rays $H\ I$ and $F\ G$ are equi-distant from the axis $D\ E$, the path of the former will be similar, though reversed, to that of the latter, and it will also meet the axis of the sphere in P. This point where the rays meet after passing through the sphere is called the *focus of parallel rays*.

The rule for finding the focus of a sphere is as follows:—

Let index of refraction $= \mu$, then

$$\frac{\mu \times \text{radius}}{2\,(\mu - 1)} = \text{the distance } O\ P,$$

and $O\ P$ — radius = the axial distance of the focus from the surface of the sphere $= R\ P$. Thus, in Fig. 2, let $O\ G =$ radius of the sphere $= 1$ inch, and $\mu =$ index of refraction $= 1.6$, then we have

$$O\ P = \frac{1.6 \times 1}{2\,(1.6 - 1)} = \frac{1.6}{1.2} = 1.33$$

and $R\ P = 1.33 - 1 = 0.33$ inches.

A careful consideration of Fig. 2, and the principles which govern the direction of the paths of the rays of light $F\ G$ and $H\ I$, will make it evident that the focus of *converging* rays would be nearer to the sphere than the focus P of parallel rays, so much so even in some cases that it might be within the sphere itself, while the focus of *diverging* rays would be further from the sphere than the point P. Should the distance from the surface of the sphere of the point of emanation of the diverging rays be equal to PR, then such rays would after refraction in the sphere emerge from it in parallel lines, just as if in the figure, P were the source of the diverging rays, then the emerging rays would be indicated by FG and HI.

AN IMPROVED REFLECTOR FOR TELESCOPES.

THE ADVANTAGES of this improved form of reflector are greater efficiency and durability. It consists of an ordinary sun shade which fits on the objective end of the telescope, and within which slides a short tube to which the elliptical silvered reflector is firmly attached round its entire periphery, at an angle of 45° with the axis of the tube, instead of being merely attached to a ring by a small tongue, said ring being fitted to the objective end of the telescope. The reflector tube is kept in place by a small stop; a portion of the sun shade is cut away, as shown in the figure, to allow the rays of light to reach the reflector, and thus illuminate the cross-hairs. By this mode of construction, solidity and efficiency are obtained; and when the reflector is withdrawn the sun shade serves its ordinary purpose, the opening being turned downwards, thus doing away with the necessity of having both attachments to the telescope.

THE SOLAR TRANSIT. IV.

WE NOW COME to the consideration of the special astronomical problems with which the surveyor has to deal. These are in the main three, namely:—

To determine a true Meridian;
To ascertain apparent Time;
To obtain the Latitude.

Various methods by which a true meridian may be determined are at his disposal, such as

1. By equal Altitudes of a star;
2. By Circumpolar stars;
3. By the Polar Star;

to which, however, we shall not refer here, as in general it will be found more convenient to make use of the sun, as the observations required are simple, although the calculations are somewhat tedious.

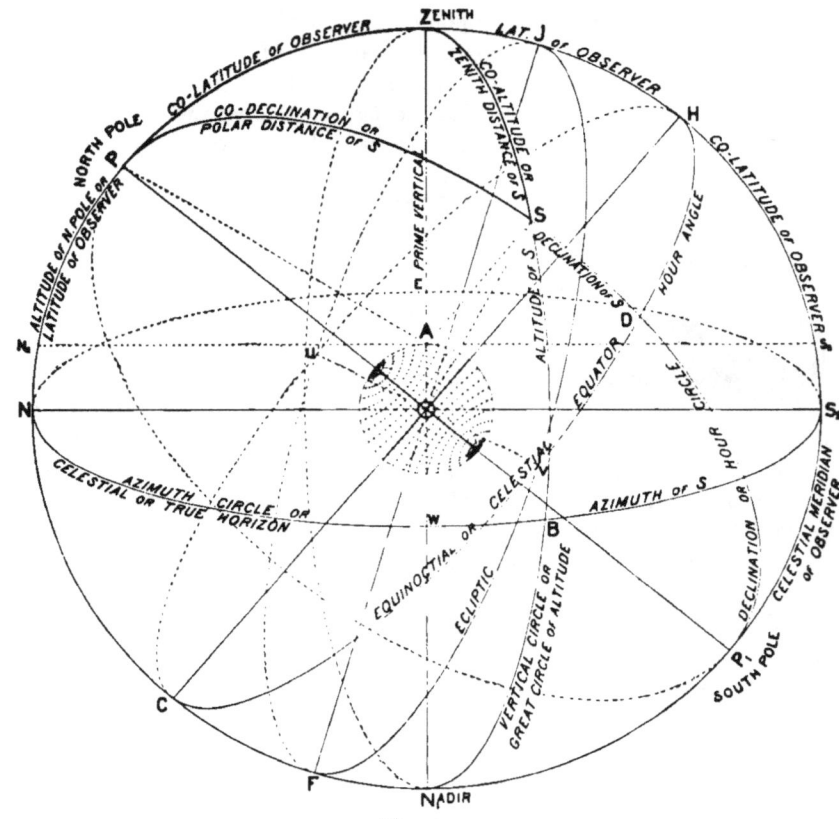

Fig. 1.

In Plate I, reproduced in Fig. 1.

the observer's co-latitude = PZ,

the Zenith Distance or co-altitude of the sun (or a star) = ZS, and

the Polar Distance or co-declination of the sun = PS,

are the three sides of the spherical triangle PZS, usually known as the *astronomical triangle*. In this triangle one side PZ, which is an arc of the observer's meridian, is common to the first and second systems of co-ordinates, while the other sides ZS and PS belong to the first and second systems respectively.

The other parts of this triangle are the angle PZS, which is the supplement of the Azimuth BZS_1;

the angle SPZ, which is the hour angle of the sun or star S; and

the angle ZSP, called the parallactic angle.

Of these six parts, certain ones can always be known, and from them the others may be computed.

The parts of the triangle PZS required to be determined for the three problems referred to are the following:—

1st. For the Meridian:—the Supplement of the Azimuth $= PZS$.
2d. For time:—the Hour Angle $= SPZ$.
3rd. For latitude:—the Co-Latitude $= PZ$.

To determine the MERIDIAN, the data given or obtainable are

1. The Latitude HZ, whence we have the Co-latitude PZ,
2. " Declination SD, " " " " Co-declination PS,
3. " Altitude SB, " " " " Co-altitude ZS,
4. " Hour Angle SPZ.

To ascertain the HOUR ANGLE the data at our disposal are

1. The Latitude HZ,
2. " Declination SD,
3. " Altitude SB,
4. " Azimuth PZS.

To obtain the Latitude, we have

1. The Declination SD,
2. " Altitude SB,
3. " Hour Angle SPZ,
4. " Azimuth PZS.

It will be seen that all these data are parts of the astronomical tri-

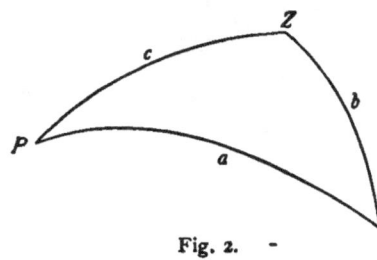

Fig. 2.

angle. In the solution of either of our problems three of them are required to be known, the computation being then performed according to the rules of spherical trigonometry. Thus, to determine the meridian we obtain the value of the angle PZS, the supplement of the Azimuth, by means of the following formula applied to the triangle ZPS.

$$\text{Cos } \tfrac{1}{2} Z = \sqrt{\frac{\text{Sin } s \times \text{Sin } (s-a)}{\text{Sin } b \times \text{Sin } c}}$$

where

$Z =$ the angle $PZS =$ the supplement of the azimuth,
$a =$ the side $PS\ \ \ =$ the co-declination,
$b =$ " " $SZ\ \ \ =$ the co-altitude,
$c =$ " " $PZ\ \ \ =$ the co-latitude,
$s = \tfrac{1}{2} (a + b + c) = \tfrac{1}{2} (PS + SZ + PZ).$

If in above formula we take $\frac{1}{\sin} = \text{cosec}$, and express the same logarithmically, we have

$$2 \log \cos \tfrac{1}{2} PZS = \log \sin s + \log \sin (s - PS)$$
$$+ \log \text{cosec } SZ + \log \text{cosec } PZ - 20.$$

EXAMPLE.* At a place in latitude 44° 12′ N, the altitude of the sun's centre, observed by means of a transit, and after the necessary corrections were made, was found to be 36° 30′, whilst its declination, taken from the Nautical Almanac and corrected for hourly change is 15° 4′ N; what is its azimuth?

The declination SD is 15° 4′, therefore the Co-declination PS	= 74° 56′
The altitude SB is 36° 30′, therefore the Co-altitude SZ	= 53° 30′
The observer's latitude is 44° 12′, therefore the Co-latitude PZ	= 45° 48′
together	= 174° 14′
whence s	= 87° 07′
and $s - PS$	= 12° 11′

The above are the necessary data, the solution being as follows,

$\log \sin s$	= 9.9994498
$\log \sin (s - PS)$	= 9.3243657
$\log \text{cosec } SZ$	= 10.0948213
$\log \text{cosec } PZ$	= 10.1445350
	39.5631718
	20.
$2 \log \cos \tfrac{1}{2} PZS$	= 19.5631718
$\log \cos \tfrac{1}{2} PZS$	= 9.7815859

whence $\qquad \tfrac{1}{2} PZS = 52° 47′ 17″.3$
and $\qquad PZS = 105° 34′ 34″.6$

which is the azimuth reckoned from the north, whence the azimuth from the south BS_1, or angle $BZS_1 = 180° - 105° 34′ 34″.6 = 74° 25′ 25″.4$.

All that is now required to bring the transit telescope into the meridian is to revolve the horizontal limb through this angle, from which the declination of the compass needle can then be easily obtained.

The sun's declination is taken from the Nautical Almanac, being given

---

* Adapted from Chamber's "Practical Mathematics."

for Greenwich mean noon. Its position thus determined is that in which it would be seen by an observer at the centre O of the earth, and is termed its *geocentric* or *true* position, whilst positions observed from the surface of the earth, as from A, are called *observed* or *apparent* positions. The declination thus obtained requires to be reduced to the corresponding declination for the place and time of observation by applying the difference for time and longitude, computed from the hourly change of declination given in the almanac.

Corrections must also be made in the altitude for refraction and parallax. As shown in Fig. 1, S is not the real position of a celestial body as seen there by an observer at A, because, owing to the increasing density of the atmosphere surrounding the earth, the rays of light, proceeding from the body S towards the earth, are bent downwards from a straight line, and their path becomes a curved one, the object being in reality nearer the horison than its apparent position, thus making its true altitude $S B$ less, and its co-altitude $S Z$, greater than that observed.

When observing the sun's altitude it is usual to direct the horizontal cross wire of the telescope upon its upper or lower limb. To this observed altitude the sun's registered semi-diameter, taken from the Nautical Almanac, must be added or substracted, according as the lower or upper limb was observed. Corrections must then be made for refraction, and when great precision is required, for contraction and parallax, (into which we shall enter more fully in a subsequent issue) in order that the geocentric or true altitude of the sun's centre may be obtained.

WORK is the product of weight into height,
    The weight to that height being lifted ;
Done slowly or fast, the same it is, quite,
    To the "underconstamblers" and gifted.
But when time and its fractions are brought into sight,
Then *work* is the wrong word, and *power* the right.

Thirty-three thousand foot-pounds by a horse
    In a minute's the usual sum ;
And sixty-six thousand foot-pounds can, of course,
    By that horse in two minutes be done ;
Then similarlee, by the Ruling of Three,
Fifty-five in a second's the tenth of a $G E E$.

J. I. B.

From letter on "Economical Speed of Steamships" in "Engineering."

A DIAMETER AND CIRCUMFERENCE SCALE.

WE DESCRIBED in a former number, (July, 1892), a steel tape for determining diameters and circumferences. The above figure shows a portion of a 12 inch fully divided boxwood scale, having on one edge a scale of inches, divided into 32nds, representing a table of diameters or circumferences, (depending upon the method of using it, as we shall show,) while the scale on the other edge gives the corresponding circumfereuces or diameters. One main division of this latter or π scale measures 3.1416 inches, and is subdivided into 128 equal parts, being equal to about 40 parts per inch, thus insuring perfect distinctness of the divisions.

The scale may be used in two ways, each graduated edge serving for either diameters or circumferences according to the method employed. Thus, if it be required to find *graphically* the length of the circumference answering to a diameter of $1\frac{1}{2}$ inches, we obtain it at once by measuring off $1\frac{1}{2}$ from the larger or π scale. If on the other hand we wish to find *arithmetically* the length of the circumference answering to the same diameter, we take the measure $1\frac{1}{2}$ from the larger or π scale, and transfer it by means of dividers or on paper, to the inch scale and at once find the circumference to be $4\frac{23}{32}$ inches. The reverse of this is as simple to work out.

This scale will be found specially useful in gearing calculations, as for example to obtain the diameter of a wheel with a given number of teeth of a required pitch; thus, what will be the diameter of a wheel with 20 teeth, the pitch being $\frac{1}{2}$ inch. We have here 10 inches circumference, which we at once find gives a diameter of $3\frac{3}{16}$ inches. This can of course be easily laid off on the drawing to other scales than the inch one, by taking the same number of fractional parts of an inch on each graduated edge of the rule.

These scales are machine divided and are U. S. Standard; they can be had with decimal divisions of an inch if desired, and in plain boxwood, or boxwood coated on the bevels with a special white substance resembling ivory, these latter being the well known PARAGON scales fully described in our issue of November, 1891.

THE DUPLEX SLIDE RULE.

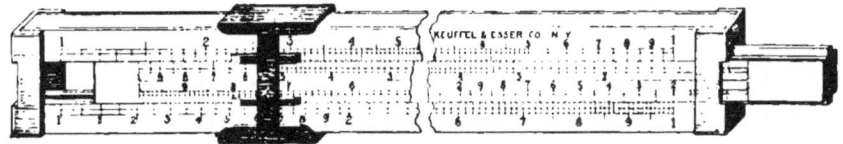

Fig. 1.

THE ABOVE FIGURE is a representation of one side of the DUPLEX SLIDE RULE, which we described in a former number of THE COMPASS, (May, 1893). The principal feature of this new slide rule is that the slide is graduated on both sides, the scales of the upper face being the same as those of the ordinary Mannheim slide rule, whilst the scales of the under face of the slide (shown in Fig. 1,) are in reversed order, the result being that when the indices are made to coincide, the coinciding numbers on the rule and slide are severally the reciprocals of each other, thus, we have on the rule 5, and opposite it on the slide 2. Now 0.2 is the reciprocal of 5, and 0.5 is the reciprocal of 2. Multiplication by the reciprocal of a number is equivalent to dividing by that number, and vice versa. The advantages of this arrangement are apparent when it is required to obtain the product of three factors, as two factors are first multiplied together by dividing by the reciprocal of one of them, the final product being then obtained by multiplying directly the first product by the third factor.

With such a slide rule, however, trigonometrical computations can only be effected by reference to a table of sines or tangents, whereas on the ordinary Mannheim slide rule, this is not necessary, as scales of sines and tangents are given on the under side of the slide. This presents, however, several inconveniences as the slide has frequently to be taken out and replaced with its under side uppermost. To obviate this and to further add to the completeness of the DUPLEX we have provided an extra slide, having on one side the ordinary logarithmic scales, and on the other side scales of sines, tangents and equal parts. When ordinary computations are to be performed, this trigonometrical slide is used, common multiplication and division being performed with one side, and the trigonometrical computations with the other, the slide meanwhile always remaining in the same position, the use of one scale or the other being effected by merely turning the rule over. To show the advantages and the simplicity of this method, let it be required to find the value of 4.5 sin² 30°.

Making all indices coincide, we set the runner to sin 30°, then bringing the right end slide index to the runner, we have over 30° the value of sin² 30°. Without moving the slide, we again set the runner to 30°, turn the rule over and bring the index to the runner, when over 4.5 on the slide we have 1.125 on the rule, which is the solution sought. The demonstration of this would be as follows:—

A ‖			‖ A		Find 1.125.
S ‖	Set R to 30°	1 to R	R to 30° ‖ B	1 to R	Over 4.5

To find the value of 4.5 tan² 30° is still simpler, thus

A ‖		‖ A		Find 1.5
S ‖		‖ B	1 to R	Over 4.5
T ‖	Set R to 30°	‖ C		
D ‖		‖ D		

The reason of this simplicity is that the square of the tangent is at once found on scale A over 30° on scale T. The same simplicity would obtain if it were required to find 4.5 $\sqrt{\sin 30°}$, the square root of sin 30° being at once got on scale D.

It will be noticed that the scale of tangents only gives angles up to 45° whose tangent is 1. To obtain the tangent of a greater angle, the complement of the angle on the slide must be brought into coincidence with the left index of the rule, when on scale D under the right index of the slide will be found the tangent required. Example:—What is the tangent of 60°?

T ‖	Set 90°—60°=30°	Under 1
D ‖	To 1	Find 1.732 = tan 60°.

The scale of sines includes angles from 34′ 23″, whose sine is 0.01, up to 90°, whose sine is 1.0, the sine of 5° 44′ 39″ which is 0.1 being found in the middle of scale A.

If the indices of the rule and slide are made to coincide, a mark will be noticed on the scale of sines coinciding with 206265 of scale A, and another one coinciding with 3438 of scale A. The first one marked " gives the value of $\frac{1}{\sin 1″}$, and the second one marked ' the value of $\frac{1}{\sin 1′}$. As the sines of very small angles are proportional to the angles themselves, their values may be easily obtained by means of these marks. Thus to find the value of 54 minutes, set the mark 34 38 of the slide opposite 54 on scale A, when over the slide index will be found 157 on scale A, the sine of 54′ being 0.0157. The value of $x \times \sin 54′$ may now be at once obtained by turning the rule over and reading the product on scale A over x on scale B.

The following table will be found very useful for determining the value of sines and tangents of different angles.

Sine or tangent 2″.062644 = 0.00001
" " 20″.62644 = 0.0001
" " 3′26″2644 = 0.001
" " 34′22″.644 = 0.01
Sine 5° 44″ 39″ = 0.1
" 90 00 00 = 1.0
Tangent 5° 42″ 38″ = 0.1
" 45 00 00 = 1.0
" 84 17 21 = 10.0

The chief value of the trigonometrical scales will, however, be found in their adaptability to the solution of triangle problems, the scale of sines being mostly used for this purpose. The well known theorem

The sides of a plane triangle are proportional to the sines of their opposite angles, that is in Fig. 2,

Side a : Sine A : : Side b : Sine B : : Side c : Sine C.

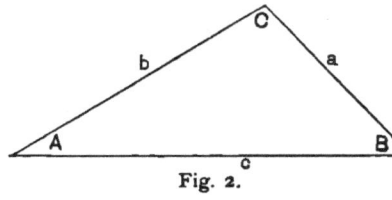

Fig. 2.

Let in the figure the side $c = 80$ feet, angle $A = 30°$ and angle $B = 40°$; we have angle $C = 180° - 70° = 110°$. Now set the known side c in coincidence with its known opposite side C, then coinciding with the angles A and B will be found the sides a and b. The angle C being more than 90°, we of course use its supplement 70° and proceed thus:

A ‖ To $c = 80$ | Find $a = 42.6$ | Find $b = 54.7$
S ‖ Set $C = 70°$ | Over $A = 30°$ | and over $B = 40°$

Should it now be wished to find the length of a perpendicular drawn from the apex of C to the base c, we have

A ‖ To $b = 54.7$ | Find 27.3 | Find 47.2
S ‖ Set 90° | Over $A = 30°$ | and over 60°

whence the perpendicular = 27.3, and the left section of the base = 47.2, the right section being 80 — 47.2 = 32.8.

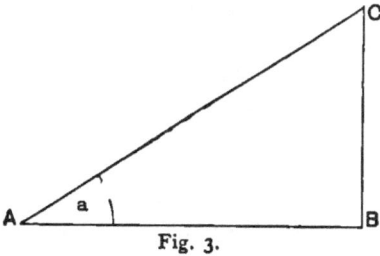

Fig. 3.

It will also be found very useful for calculating latitudes and departures in surveying, thus in Fig. 3, let distance $AC = 60$ feet, and course $a = 30°$, then

$$\begin{array}{l|ll}A\,\|&\text{To distance}=60\;|\;\text{Find lat.}=30\;|\;\text{Find dep.}=52\\ \hline S\,\|&\text{Set }90°\qquad\quad\;|\;\text{Over }a=30°\;|\;\text{Over }60°\end{array}$$

Then to find the area of the triangle $A\,B\,C$,

$$\begin{array}{l|ll}C\,\|&\text{Set }2\qquad\;\;|\;\text{Under lat.}=30\\ \hline D\,\|&\text{To dep.}=52\;|\;\text{Find area}=780\text{ sq. feet.}\end{array}$$

The DUPLEX Slide Rule may now be purchased with one or two slides as desired. The addition of the trigonometrical slide will we are confident, further increase the popularity of this valuable instrument.

DRAWING INSTRUMENTS. I.

"PENNY WISE AND POUND FOOLISH" is an old English maxim applied to those who object to pay the price for a really good article, hoping (although often with a certain feeling of distrust which they would not care to acknowledge) that the cheaper article will after all give them satisfaction. So it is in almost every thing which surrounds us,—our clothes, our homes, our victuals, and countless other objects. We have always maintained that *the best is always the cheapest in the end.*

We have already referred to this point in our pages, as applied to the selection of drawing instruments, and knowing its importance, we reiterate the advice given, namely, that if it is desired to do good and accurate work, the best instruments procurable should be used. Why? Because in mechanical or architectural drawing, just as in arithmetical computations, accuracy is the chief desideratum, and from our own experience this essential is, except with great patience, almost wholly unobtainable with second class instruments. We know that with care and considerable waste of time, many instruments, even though they be of inferior quality, can be made to do very good work, but this possibility is after all only temporary, as after a time the wearing of their parts renders them absolutely unfit for such. What advantage, therefore, is in reality gained by the temporary moderate outlay for cheap instruments when it must assuredly be superseded by a future greater one? Our opinion is decidedly and emphatically, none,—but on the contrary, loss and annoyance.

What follows is written in defense of the position we hold and with the desire to give some information as well as a few useful hints, so that disappointment may not follow the acquisition and use of drawing instruments, and with this object in view we ask our readers to follow us in making a careful comparison of a few instruments of different qualities.

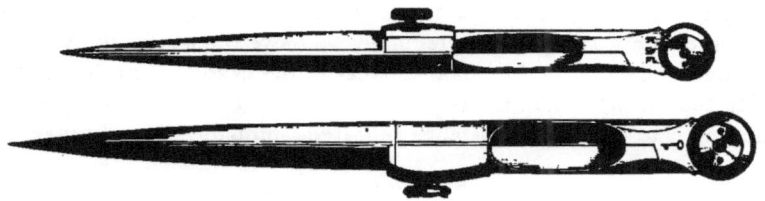

We shall begin with two German silver plain dividers or compasses, one, an honest, cheap instrument, and the other, one of the best quality. We notice then,

1st. The weight of the former is nearly half as much again as that of the latter.

2nd. The breadth and thickness of the legs of the former are at least one-fifth greater than those of the latter.

3rd. The quality of the German silver of the better instrument is clearly of the best, while that of the cheaper one is of a lower grade. The metal of the one will also be found to be harder than that of the other. The general appearance of the two shows this, but that it is so may be sufficiently demonstrated by attempting to bend them; in one case this can be done comparatively easily, while the resistance offered by the other to the attempt will be found to be considerable. Of course this difference will be much more noticeable in cheap instruments whose form and *dimensions* are made similar to those of the highest grade, as in such there is no extra quantity of metal added to compensate for what is lacking in quality. The main proof, however, of our assertion lies in the use of the instruments, the wear and tear of the frictional parts being much greater and much sooner discernible in the one than in the other.

4th. If carefully examined, the finish of the one will be seen to be finer than that of the other.

5th. If the heads are examined, it will be noticed that the surfaces of the tongue and lugs of the superior instrument fit perfectly together, however much the dividers may be opened, whilst those of the other instrument will probably present interstices of greater or lesser apparence between the three parts or plates of the head, showing that all their surfaces are not true and parallel, or that the tongue has not been properly fitted to the cavity in which it works. Further, in opening the dividers, a great difference will be observed in the smoothness with which this can be done, unequal friction of the parts, with consequent jerkiness being evident in one case, while in the other the operation is performed easily and smoothly from beginning to end without the least effort. The importance of this point cannot be over-estimated when it is desired to take off measurements from a scale or plan with great accuracy. With the best instruments variations as fine as $1/_{100}$th of an inch may be taken off with a gentle, steady pressure of the forefinger upon the leg, whereas with the cheaper dividers the pressure required to move the leg, or to overcome some unevenness of the frictional surfaces of the head, will probably close the leg too much, so that it has to be opened out again, and the operation of setting it to the correct distance repeated—probably several times.

GLOSSARY AND DEFINITIONS OF TERMS EMPLOYED IN SURVEYING, ASTRONOMY, ETC. V.

DIAGRAM. Gr. *diagramma*, from *dia*, through, and *graphein*, to draw or write. A drawing or figure which serves to present in visible form the details of a mathematical or other demonstration.

DIAMETER. Gr. from *dia*, through and *metron*, measure. A straight line which cuts a circle or sphere in two equal halves by passing through its centre and meeting the circumference on opposite sides. The term is also applied to squares and some other figures.

DIAPHRAGM. Gr. *diaphragma*, from *dia*, through, and phragnunai, to fence or inclose. In a telescope a diaphragm is a thin partition placed across and filling up its tube, with the exception of a certain circular portion in the centre, through which the rays of light pass, the peripheral solid portion cutting off the outer rays, thereby adding to the clearness and distinctness of the image produced by the inner rays. The cross hairs in the telescope of a surveyor's transit or level are attached to an adjustable diaphragm.

DIATHERMIC. Gr. *dia*, through, and *therme*, heat. Bodies are not equally pervious to light and heat, thus black mica, obsidian, and black glass in thin laminæ, although impervious to the light, are pervious to the heat of the solar rays.

DIFFRACTION. Lat. *dis*, apart, and *frangere*, to break. When light from a luminous point falls divergently upon an opaque body, the edges of this body bend the rays which pass in contact with them out of their course both inwards and outwards. This visible effect produced by the obstruction is called the diffraction of light.

DIOPTRIC. Gr. *di*, for *dia*, through, and *optein*, to see. Pertaining to dioptrics, which is that branch of optical science which treats of the laws of refraction of light when passing from one medium into another, as catoptrics treats of reflected rays.

DIPLEIDOSCOPE. Gr. *diplos*, double, *eidos*, image, and *skopein*, to view. An instrument composed of a combination of mirrors or a prism by means of which the sun's reflected rays produce two images, indicating when they coincide the transit of the sun's centre over the meridian.

DISTORTION. Lat. *distorquere, distortum*, from *dis*, apart, and *torquere*, to turn about. Used in optics to designate the deformity of the images of objects produced by a lens, by reason of the varying distances from the axis of the lens of the different portions of the object.

DIVERGE. Lat. *dis*, apart, and *vergere*, to bend, turn, or incline. Diverging lines or rays are those which proceed from a given point in different and extending directions, becoming more and more separated from one another as they recede from their point of origin.

DYNAMETER. Gr. *dunamis*, power, and *metron*, measure. An instrument consisting of a compound microscope with a finely divided scale for determining the magnifying power of telescopes.

DYNAMICS. Gr. *dunamis*, power. That branch of mechanics which treats of forces in motion, producing power and work.

ECCENTRIC. Lat. *ex*, out of, and *centrum*, centre. Said of circles corresponding more or less, and yet not having a common centre. If the axis of revolution of the different sockets or sleeves, as well as of the limbs and verniers of a transit do not coincide, these various parts are said to be eccentric, and they do not consequently give correct results. The eccentricity of an ellipse is the distance from either focus to the centre.

ECCENRTOLINEAD. Lat. *ex*, out of, *centrum*, centre, and *linea*, a line. An instrument by means of which lines may be drawn to the circumference of a circle, these lines having their origin at a given lateral distance from its centre, as the sides of the spokes of a wheel.

ECLIPSE. Gr. *ekleipsis*, from *ek*, out, and *leipein*, to leave. When one heavenly body passes between two other ones, the rays of light which proceed from the luminous body are intercepted, thus producing an eclipse.

ECLIPTIC. Gr. *ekleiptikos*, belonging to an eclipse. The great circle of the sphere which the sun appears to travel over from west to east by reason of the earth's annual motion in its orbit; it is consequently the real path of the earth as seen from the sun. An eclipse of the moon can only take place when that luminary is on the ecliptic, hence the derivation.

EIDOGRAPH. Gr. *eidos*, form, and *graphein*, to describe or draw. An improved form of pantograph for reproducing copies of drawings on an enlarged or diminished scale.

ELLIPSE. Gr. *elleipsis*, a leaving or defect. A plane curve such that the sum of the distances of any point on its periphery from two given points within the curve, called the foci, is always the same. Any oblique section of a cylinder is an ellipse.

"COPYRIGHT, 1892, BY WILLIAM COX, NEW YORK."

A Monthly Journal for Engineers, Surveyors, Architects, Draughtsmen and Students.

Vol. II.   JANUARY 1, 1894.   No. 6.

THE SOLAR TRANSIT. V.

Fig. 1.

We now come to the method followed for ascertaining the Solar Hour Angle and computing from it local time. As in the example given in our last number for determining the meridian, the necessary data are the latitude and the sun's declination and altitude, by means of which the value of the angle SPZ is obtained. Changing the lettering in our last formula, we have

$$2 \log \cos \tfrac{1}{2} SPZ = \log \sin s + \log \sin (S - SZ)$$
$$+ \log \cosec PS + \log \cosec PZ - 20,$$

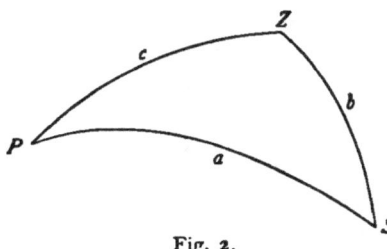

Fig. 2.

whence we obtain the hour angle SPZ and local time. The following example will show how simple is the instrumental work required, and at the same time the necessary calculations.

EXAMPLE.* At a place in latitude 39° 54′ N, and longitude 80° 39′ 45″ W., on May 8, 18.., at $5^h 30^m 32^s$ P.M. by the watch, the altitude of the sun's lower limb, observed by a transit, was found to be 15° 40′ 57″; required local time and the error of the watch.

1. The latitude is known to be 39° 54′, therefore

$$\text{Co-latitude } PZ = 50° 06'.$$

2. The sun's declination by Nautical Almanach, for Greenwich mean noon.......................... = 17° 4′ 36″
The longitude is equivalent in time to $5^h 22^m 39^s$
The given time.................. = 5 30 32
                                   ―――――――
                                   10 53 11
Increase in sun's declination per hour = 40″.37, which gives for $10^h 53^m 11^s$...............   7   19
                                                              ―――――――
Therefore sun's declination at time of observation.. = 17° 11′ 55″

whence

$$\text{Co-declination } PS = 72° 48' 05''.$$

3. The observed altitude of the sun's lower limb.. = 15° 40′ 57″
Sun's semi-diameter by Naut. Al................ = 0 15 52
Sun's parallax.................................. = 0   0 08
                                                   ―――――――
                                                   15 56 57
Deduct :—Refraction............... 0° 03′ 21″
         Contraction.............. 0 00 03
                                   ―――――――
                                                    0 03 24
                                                   ―――――――
True altitude of sun's centre...................... = 15° 53′ 33″

whence

$$\text{Co-altitude } SZ = 74° 06' 27''.$$

Having thus obtained the necessary data we now proceed to obtain the value of the Hour Angle SPZ as follows.

---

* Adapted from Chamber's "Practical Mathematics."

Co-latitude PZ............ = 50° 06′ 00″
Co-declination PS......... = 72 48 05
Co-altitude SZ............ = 74 06 27
─────────────
197 30 16

The half sum $s =$ 98° 30′ 16, and
$s - SZ =$ 24 23 49

We now have
log sin s................. = 9.9951982
log sin $(s - SZ)$.......... = 9.6160088
log cosec PS.............. = 10.0198668
log cosec PZ.............. = 10.1151111
─────────────
39.7461849
20.
─────────────

2 log cos ½ SPZ......... = 19.7461849

whence ½ $SPZ =$ 41° 42′ 09″.5
and $SPZ =$ 83° 24′ 19″

which is the hour angle which we reduce to time thus,

83° = 332 minutes = 5ʰ 32ᵐⁱⁿ.
24′ = 96 seconds = 1 36ˢᵉᶜ.
19″ = 76 thirds = 1.27
─────────────

Apparent time at place of observation = 5ʰ 33ᵐ 37ˢ.27

We now proceed to reduce this apparent time to local mean time, and to compare same with the watch, as follows:—

Local apparent time...................... 5ʰ 33ᵐ 37ˢ.27
Equation of time at Greenwich mean
  time........................ 3ᵐ 41ˢ.57
Difference for 1 hour = 0ˢ.139
  "   "   5ʰ 22ᵐ 39ˢ longitude.. 0 0.73
                                    ─────────
                                            3 42.30
                                    ─────────
Mean time at place of observation........... 5ʰ 29ᵐ 54ˢ.97

Time by watch............... 5ʰ 30ᵐ 32ˢ
Local mean time............. 5 29 55
                            ─────────
Difference = 0 0 37

The watch is, therefore, 37 seconds fast on local mean time.

The equation of time as above is taken from the Nautical Almanach in which it is given for daily noon with hourly differences. The following table will be found near enough for the surveyor's general requirements.

TABLE OF DIFFERENCES to be *added* to, or *subtracted* from, APPARENT TIME to obtain MEAN TIME.

Date	Minutes	Date	Minutes	Date	Minutes	Date	Minutes
Jan. 1	ADD 4	Mar. 27	ADD 5	Aug. 14	ADD 4	Oct. 23	SUBT. 16
" 3	" 5	" 30	" 4	" 19	" 3	Nov. 14	" 15
" 5	" 6	Apr. 3	" 3	" 23	" 2	" 19	" 14
" 7	" 7	" 6	" 2	" 27	" 1	" 23	" 13
" 9	" 8	" 10	" 1	" 30	" 0	" 26	" 12
" 11	" 9	" 14	" 0	Sept. 3	SUBT. 1	" 29	" 11
" 14	" 10	" 18	SUBT. 1	" 6	" 2	Dec. 2	" 10
" 17	" 11	" 22	" 2	" 9	" 3	" 5	" 9
" 21	" 12	" 28	" 3	" 12	" 4	" 7	" 8
" 25	" 13	May 5	" 4	" 14	" 5	" 9	" 7
" 29	" 14	" 24	" 3	" 17	" 6	" 11	" 6
Feb. 8	" 15	June 2	" 2	" 20	" 7	" 13	" 5
" 14	" 14	" 8	" 1	" 23	" 8	" 15	" 4
" 24	" 13	" 13	" 0	" 26	" 9	" 17	" 3
Mch. 2	" 12	" 18	ADD 1	" 29	" 10	" 19	" 2
" 7	" 11	" 22	" 2	Oct. 2	" 11	" 21	" 1
" 11	" 10	" 27	" 3	" 5	" 12	" 23	" 0
" 14	" 9	July 2	" 4	" 9	" 13	" 26	ADD 1
" 18	" 8	" 8	" 5	" 13	" 14	" 28	" 2
" 21	" 7	" 15	" 6	" 17	" 15	" 30	" 3
" 24	" 6	Aug. 7	" 5				

The corrections for refraction for altitudes from 10° to 80° may be taken from the following table; and here it will be well to note the following points:

(1). When observed or apparent altitude is to be reduced to true altitude, the refraction must be *deducted*, because it makes the observed object appear *higher* than it really is, but (2) when the true altitude of an object is known and its apparent altitude is sought, the refraction must be *added* to bring the object up to the angular position in which it will be visible or apparent if viewed through a telescope whose angle of elevation is equal to the true altitude plus refraction.

TABLE OF MEAN REFRACTION CORRECTIONS.*

Barometer, 30 inches. Thermometer, 50° Fahr.

Altitude	Refraction.	Altitude	Refraction.	Altitude	Refraction.	Altitude	Refraction.
° ′	′ ″	° ′	′ ″	° ′	′ ″	° ′	′ ″
10 0	5 19.2	16 40	3 12.2	26 0	1 58.9	42 0	1 4.7
20	5 9.3	17 0	3 8.3	30	1 56.4	43 0	1 2.4
40	5 0.0	20	3 4.6	27 0	1 53.9	44 0	1 0.3
11 0	4 51.2	40	3 1.0	30	1 51.5	45 0	0 58.2
20	4 42.9	18 0	2 57.5	28 0	1 49.2	46 0	0 56.2
40	4 35.0	30	2 52.4	30	1 47.0	47 0	0 54.3
12 0	4 27.5	19 0	2 47.7	29 0	1 44.8	48 0	0 52.5
20	4 20.4	30	2 43.1	30	1 42.7	49 0	0 50.6
40	4 13.6	20 0	2 38.8	30 0	1 40.6	50 0	0 48.9
13 0	4 7.2	30	2 34.6	31 0	1 38.7	52 0	0 45.5
20	4 1.0	21 0	2 30.7	32 0	1 33.0	54 0	0 42.3
40	3 55.2	30	2 26.9	33 0	1 29.5	56 0	0 39.3
14 0	3 49.5	22 0	2 23.3	34 0	1 26.2	58 0	0 36.4
20	3 44.2	30	2 19.8	35 0	1 23.1	60 0	0 33.6
40	3 39.0	23 0	2 16.4	36 0	1 20.1	62 0	0 31.0
15 0	3 34.1	30	2 13.3	37 0	1 17.2	64 0	0 28.4
20	3 29.4	24 0	2 10.2	38 0	1 14.5	66 0	0 25.9
40	3 24.8	30	2 7.2	39 0	1 11.9	86 0	0 23.6
16 0	3 20.5	25 0	2 4.4	40 0	1 9.4	70 0	0 21.2
20	3 16.3	30	2 1.6	41 0	1 7.0	80 0	0 10.3

The correction for the sun's parallax may be taken from the following table, intermediate values being obtained by interpolation or by means of the following formula which gives very near results and is very simple.

$$\text{Sun's Parallax in seconds} = 8.8 \text{ Cosine of sun's altitude.}$$

SUN'S PARALLAX IN ALTITUDE.

Altitude	Parallax	Altitude	Parallax	Altitude	Parallax	Altitude	Parallax
0°	8″.80	25°	7″.97	50°	5″.66	75°	2″.28
5	8.77	30	7.62	55	5.05	80	1.53
10	8.57	35	7.21	60	4.40	85	0.77
15	8.50	40	6.74	65	3.72	90	0.0
20	8.27	45	6.22	70°	3.01		

* Arranged from "Spherical and Practical Astronomy" by Wm. Chauvenet.

Having described and explained some of the astromical problems with which the surveyor has to deal, and shown their relationship to the astronomical triangle, we shall in our next describe the Transit with Solar Attachment, and then explain how the various parts of this triangle are solved instrumentally in virtue of the special construction of the attachment. We also give in this number certain data required for the month of January, and shall continue to publish them monthly throughout the year, so that our readers may have at hand every means for following up their investigations.

RAILROAD CURVES.

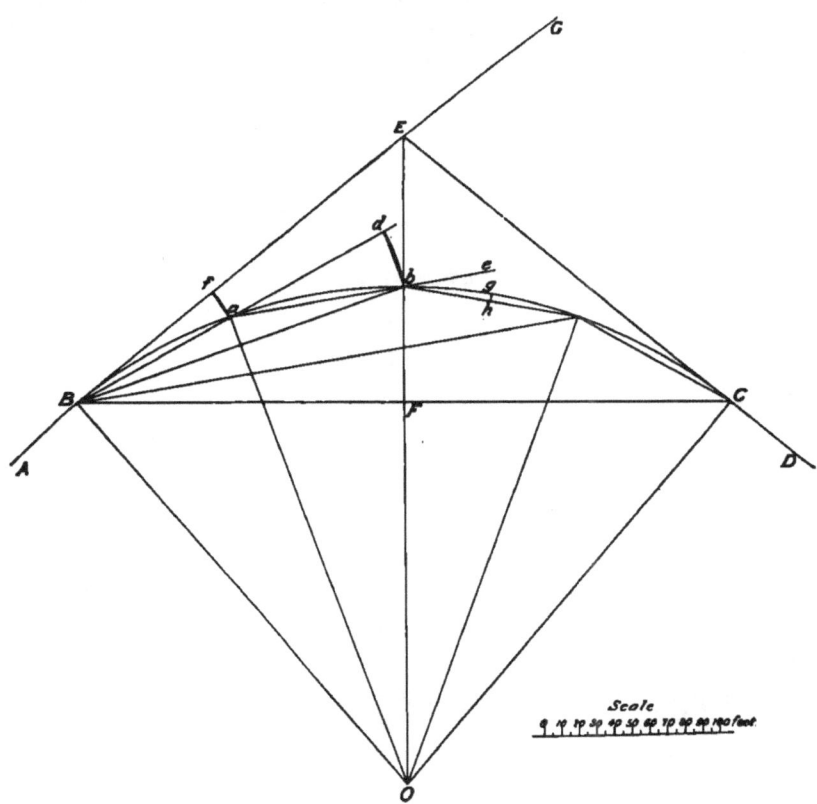

RAILROAD CURVES are designated by the angles which are subtended by a uniform chord 100 feet long, as a *one-degree*, *two-degree* curve, etc.

The angle subtended by an *arc* of 100 feet is in inverse proportion to the length of the radius, thus the radius of an arc subtending

1° is 5730 feet (exactly 5729.6)
2° " 2865 "
3° " 1910 " etc.

As, however, the chord of a curve is shorter than the arc, it is clear that as the degree of curvature becomes greater, the radii of curves whose chords are uniformly 100 feet will also be somewhat longer than those of uniform arcs of 100 feet; thus we have

Curvature 20°, Radius of 100 ft. arc = 286.5 ft.
" 20°, " " 100 " chord = 287.9 "

When, however, the degree of curvature is not great, it is usual to consider that the radius is also inversely proportional to the degree of curvature for uniform chords of 100 feet, in which case the radius may be found by dividing 5730 by the degree of curvature, and the degree of curvature obtained by dividing 5730 by the radius; thus,

$$\text{Radius} = \frac{5730}{\text{No. of degrees}}, \text{ and}$$

$$\text{Degree of Curvature} = \frac{5730}{\text{Radius}}.$$

The exact radius of any curve may be found by

$$\text{Radius} = \frac{\tfrac{1}{2} \text{ Chord}}{\text{Sin } \tfrac{1}{2} \text{ Angle}},$$

which gives for chords of 100 feet

$$\text{Radius} = \frac{50}{\text{Sin } \tfrac{1}{2} \text{ Angle}}.$$

The above figure represents two straight lines $A\ G$ and $D\ E$ united by the curve $B\ a\ b\ c\ C$. Without entering into particulars of methods of laying out curves, we now, in response to an enquiry, designate the different functions of the railroad curve, adding the principal formulæ by means of which their values are obtained. We *assume* that the chords $B\ a$, $a\ b$, $b\ c$ and $c\ C$ are each 100 feet long. We have then as follows:

Beginning of curve, designated $B.\ C.$, } = point B when
 or Point of curve,   " $P.\ C.$ }   proceeding from A.

End of curve, designated $E.\ C.$, } = point C.
 or Point of tangent " $P.\ T.$ }

Point of Intersection of tangents, designated $P\ I$, = point E.

Apex Distances or Tangents to the curve = $B\ E$ = $C\ E$.

Total Deflection Angle or Angle of Intersection $= G\,E\,C\,(= B\,O\,C)$.

Total Central Angle $= B\,O\,C\,(= G\,E\,C)$.

Total Tangential Angle $= G\,B\,C\,(= \frac{1}{2}\,G\,E\,C = B\,O\,E)$.

Chord Deflection Angle $= d\,a\,b = e\,b\,c,\,(= a\,O\,b,$ etc.$)$

Chord Central Angle $= B\,O\,a = a\,O\,b,$ etc.

Single Tangential Angle $= f\,B\,a,\left(= \dfrac{a\,O\,b}{2},\text{ etc.}\right)$

Apex Angle $= B\,E\,C$.

Tangential Distance $= a\,f$.

Deflection Distance $= b\,d$.

External Secant $= E\,b$.

Radius of Curve $= B\,O = b\,O$.

The following are some of the formulæ for obtaining the values of these various functions, the Total Deflection Angle $G\,E\,C$ being generally a known quantity.

1. Apex Distance or Tangent $B\,E =$ Rad $O\,B \times \tan E\,B\,C$.

2. Radius of Curve $O\,B = \dfrac{B\,E}{\tan B\,O\,E} = B\,E \times \cot B\,O\,E,$

$$= \dfrac{B\,C}{2\sin B\,O\,E}$$

4. Long Chord $B\,C =$ Rad $O\,B \times 2\sin B\,O\,E$.

5. Secant $O\,E =$ Rad $O\,B \times \sec B\,O\,E$.

6. External Secant $E\,b = O\,E -$ Radius.

$= B\,E \times \tan \frac{1}{2}\,E\,B\,C$.

7. Tangential Distance $a\,f = \sin \frac{1}{2}\,a\,B\,f \times 2\,B\,a$.

8. Deflection Distance $d\,b = \dfrac{a\,b^2}{\text{Radius}}$

$= \sin \frac{1}{2}\,b\,a\,d \times 2\,a\,b$.

9. Sine Tangential Angle $a\,B\,f = \dfrac{\frac{1}{2}\,B\,a}{\text{Radius}}$.

10. Deflection Angle $b\,a\,d = 2$ Tangential Angle $a\,B\,f$.

11. Middle Ordinate $g\,h =$ Rad $- \sqrt{\text{Rad}^2 - \frac{1}{2}\,\text{Chord}^2},$

$=$ Rad $\times (1 - \cos \frac{1}{2}\,b\,O\,c)$.

12. Number of 100 ft. Chords in curve $\Big\} = \dfrac{G\,E\,C}{b\,a\,d}$.

Tables are published in Keuffel & Esser Co.'s Field Books, which simplify considerably the Railroad Engineer's calculations. One of them gives the Apex Distance or Tangents $B\ E$ and $E\ C$ and the External Secants $E\ b$ for curves of 5730 feet radius with Total Deflection or Central Angles of 1° to 120°. The Apex Distances are obtained by the formula $5730 \times \tan \frac{1}{2} BOC$ and the External Secants by $(5730 \times \sec \frac{1}{2} BOC) - 5730$. Being bound up with the Field Book the engineer has always at hand all that he requires in the way of tables and is not obliged to carry continually in his pocket a more or less cumbersome book of reference.

The following example will give some idea of the method of using this table.

Let, in the figure, the Total Deflection Angle $G\ E\ C$ be 80°, and let it be required to join $A\ G$ and $D\ E$ by a curve which shall pass through the point b, and let $E\ b$ be 87.5 feet.

From the table we find that the External Secant of a curve whose central angle is 80° and radius 5730 feet, is 1749.9 feet. Instead therefore of the 100 foot chords subtending Chord Central Angles of 1°, they should subtend angles of $\frac{1749.9}{87.5} = 20° = B\ O\ a = a\ O\ b$, etc.

Similarly, from the table we find that the Apex Distance or Tangent for a 1° curve is 4807.7 feet, therefore for a 20° curve, the Apex Distances $B\ E$ and $C\ E$ would be $\frac{4807.7}{20} = 240.2$ feet.

The number of chords in the curve will be $\frac{80°}{20°} = 4$ chords of 100 feet each.

From another table in the Field Book we now obtain the following:

$\qquad$ Radius of curve $B\ O = 287.9$ feet.

$\qquad$ Deflection Distance or Chord Deflection $\}$ $b\ d = 34.73$ ft.

$\qquad$ Tangential Distance or Deflection. $\}$ $a\ f = 17.37$ ft.

$\qquad$ Middle Ordinate $g\ h = 4.374$ ft.

$\qquad$ Chord Deflection Angle $d\ a\ b = 20°$.

$\qquad$ Single Tangential Angle $f\ B\ a = \frac{d\ a\ b}{2} = 10°$.

We have thus the chief distances and angles by means of which the curve can now be laid down, the method of computation being similar in other cases when different data are given from which to calculate the various functions.

The table may also be used for obtaining the natural tangent of angles by dividing the tabular tangent of twice the given angle by 5730; the quotient is the natural tangent sought. Natural External Secants may be found in the same way.

LOGARITHMIC CROSS-SECTION PAPER.

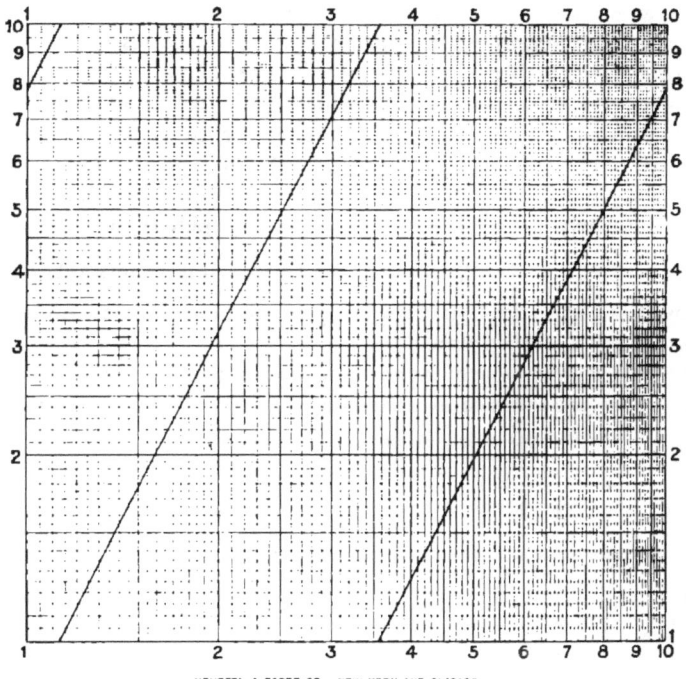

THE ABOVE FIGURE represents a sheet of cross-section paper in which the distances or spaces between the consecutive lines, instead of being all equal, or similar to those of a scale of equal parts, are logarithmic ones, the same as those of an ordinary slide rule.

An equation of the first degree having two variable quantities, such as $A = Cn$, in which A and n are variable quantities, while C is a constant, or in other words, the successive products of two factors of which one is a variable one and the other a constant, may be represented upon equally-divided cross-section paper, by means of a *straight line*. Thus, if we give to C the constant value of π, and let n represent a series of diameters of circles, then A will be the corresponding series of circumferences. The graphic representation of this equation would be as follows:—the abscissœ n are laid off on the horizontal axis X, whilst the corresponding ordinates A are laid off on the vertical axis Y, the locus of the equation being the inclined straight line proceeding from the point of origin and representing the given equation $A = \pi n$.

If, however, we take an equation of the second degree having three variables, such as $A = xy$, or in other words the successive products of two variable factors x and y, we shall find that the locus of the equation will be represented by a *curved line* instead of a straight line. Thus, to obtain a graphic representation of the squares of a series of numbers such as n^2, $(n + 1)^2$, $(n + 2)^2$, etc., (which is equivalent to the products of, say 2×2, 3×3, 4×4, etc., in which both factors are variable), the various products or squares would have to be independently plotted by means of previously computed data, while the line passing through the points thus plotted, (the locus of the equation) would be found to trace a curve. Similarly if it were wished to make a graphic representation of the areas of circles, $= \frac{\pi}{4} d^2$, in which the factor $\frac{\pi}{4}$ is a constant, and d^2, is composed of two variable factors, the plotting of such areas would also be represented by a curved line.

The great advantage of logarithmic cross-section paper, as shown in the figure. is that the locus of equations of the second degree, of the form of
$$A = n^2, A = C n^2, A = C \times xy,$$
$$A = n (n \pm 1), \text{ etc.}$$
is represented by a straight line. Thus, the figure is a graphic representation of diameters and areas of circles, the formula being Area $= \frac{\pi}{4} d^2$, which is equivalent to $A = C n^2$ as above, where C is a constant equal to 0.7854. Here the diameters are laid off on the horizontal axis, being numbered from 1 to 10, whilst the areas are laid off on the vertical axis and are likewise numbered from 1 to 10. As in the case of the slide rule, the value of the initial 1 of each scale may vary, being according to the circumstances of the case equal to 0.1, 0.01, 10, 100, etc., all the other figures having necessarily proportionate values. Thus, to examine the figure a little more closely, we have along the bottom horizontal axis a scale of diameters, and along the left hand vertical axis, a scale of areas. To find the area of a circle whose diameter is 2 inches, we follow the vertical line marked 2 on the axis X until it intersects the inclined line, then from this point of intersection follow by estimation a continuous horizontal line until it meets the left hand vertical scale or axis Y, where we read 3.1416.

It will be noticed that the inclined line or locus of the equation is divided into three sections, as follows:—

(1.) 0.7854, the area of a circle whose diameter is 1.0000
to 1.0000, " " " " 1.129..

(2.) 1.0000, " " " " 1.129..
to 10.0000, " " " " 3.569..

(3.) 10.0000, " " " " 3.569..
to 78.5400, " " " " 10.0000

The values to be attached to the scale of areas are easily ascertained, when it is remembered that the square of 10 is 100; thus, if the area of a circle whose diameter is 20 is required, the area will be necessarily between 300 and 400 instead of between 3 and 4 as in the above example, so that instead of 3.1416 as before, we now read 314.16; while to find the diameter of a circle whose area is 31.416, we follow the estimated horizontal line 3.1416 to its intersection with the *third* inclined line, then follow the vertical downwards to the scale of diameters where by estimation we read 6.324, the diameter required. It will be thus seen that the different values to be attached to the scales of diameters and areas follow precisely the same rules as for the slide rule.

To lay down the locus of an equation we proceed exactly as if we were plotting by means of co-ordinates. Thus, to determine the locus of the equation $A = \dfrac{\pi}{4} d^2$, we *compute* the exact areas for two or three diameters, then lay off these diameters on the axis of x or axis of abscissœ, and their corresponding areas on the axis of y or axis of ordinates. From the different points thus obtained draw horizontal and perpendicular lines, —their points of intersection will be points in the locus of the equation. Having in this way drawn one inclined line, others to complete the scale of abscissœ from 1 to 10, require merely to be drawn parallel to it, their point of origin being determined either by calculation or by measurement.

In conclusion, to show on ordinary cross-section paper the products of a series of factors by means of a *straight line*, these products are limited to the formation of a series of numbers in arithmetical progression, having a *common difference*, as 1π, 2π, 3π, etc., the common difference being π.

With logarithmic cross-section paper, however, we can also represent by means of a straight line the consecutive products of several variable factors, provided the products form a series of numbers whose *differences* are in arithmetical progression, such as:—

Formula.	*Series of Products.*	*Differences.*
$A = n^2$	1, 4, 9, 16, 25, etc.	3, 5, 7, 9, etc.
$A = n(n+1)$	2, 6, 12, 20, 30, etc.	4, 6, 8, 10, "
$A = Cn^2$ where $C = \dfrac{\pi}{4}$	0.7854, 3.1416, 7.0686, 12.566,..	$3\dfrac{\pi}{4}$, $5\dfrac{\pi}{4}$, $7\dfrac{\pi}{4}$ "
$A = C \times 3n^2$ where $C = 7$	21, 84, 189, 336, 525,..	63, 105, 147, 189 "
$A = 4n^2 + 5n - 2$	7, 24, 49, 82, 123,..	17, 25, 33, 41 "

We may also represent by a straight line the powers and roots of a consecutive series of numbers, as well as many other formulæ used in engineering, hydraulics, etc. For purposes of computation, therefore, this cross-section paper will be of great use to the engineer, who will thus be enabled to prepare and have at all times at hand a set of graphic tables specially adapted to the various calculations necessitated by the particular work in which he is engaged.

The figure is one-third the natural size; the sheets are about 11 inches square, of good paper, and clearly printed, so that they may long retain their usefulness. For price, see cover of present issue.

A GYROSCOPE ARTIFICIAL HORIZON.

IN FORMER NUMBERS of THE COMPASS (August and December, 1892), we described the artificial horizon and the method of using it for ascertaining altitudes. *Terra firma* is a necessary condition of the operation referred to, but we transcribe from *The Railroad Gazette* the following description of an artificial horizon which may be used at sea, even in rough weather.

"An instrument recently patented by Capt. J. N. Rowe and C. E. Crane, of Seattle, Wash., will be of interest to navigators and engineers. Observations at sea for latitude and longitude depend upon a correct vision of the natural horizon or upon the unstable surface of a balanced dish of mercury, the former of which cannot be used in fogs or storms nor the latter in a rough sea. This new instrument may be used on deck or at the crosstrees and at any time the sun or stars are visible. The artificial horizon consists of a highly polished disc forming the top of a truncated hollow cone 2 inches in depth, flaring at the bottom, which may revolve on a steel pin for a pivot, much like a common tea cup and saucer inverted and balanced upon a pencil. The pivot can be lowered and this female cone let down upon a male truncated cone that is connected with machinery and operated by a crank.

When the lower cone is rotated, the friction between the cones causes the upper one and its disc to revolve at a very high speed, 3000 revolutions a minute, when it is raised upon the pivot by a lever. The centre of gravity being below the point of the pivot, the axis of the cone assumes a vertical position, and the disc a horizontal position, and the gyroscopical action of the cone and disc maintains it in that position, though the pivot may be inclined within the limits of the cone. It is used when revolving thus freely. The principle is the same as is employed by jugglers to balance an inverted bowl on a pointed stick.

The Navy Department has given the instrument a trial on the U. S. monitor Monterey, and it has received high praise from its officers. The instrument is also valuable to determine at what moment a gunboat is level, that the signal may be given for firing the guns, and it may be used in the conning tower. The instruments are made of aluminum-bronze."

"*UNEXPLAINED*" *MAGNETIC VARIATIONS*.

The following cases are communicated to recent numbers of *Engineering News*, and as they may interest some of our readers, we reproduce them.

1. By Edward P. Adams, L. H. Surveyor, 1st and 2d Dists., Stockton Springs, Me.

"While running out the magnetic bearings according to an old deed at this station, I discovered an unsuspected cause of error in reading the needle of the transit. Noticing a movement of the needle when I changed my position from side to front of instrument, I investigated the cause and found it to be the small stiffening piece in the point of my necktie. It is only $3\frac{1}{2}$ inches long, $\frac{1}{4}$ in. wide and 1-50 in. thick, but it has more effect on the needle than a 100 foot steel tape or a hatchet at the same distance. As it is covered with paper, it is innocent looking enough; but it obliged us to spend half a day in correcting our work. I send the little piece inclosed. It is evidently magnetized steel. When one end was held close to the box, it moved the needle through 90°. The similar piece in each of a dozen other neckties had no effect or moved the needle only one or two degrees."

2. Frank Bruen, Civil Engineer, Dayton, Ohio.

"While reading the letter of Mr. Edward P. Adams, published in your issue of Nov. 30, upon "Unexplained Magnetic Variation," I was reminded of another source of error discovered some time ago. It is the steel stiffening in some Derby hat rims. While my hat had no effect upon the needle, that of an assistant drew the needle perhaps 45°."

GLOSSARY AND DEFINITIONS OF TERMS EMPLOYED IN SURVEYING, ASTRONOMY, ETC. VI.

ELONGATION. Low Lat. *elongare*, from *e*, out or forth from, and *longe*, a long way off. The angular distance of Polaris, the pole star, due east or west of the true pole, being 1° 15' 26" on January 1, 1894, with an annual decrease of 18.9". An observation of Polaris at elongation is a very simple method for determining the meridian. Is also used in reference to other circumpolar stars.

EQUATION. Lat. *æquare*, to make level or equal, from *æquus*, level, equal. In mathematics an equation is the expression of equality between two quantities or sets of quantities, and is designated by $=$ placed between them, as $a + b = x - y$.

EQUATION OF TIME. In Astronomy, the difference between Apparent Solar Time derived from the apparent motions of the sun, and Mean Solar Time, as it would be obtained from a fictitious or imaginary sun whose motions are supposed to be perfectly regular and uniform, is termed the equation of time. Clocks are regulated by mean solar time, and in consequence of the variation in the intervals of time between successive passages of the sun across a given meridian, the expression is used "Sun after clock" or "Sun before clock." A "table of differences to be added to, or subtracted from, apparent time to obtain mean time," will be found in the present number, Art. "The Solar Transit."

EQUATOR. Lat, *æquare*, as above. The terrestrial equator is an imaginary circle going round the earth midway between the poles, its plane being perpendicular to the earth's axis. The celestial equator, $C\ V\ H$, Plate I, is that great circle whose plane is perpendicular in all directions to the axis of the heavens, and passes through the centre of the earth. It coincides with the plane of the terrestrial equator produced to the inner surface of the celestial sphere. When the sun is in the equator the days and nights are of equal duration, hence it is also called the equinoctial.

EQUATORIAL. An astronomical instrument provided with a telescope whose chief axis of rotation, or polar axis, is parallel to the earth's axis, while a secondary axis of rotation, called the declination axis, is perpendicular to it. The telescope is secured at right angles to the upper end of the declination axis, and is consequently parallel to the polar or earth's axis, and can be by a combination of the two motions of rotation directed upon any celestial body, such body being then maintained in the field of view for prolonged observation by means of a clock which moves the telescope in right ascension.

EQUINOCTIAL. Lat. *æquus*, equal and *nox*, night. See EQUATOR

EQUINOX. The two points of intersection of the great circle of the ecliptic with the celestial equator are called the equinoxes. The vernal or spring equinox is that point where the sun crosses the equator northwards on March 21, and the autumnal equinox is the point where the sun crosses the equator southwards on September 21, thus forming the alteration of the seasons. These points are shown by U and V on Plate I.

FIDUCIAL. Lat. *fiducia*, trust, confidence. Any data, such as a point, line, benchmark, meridian, etc., whose determined positions are known to be reliable and correct, and may consequently be used in determining other points, etc., are said to be fiducial.

SOLAR EPHEMERIS, JANUARY 1894.
For Greenwich Apparent Noon.

Day of Week	Day of Month	The Sun's Apparent Declination	Difference for 1 Hour	Equation of Time to be added to Apparent Time	Day of Month	Refraction * Correction Latitude 40°
		° ′ ″	″	m s		
Mon.	1	S 22 59 21.9	+ 12.76	3 52.72	1 to 3	1 h. 1′ 58″
Tues.	2	22 54 1.9	13.90	4 20.90		2 2 16
Wed.	3	22 48 14.7	15.04	4 48.71		3 3 04
Thurs.	4	22 42 0.2	16.17	5 16.14		4 0 23
Frid.	5	22 35 18.6	17.29	5 43.16		
Sat.	6	22 28 10.2	+ 18.41	6 9.73	4 to 8	1 h. 1′ 54″
Sun.	7	22 20 35.2	19.51	6 35.82		2 2 11
Mon.	8	22 12 33.7	20.60	7 1.40		3 2 59
Tues.	9	22 4 6.1	21.68	7 26.44		4 6 01
Wed.	10	21 55 12.5	22.76	7 50.92	9 to 13	1 h. 1′ 51″
Thurs.	11	21 45 53.4	+ 23.82	8 14.80		2 2 07
Frid.	12	21 36 8.8	24.87	8 38.06		3 2 51
Sat.	13	21 25 59.3	25.91	9 0.68		4 5 40
Sun.	14	21 15 24.9	26.93	9 22.63	14 to 18	1 h. 1′ 46″
Mon.	15	21 4 26.2	27.94	9 43.89		2 2 01
Tues.	16	20 53 3.4	+ 28.95	10 4.45		3 2 40
Wed.	17	20 41 16.8	29.94	10 24.29		4 5 00
Thurs.	18	20 29 6.7	30.91	10 43.40	19 to 23	1 h. 1′ 42″
Frid.	19	20 16 33.6	31.86	11 1.77		2 1 56
Sat.	20	20 3 37.6	32.80	11 19.38		3 2 31
						4 4 35
Sun.	21	19 50 19.2	+ 33.73	11 36.22	24 to 28	
Mon.	22	19 36 38.7	34.65	11 52.30		1 h. 1′ 37″
Tues.	23	19 22 36.5	35.55	12 7.61		2 1 50
Wed.	24	19 8 12.9	36.42	12 22.13		3 2 22
Thurs.	25	18 53 28.2	37.29	12 35.88		4 4 07
Frid.	26	18 38 22.8	+ 38.14	12 48.83	29 to Feb. 2	1 h. 1′ 32″
Sat.	27	18 22 57.1	38.98	13 0.98		2 1 44
Sun.	28	18 7 11.5	39.81	13 12.35		3 2 13
Mon.	29	17 51 6.3	40.62	13 22.91		4 3 41
Tues.	30	17 34 41.9	41.41	13 32.68		
Wed.	31	17 17 58.7	42.18	13 41.64		

* By permission from "The Theory and Practice of Surveying", by Prof. J. B. Johnson, C. E.

In this column the hours are counted each way from noon; thus, 9 A. M. and 3 P. M. would each correspond to the 3d hour in the table. The hourly corrections are exact for the middle day of the five-day period corresponding to any given set of hourly corrections. For other days interpolations can be made where extreme accuracy is required.

A Monthly Journal for Engineers, Surveyors, Architects, Draughtsmen and Students.

Vol. III.   FEBRUARY 1, 1894.   No. 7.

VERNIERS. V.

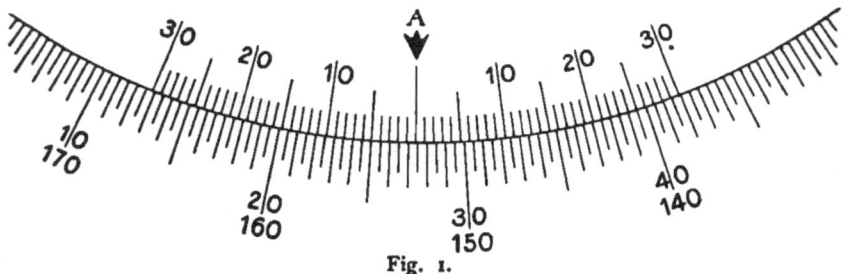

Fig. 1.

WE CONCLUDE these articles on Verniers by presenting those usually employed in connection with the graduations of the horizontal and vertical limbs of an Engineer's Transit. Clear and distinct graduations and well-combined verniers are in such instruments of great importance, and as the least count or reading can be obtained by different combinations of scale and vernier, it is essential that the one affording the greatest facilities for accurate reading should be selected.

Fig. 1 represents the usual method of graduating the horizontal limbs of Engineers' Transits, with the corresponding vernier. It is an ordinary *double direct* vernier, that is, two simple verniers conjoined, each one reading outwards from the centre zero division, the scale of the vernier to be used being determined by the numbering of the limb, thus for the inner set of figures of the limb, numbered from 10° to 40° towards the right, the right-hand scale of the vernier must be used, whilst the outer set of figures of the limb from 140° to 170° is read by the left-hand vernier scale.

The limb is divided to half-degrees, and each scale of the vernier is divided into 30 equal parts, 29 divisions of the limb corresponding to 30 divisions of the vernier, so that the least count or reading of the vernier is 30 minutes ÷ 30 = single minutes. The figure reads 27°00′ + 25′ = 27°25′ from left to right and 152°30′ + 05′ = 152°35′ from right to left.

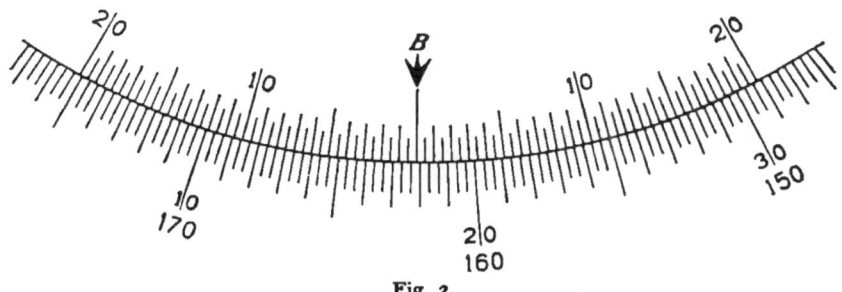

Fig. 2.

This is a double direct vernier similar to Fig. 1, but with finer divisions; it also reads from the centre to the right and to the left, according to the direction followed on the horizontal limb. The limb is graduated to thirds of a degree or 20 minutes, while each scale of the vernier is divided into 40 equal parts, and 40 vernier divisions correspond to 39 limb divisions, thus giving a least count or reading of 20 minutes or 1200 seconds ÷ 40 = 30 seconds.

The figure reads 17°40′ + 12′30″ = 17°52′30″ from left to right, and 162°00′ + 7′30″ = 162°7′30″ from right to left.

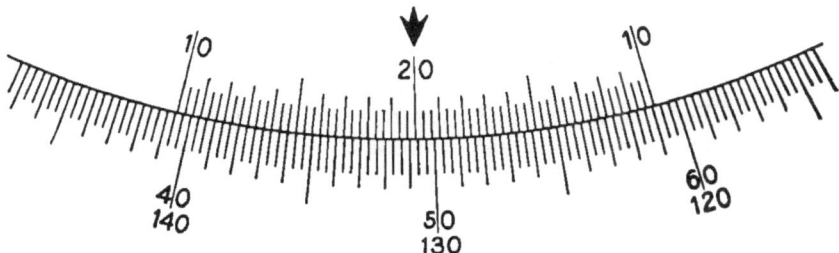

Fig. 3.

Figure 3 also represents part of the horizontal limb of an Engineer's Transit, finely divided for the best work. As the space which can be taken up on the horizontal limb for the vernier is usually about 30 degrees, and as a double vernier to read as fine as Fig. 3 would require 40 degrees, this vernier is a *double-folded* or *crossed* one, similar to the one described on page 30, reading from the centre arrow or zero to either of the extreme divisions, and then, if no coinciding lines have been found, proceeding from the opposite extreme division to the same centre division marked 20, until lines on the vernier and scale are found which coincide, such vernier line being the reading. The direction in which the vernier is read is in principle the same as that stated for Fig. 1.

The limb is divided into equal parts of 20 minutes each, whilst the vernier is composed of 60 equal parts, and 59 divisions of the limb = 60 divisions of the vernier, so that the least count or reading of the vernier is 20 minutes or 1200 seconds ÷ 60 = 20 seconds. The figure reads 49°00′ + 14′20″ = 49°14′20″ from left to right and 130°40′ + 5′40″ = 130°45′40″ from right to left.

Sometimes, when it is required to read to 20 seconds, the limb is divided to quarter-degrees or 15 minutes, and the vernier is composed of 45 equal parts corresponding to 44 divisions of the limb, whence 15 minutes or 900 seconds ÷ 45 = 20 seconds. This arrangement appears to be rather crowded and does not so readily fulfil the essential condition of accurate reading referred to.

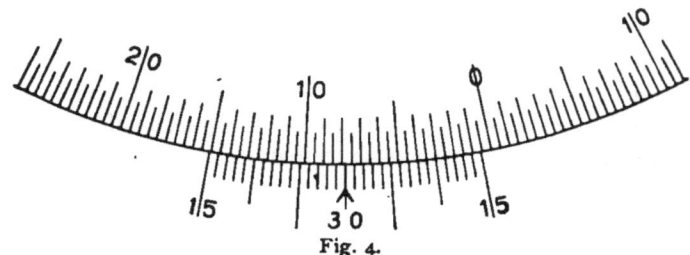

Fig. 4.

Fig. 4 represents a portion of the vertical limb or arc of an Engineer's Transit. As in Fig. 3, the space usually available for the vernier is very limited, so that a double folded vernier is indispensable; its main features are similar to those of Fig. 3, and the method of reading also the same.

The limb or arc is graduated to half-degrees, and the vernier is divided into 30 equal parts, 29 divisions of the vertical limb being equal to 30 divisions of the vernier, so that the least count or reading of the vernier is 30 minutes ÷ 30 = single minutes. The figure shows that the telescope is depressed, the eye-piece being to the right; the angle is 7°30′ + 21′ = 7°51′, read from right to left.

DRAWING INSTRUMENTS. II.

WE NOW COME to the consideration of that important point in the manufacture of drawing instruments, namely the materials of which they are made, to which are closely allied, and upon which largely depend their graceful form, general appearance, and above all their serviceableness and durability. The metals usually employed are German silver and steel in the best and medium qualities of instruments, and brass and iron in the cheapest ones, although in some exceptional cases, unknown and unappreciated in this country, brass is also used for the finest grades.

The quality of German silver is determined by two important considerations, namely, the proportions of the different ingredients of which the alloy is composed, and the density or toughness of the metal, which is mainly dependent upon the method of treatment. The best German silver approaches in color the peculiar whiteness of standard silver, whilst inferior alloys (also called German silver) vary in accordance with the metals which enter into their composition. And here it should be clearly understood, that the color is, as a general rule, no criterion of the quality of the metal, as this depends so largely upon the addition of foreign metals to the pure alloy, such being generally selected with the intention of rendering it more ductile and consequently more easily manipulated, thus lessening the cost of workmanship.

Another point, as important as the composition of the alloy, is the mode of treatment, as upon this largely depend its essential qualities of hardness and stiffness. The parts of instruments, into whose construction it enters, may be treated in three different ways:

1st, merely cast and polished;

2d, cast and hammered, or coined in dies and submitted to pressure; or,

3d, the alloy may be first *rolled* into plates, out of which the several parts are then cut and filed to shape.

It will be readily conceived that these different processes give to the metal a varying degree of density and consequent hardness, the latter method being naturally greatly superior to the two others.

It follows therefore that according to the method of treatment adopted, we may have three grades of instruments, (all made of the same alloy, but treated in each case in a different manner), each one varying in density, and consequently possessing the qualities of serviceableness and durability in a different degree. The importance to be attached to the density of the metal is greater than would be at first supposed. Rigidity in the legs of a pair of dividers or compasses is of paramount importance. Now this rigidity can only be obtained by making the *quantity of metal in a given piece proportionate to its density*, hence, when the piece is merely cast and polished, a greater thickness of metal is required to give the necessary rigidity, thus adding not only to the weight of the instrument, but also to its uncouth appearance. If, however, the metal used be first rolled and then cut and filed to the required shape, a much smaller amount of metal will possess all the rigidity desired, thus allowing of graceful form and proportionate lightness being combined in the design of the instrument, which will be both serviceable and durable.

Rigidity is however not the only consideration, as the toughness and hardness of the metal also play a very important part, especially in the joints, whose surfaces are subject to continual friction, which, in the case of an instrument made of soft metal, will soon wear them away and render the instrument worthless.

Another point which is influenced by the method of treatment, to which the German silver is subjected, and which principally affects the buyer of instruments, as it enters very largely into the question of cost, is the subsequent labor bestowed upon their manufacture. To work up the hard rolled plate metal not only demands more time and labor on the part of skillful and highly paid workmen, than the mere smoothing up by an inferior workman of a casting made in accordance with the first process, but the extra wear of tools caused by the greater hardness of the metal is also an item of expenditure, which cannot be left out of consideration when calculating cost.

Further, the steel used in these instruments may be of the highest or of an inferior quality, while in the cheapest instruments the steel is in most cases replaced by iron. The mode of treatment also varies, only the best methods being adopted where a high grade instrument is required; in the very best the finest steel alone is used, all the parts being hand-forged and the points very carefully tempered.

When these various features:—quality of the alloy and its mode of treatment; use of iron or steel, tempered or untempered; skilled or cheap workmanship, are all taken into consideration, it will be evident that a very great and real difference exists between the qualities of the various grades of instruments, this difference being often considered by the uninitiated as imaginary, as it is not apparent to him on mere examination. It exists however, and actual and continuous USE of the *best* instruments, and similar use of a lower grade, will make the difference evident, whilst the annoyance resulting from the use of a tool, imperfect in quality and construction, will convince the most sceptical.

Another point, which is also of great importance, as it is often deceptive and leads to a wrong appreciation of an instrument, must also be considered; we refer to the finish, but must reserve its consideration for our next.

ALUMINIUM DRAWING INSTRUMENTS.

IT IS GRADUALLY becoming evident that many of the thousand and one suggested applications of aluminium will not be realized in practice unless some method of modifying the nature of the metal without increasing its weight is discovered. It was generally thought that aluminium drawing instruments would show a decided improvement over those of ordinary make, but these anticipations do not appear to be borne out in practice. One prominent firm of mathematical instrument makers having made a number of experiments, states that instruments of any delicacy or which have joints or wearing surfaces made of this metal or any alloy containing it in sufficient quantity to have an appreciable effect upon the weight, are inferior in stiffness and wearing qualities. Pure aluminium is very soft, it possesses no wearing qualities, it is readily bent and cut, and its surface is easily rubbed or worn off, being somewhat like lead in these respects. Alloying it with silver, copper and various other metals somewhat improves it, but not until the percentage of the latter neutralizes the advantage of the light weight claimed for it. They further refer to the fact that the surface of aluminium is so easily abraded that it soils the hands and paper, while it has also a greasy, unpleasant feel which becomes very objectionable. Set-squares have been largely made in aluminium, and these appear to be an improvement upon the old-style wood triangles. In this case, however, it has become necessary to coat the suface either with silver or some varnish, either black or transparent.—*The Mechanical World.*

(We present the above to our readers because it expresses in the main what have been from the first our own views on the subject of aluminum and its unsuitability for drawing and other instruments. We should, however, have expected that a "prominent firm of instrument makers" would have been more consistent than to even appear, as stated by our English contemporary, to recommend the use of such a very soft material for set-squares, in which toughness combined with a certain degree of elasticity are necessary qualities. We regret that we cannot on this point agree with the firm in question as we consider that for such instruments aluminum is bad, wood is fair, and hard black rubber is good; and we believe the experience of those who have *used*, not merely manufactured, tools made of each will bear us out. It seems as if a lingering desire remained, despite the lessons of experience, in the minds of some manufacturers to force this metal into some kind of use, believing probably that the public would be allured by the enticing appearance of articles into whose composition it enters. A word to the wise.... ED.)

LIGHT: ITS REFLECTION AND REFRACTION. XIII.

WE NOW COME to the consideration of refraction as it affects convex lenses. The principle is the same as in the case of a sphere, examined in a previous number, its application being as shown in Fig. 1.

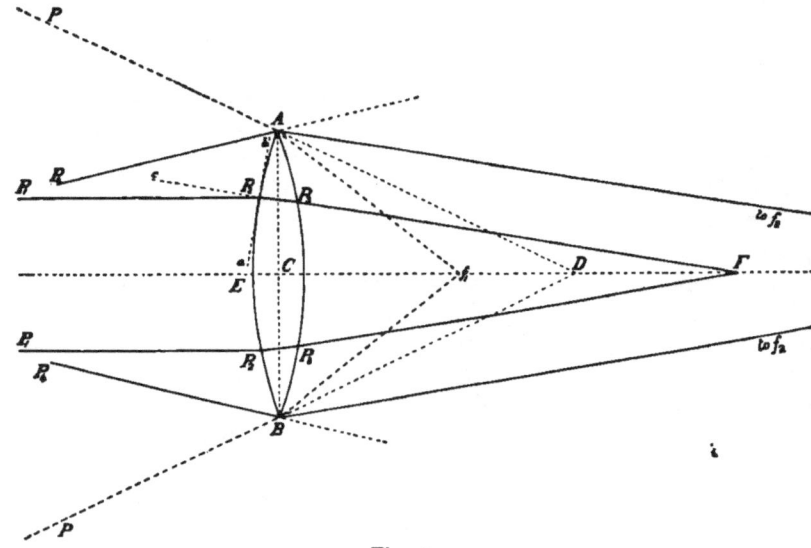

Fig. 1.

Let AB be a double convex lens, the radius of each surface being the same, and let $P_1 P_2$, $P_1 P_2$ be parallel rays of light falling upon the lens. To analyze their path let us follow the upper ray $P_1 P_2$. The point P_2 where the ray strikes the lens must be considered as part of a plane ab, tangent to the surface of the lens at this point. The index of refraction of the lens being known, the direction of the path $P_2 P_3$ of the ray through it can be calculated and graphically set out exactly as shown in Fig. 2, page 66; or we may proceed as follows. If we suppose the index of refraction of the lens to be 1.5, the sine of the angle of incidence will be to the sine of the angle of refraction as 1.5 is to 1.0. Let the angle of incidence formed by the ray $P_1 P_2$ with the normal $P_2 c$, that is, with a perpendicular to the plane ab, be 10°, the sine of this angle being 0.1736. We then have

Sine Angle Incidence : Sine Angle Refraction : : 1.5 : 1.0

whence   Sine Angle Refraction $= \dfrac{\text{Sine Angle Incidence} \times 1.0}{1.5}$

$= \dfrac{0.1736 \times 1.0}{1.5} = 0.1157 =$ Sine of 6° 39′.

The course of the ray of light through the lens or $P_2 P_3$ will be, therefore, at an angle of 6° 39′ with the normal. On emerging from the lens, the sine of the angle of incidence will be to the sine of the angle of refraction as 1.0 is to 1.5. Calculating the angles with the normal as before, we obtain the direction of the emerging ray from P_3 to F in the axis of the lens CF. If we follow in a similar manner the course of the lower parallel ray $P_1 P_2$ through the lens we shall find that it also strikes the axis of the lens at the point F. This point F is called the *Focus of Parallel Rays* or the *principal focus* of the lens, and is the point always referred to when speaking of the focus of a lens, unless some other focus be specified or distinctly implied. The distance CF from the *optical centre* of the lens to its principal focus is called the *principal focal distance* or the focal distance. If the course of other parallel rays is similarly calculated and followed they would, if the surfaces of the lens are truly spherical, also be found to converge and meet in the point F.

If instead of parallel rays we now suppose them to be converging rays as PA and PB, which, if not interrupted, would meet at D in the axis of the lens, we should find if the same method of calculating the refraction be observed, that they would converge more rapidly than parallel rays and meet at some point f, between the principal focus F and the surface of the lens, this point varying with the degree of convergence of the unintercepted rays, being nearer the lens the greater the degree of convergence and nearer the principal focus the more they approach a state of parallelism. The two points of convergence, D for unintercepted rays, and f_1 for rays which are refracted by the lens, are called *conjugate foci*, and their respective positions vary, the one with the other.

If we now examine the path of divergent rays such as $P_4 A$ and $P_4 B$ we shall find that their course is governed by identically the same principles, but that instead of their focus being between the surface of the lens and the principal focus, it will be beyond the latter at some point f_2, the distance between F and f_2 varying with the degree of divergence of the unintercepted rays. If the point of emanation of these diverging rays be equidistant from the centre of the lens with CF, then these rays, when refracted by the lens, will be parallel, thus giving an exact reversion of our first illustration of parallel rays.

The position of the points F, or the focal distance for parallel rays may also be ascertained by calculation.

The formula for double convex lenses is

$$CF = \frac{R\,r}{(\mu-1)(R+r)} \quad \dots \dots \dots \dots \dots (1)$$

where $CF =$ Focal length or distance of the focus from the optical centre of the lens.

$R =$ Radius of the near surface of the lens, or the side upon which the rays of light fall.

$r =$ Radius of the off surface of the lens or the side from which the rays emerge.

$\mu =$ Index of Refraction.

To obtain the position of the optical centre of a double convex lens, we have

$$C E \frac{R\ T}{R + r} \quad \dots\dots\dots \dots\dots\dots\dots\dots (2)$$

where $C E =$ Distance of C from the near surface of the lens.

$T =$ Thickness of the lens at the centre, that is, on the axis of the lens.

As the radius of the curved surfaces may not always be known, we give the following method for ascertaining it,

$$\text{Radius} = \tfrac{1}{2}\left(\frac{C B^2}{C E} + C E\right) \quad \dots\dots (3)$$

where $C B =$ half the diameter of the lens.

$C E =$ half the thickness of the lens at its centre.

Suppose $A B$ the diameter of the lens to be $1\tfrac{1}{2}$ inches, and its thickness to be $\tfrac{1}{4}$ inch, we have by (3)

$$\text{Radius} = \tfrac{1}{2}\left(\frac{0.75 \times 0.75}{0.125} + 0.125\right)$$

$$= 2.31 \text{ inches.}$$

This of course supposes that the radius of curvature of each face is the same. Where they vary, the radius must be calculated separately by the formula for each surface.

By means of formula (2) we now obtain the distance of the optical centre of the lens from its near surface thus:

$$\text{Distance } C E \frac{2.31 \times 0.25}{2.31 + 2.31} = 0.125 \text{ inches,}$$

or in the centre of the lens, as is always the case when the radii of the two surfaces are equal.

We now by means of formula (1) find the focal length thus, assuming the Index of Refraction to be 1.5,

$$C F = \frac{2.31 \times 2.31}{(1.5 - 1) \times (2.31 + 2.31)}$$

$$= 2.31 \text{ inches.}$$

It will thus be seen that in the case of equally convex lenses (when the two radii are equal) that the focal distance is equal to the radius, *if the index of refraction is* 1.5. For other indices it will vary being for a higher index nearer the lens, and for a lower index further from the lens.

BOOKS RECEIVED.

STATISTICS OF PUBLIC LIBRARIES IN THE UNITED STATES AND CANADA, by Weston Flint, Statistician of the Bureau of Education, being Circular of Information No. 7, 1893, of the Bureau of Education.

Although chiefly a compilation of Statistics, there is a very interesting introduction by Mr. W. T. Harris, Commissioner of Education. We find that from 1885 to 1891 there has been an increase of 817 libraries of over 1,000 volumes, the increase in the number of volumes being 12,111, 280, the rate of this increase having been naturally the greatest in the North Atlantic Division.

THE WIDENING USE OF COMPRESSED AIR, by Whitfield Price Pressinger, of the Clayton Air Compressor Works, New York.

This is a reprint in pamphlet form of an article which appeared in a recent number of *The Engineering Magazine*, and is interesting at the present time when the problem of the economic and efficient transmission of power engages so much attention. We here see what progress has been made, and to how many different uses, and in how many ways the transmission of means of compressed air is to-day applied.

THE EXPERT CALCULATOR, by John D. Haney, B. S. is a compendium of short-cuts in figures and useful business information.

The arrangement of this little book of 126 pages is very convenient, the subject divisions being given on the front cover, to each of which is given a consecutive number (from 1 to 17). The subject matter is then at once found by an index arrangement of the whole book. Amongst other instructive matter will be found a very good table of Useful Multipliers, Constants and Reciprocals. The low price of this book bound in leather (50 cents) places it within reach of all.

THE MECHANICAL WORLD POCKET DIARY AND YEAR BOOK FOR 1894. This is the seventh year of publication of this book which contains a collection of useful notes, illustrations, and formulæ, arranged for the use of Engineers, Draughtsmen, Mechanics, Manufacturers and others, by Chas. N. Pickworth, Editor of *The Mechanical World*, a weekly paper which, although published in England, appreciates and frequently lays before its readers the cream of what is being done and written in this country.

THE SOLAR TRANSIT. VI.

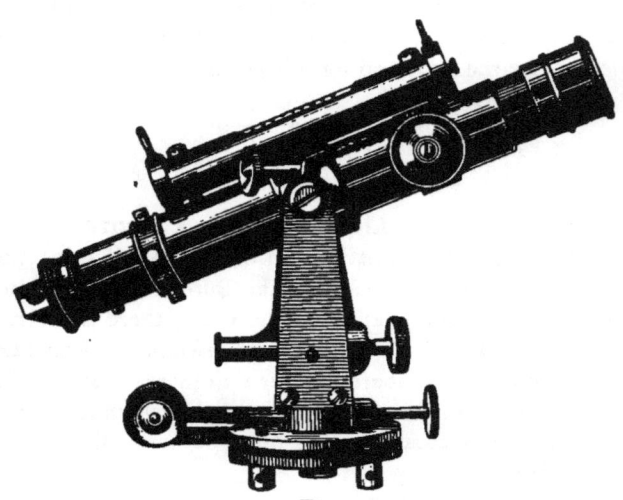

Fig. 1.

THE SOLAR ATTACHMENT shown in Fig. 1, consists of a small telescope, 6 inches long, with prismatic eye-piece and colored glass at object end, mounted in standards which revolve upon a vertical axis, the axis being adjustable to the upper part of the transit telescope. The small or SOLAR TELESCOPE is capable of being rotated in altitude and azimuth like the transit telescope, accurate adjustments to any required position being obtained by means of two clamps and tangent screws. The vertical axis of the solar telescope, called the POLAR AXIS, can also be inclined so as to make it correspond to the earth's axis of rotation by means of the telescope and vertical circle of the transit and the small level which surmounts the solar telescope. This level is provided with two small pointers, so placed that when the shadow of the smaller one is thrown upon the larger one, the sun will appear in the field of view of the solar telescope, thus affording a ready means of approximately directing the instrument to that luminary. The cross hairs in the solar telescope are six in number, three vertical and three horizontal ones, so spaced as to form a square which incloses the sun's image, while the intersection of the two middle hairs indicates the line of collimation.

We will first explain the principles of this attachment by assuming that the true meridian is already known. Before doing so, however, it is necessary to state what is the meaning of the MERIDIAN ALTITUDE of the sun. Let it be supposed that in Plate 1 the sun is on the intersection of the ecliptic and the celestial meridian, that is, at the point J; the declination is therefore JH and the co-latitude is HS_1. As in this case the celestial meridian and the sun's great circle of altitude are one and the same, and as altitude is the angular elevation of a body measured upwards from the horizon on the circle of altitude, then JS_1 must be the altitude of the sun, which is, however, designated in such a case as the sun's meridian altitude. It is clear that the measure of this angle can only be taken once a day, and that at noon, and the sun can only be in the position of J on the 21st of June, when its declination is greatest or 23° 27'.3. If the sun were below the equator, the declination, instead of being measured upwards, from H to J would have to be measured downward from H toward S_1, so that the meridian altitude would be less than the co-latitude by the amount of the declination. We have therefore

$$\left.\begin{array}{r}\text{Sun's Meridian}\\ \text{Altitude}\end{array}\right\} = \text{Co–latitude} \pm \text{Declination,}$$

according as the sun's declination is North or South. When the sun is in the equinoctial (at V or U) on March 21 and September 21, the sun's declination is zero, so that its meridian altitude is on those days equal to the complement of the latitude.

To find by calculation and instrumentally the position of the sun when on the meridian, all that is required is evidently, from what precedes, to elevate the telescope of a transit at noon to the extent of the co-latitude of the place of observation, *plus* or *minus* the sun's declination corrected for refraction, and then to direct it due south, when the sun would appear in the field of view. If the telescope could now be made to revolve upon an axis parallel to the earth's axis, and if the sun's declination were *constant* throughout the day, then if the telescope were revolved as supposed in the direction of the sun's apparent motion in the heavens, this luminary would be kept constantly in the field of view.

Such an instrument in principle is the solar transit, as the transit telescope, when elevated to the extent of the observer's co-latitude, represents the equator, the vertical axis of the solar attachment is parallel to the earth's axis, and the solar telescope sets off with the transit telescope the angular value of the sun's declination.

Figures 2, 3 and 4, in conjunction with Plate 1, will enable the principles and mode of use to be clearly understood.

We will assume that the sun's corrected declination at the time of observation has been ascertained to be 20° South, and that the latitude of the place is 40°. The following are the various steps to be followed:

1. Elevate the transit telescope the amount of the declination, to which the refraction has been previously algebraically added, by means of the vertical arc, as shown in Fig. 2, where NOE is the declination angle = 20°. When the declination is North, the transit telescope must be depressed, thus *adding*, in the succeeding operations, the declination to the co-

latitude, in order to obtain the meridian altitude, whereas elevating the telescope deducts the declination from the co-latitude. Note that E and e in the figures are the eye pieces of the two telescopes.

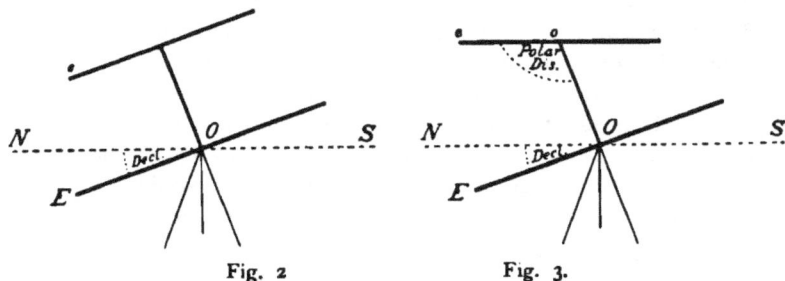

Fig. 2   Fig. 3.

2. Level the solar telescope by means of its attached level, taking care that it has been previously brought exactly into the vertical plane of the transit telescope, as shown in Fig. 3. The angle $O\,o\,e$ is then the polar distance of the sun, or the co-declination $= S\,P$ of the astronomical triangle, $= 90° + 20° = 110°$.

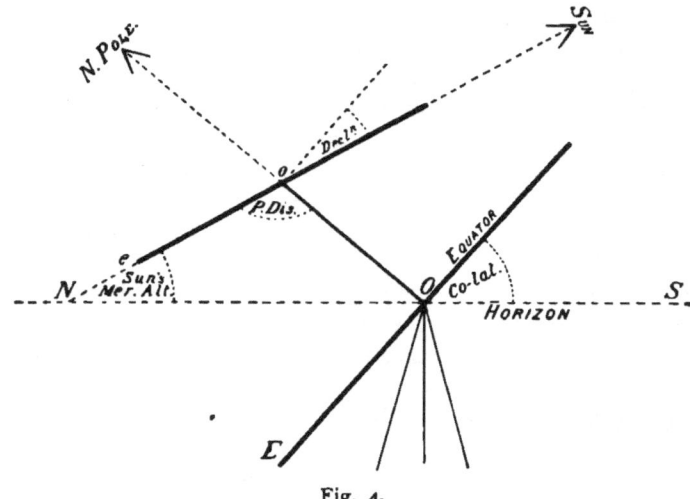

Fig. 4.

3. Without disturbing the solar telescope, elevate the transit telescope by means of its vertical arc the amount of the co-latitude $= 50°$, as shown in Fig. 4. The angle $O\,N\,o$ now formed by the solar telescope and the horizon is the meridian altitude of the sun $= 50° - 20° = 30°$.

4. Direct the transit telescope due south, and at noon the sun will be seen in the field of view of the solar telescope.

Care must always be taken during the several operations that no previously adjusted part is disturbed, for which purpose it is safest to clamp the several axes immediately after they have been set.

As previously shown, if the declination were constant throughout the day, the solar telescope could now be revolved upon its polar axis and the motion of the sun followed, thus keeping it continually in the field of view, both before and after noon, but as the declination varies every hour, the instrument has to be adjusted for observation at a specified time, previously determined and for which the declination has been calculated. How this is done will be explained in a future number. The present example is merely given to simplify and illustrate the main principles upon which the construction of this valuable attachment depends.

It will have been noted that in our table of the Solar Ephemeris for January, the Refraction Corrections are given for Latitude 40°. The following table of co-efficients or multipliers will give corresponding corrections for any other latitude, thus if the correction for latitude 40° is 1' 58", it will be 1' 58" $\times$ 1.42 = 2' 47" for latitude 50°.

TABLE OF LATITUDE COEFFICIENTS.

Lat.	Coeff.	Lat.	Coeff.	Lat.	Coeff.	Lat.	Coeff.
15°	0.30	24°	0.48	33°	0.75	42°	1.08
16	0.32	25	0.50	34	0.78	43	1.12
17	0.34	26	0.53	35	0.82	44	1.16
18	0.36	27	0.56	36	0.85	45	1.20
19	0.38	28	0.59	37	0.89	46	1.24
20	0.40	29	0.62	38	0.92	47	1.29
21	0.42	30	0.65	39	0.96	48	1.33
22	0.44	31	0.68	40	1.00	49	1.38
23	0.46	32	0.71	41	1.04	50	1.42

GLOSSARY AND DEFINITIONS OF TERMS EMPLOYED IN SURVEYING, ASTRONOMY, ETC. VII.

FILAR MICROMETER. Lat. *filum*, thread, *micros*, small and *metron*, measure. An instrument provided with a microscope, by means of which accurate measurements of small distances or angles may be obtained, which could not be had with a vernier scale.

Focus. Lat. *focus*, a hearth or fireplace. A meeting point or point of concentration. In optics, the point where converging rays of light, passing through a lens, meet. Hence, to focus, is the adjustment of a lens in such a manner that the rays of light passing through it may be concentrated upon a desired point. In mathematics, foci are certain fixed points whose position is governed by the nature of the curves to which they are related, thus an ellipse is a curve such that the sum of the distances from the two foci within the curve to any point in the curve is always the same.

GEOCENTRIC. Gr. *ge*, the earth, and *centron*, the centre. In astronomy the position of a celestial body as it would be seen by an observer at the centre of the earth is said to be its geocentric position, in opposition to its *apparent* position as seen by an observer on the surface of the earth. The difference of altitude of a body S observed from these two positions A or O (Plate 1) is the angle $A S O$, this difference being called *parallax*.

GEODESY. Gr. *ge*, the earth, and *daiein*, to divide. Geodetic surveying is the determination of the absolute position of points on the earth's surface, as regards their latitude, longitude, and elevation above the sea level, as well as the exact position of these points relatively to each other. The best instruments and the most precise methods are necessarily used.

GONIOMETER. Gr. *gonia*, an angle, and *metron*, measure. An instrument used for measuring angles. The term is not much employed in English except as referring to an instrument for measuring the angles of crystals. The French frequently apply the word to that class of instruments known as Staff Heads.

GNOMON. Gr. *gnomon*, one that knows, the index of a sun-dial. The style or pin of a sun dial whose shadow cast upon the dial by the sun, indicates the hour of the day.

GRADIENTER. Lat. *gradiens*, p. pr. of *gradi*, to step, to go. A modification of the ordinary clamp and tangent screw applied to the axis of the telescope of an engineer's transit, by which revolutions and parts of a revolution of the tangent screw may be noted. The pitch of the screw and the length of the clamp arm are so determined that one revolution of the micrometer head with which the tangent screw is provided, shall indicate a given elevation or depression of the telescope, expressed in terms of the relation of the vertical to the horizontal distance, usually 1 in 50 or 1 in 100. By this arrangement distances to, and heights of inaccessible objects may be measured easily and with considerable accuracy.

GRAPHIC. Gr. *graphikos*, from *graphein*, to write, describe. A representation of mathematical demonstrations and formulæ and scientific analyses or investigations by means of lines, curves or other figures, which appeal directly to the eye.

SOLAR EPHEMERIS, FEBRUARY 1894.
For Greenwich Apparent Noon.

Day of Week	Day of Month	The Sun's Apparent Declination			Difference for 1 Hour	Equation of Time *to be added* to Apparent Time		Day of Month	Refraction * Correction Latitude 40°		
		°	′	″	″	m	s				
Thurs.	1	S 17	0	57.1	+ 42.94	13	49.80		1 h.	1′	26″
Frid.	2	16	43	37.5	43.68	13	57.15	3	2	1	37
Sat.	3	16	26	0.3	44.41	14	3.69	to	3	2	04
Sun.	4	16	8	6.0	45.12	14	9.42	7	4	3	21
Mon.	5	15	49	55.0	45.80	14	14 34				
									1 h.	1′	21″
Tues.	6	15	31	27.6	+ 46.47	14	18.46	8	2	1	31
Wed.	7	15	12	44.5	47.12	14	21.75	to	3	1	56
Thurs.	8	14	53	45.9	47.75	14	24.24	12	4	3	04
Frid.	9	14	34	32.4	48.37	14	25.92				
Sat.	10	14	15	4.4	48.97	14	26.81		1 h.	1′	16″
								13	2	1	25
Sun.	11	13	55	22.2	+ 49.54	14	26.90	to	3	1	48
Mon.	12	13	35	26.5	50.10	14	26.21	17	4	2	47
Tues.	13	13	15	17.5	50.64	14	24.74		5	8	39
Wed.	14	12	54	55.7	51.17	14	22.51				
Thurs.	15	12	34	21.6	51.67	14	19.53		1 h.	1′	12″
								18	2	1	20
Frid.	16	12	13	35.5	+ 52.16	14	15.81	to	3	1	40
Sat.	17	11	52	37.8	52.63	14	11.37	22	4	2	31
Sun.	18	11	31	29.0	53.08	14	6.22		5	6	49
Mon.	19	11	10	9.4	53.53	14	0.38				
Tues.	20	10	48	39.5	53.96	13	53.86		1 h.	1′	07″
								23	2	1	15
Wed.	21	10	26	59.6	+ 54.37	13	46.70	to	3	1	33
Thurs.	22	10	5	10.0	54.76	13	38.90	27	4	2	18
Frid.	23	9	43	11.2	55.13	13	30.49		5	5	29
Sat.	24	9	21	3.5	55.49	13	21.48				
Sun.	25	8	58	47.4	55.83	13	11.89		1 h.	1′	03″
								28	2	1	10
Mon.	26	8	36	23.2	+ 56.16	13	1.75	to	3	1	27
Tues.	27	8	13	51.2	56.48	12	51.06	M'ch.	4	2	06
Wed.	28	7	51	11.9	56.78	12	39.86	4	5	4	39

* By permission from "The Theory and Practice of Surveying", by Prof. J. B. Johnson, C. E.

In this column the hours are counted each way from noon; thus, 9 A. M. and 3 P. M. would each correspond to the 3d hour in the table. The hourly corrections are exact for the middle day of the five-day period corresponding to any given set of hourly corrections. For other days interpolations can be made where extreme accuracy is required.

"COPYRIGHT, 1892, BY WILLIAM COX, NEW YORK."

A Monthly Journal for Engineers, Surveyors, Architects, Draughtsmen and Students.

| Vol. III. | MARCH 1, 1894. | No. 8. |

PATTERN MAKER'S SHRINKAGE RULES.

PRACTICAL MACHINISTS are not quite agreed as to the exact amount of shrinkage to be allowed for when making patterns to be cast in different metals, although we believe the following are in this country the generally accepted quantities:—

Cast Iron	$1/8$	inch per foot.
Brass	$3/16$	" "
Lead	$1/8$	" "
Tin	$1/12$	" "
Zinc	$3/16$	" "

As it is impracticable in the case of patterns of small dimensions to take the measurements from an ordinary rule and to separately add on the amount of shrinkage, (which, whether calculated or taken from a special scale is by itself an almost immeasurable quantity), and in the case of large patterns both tedious and uncertain, the customary, and we believe the most convenient and reliable method is to have a rule so graduated that every measurement taken off *includes per se* the proportionate allowance for shrinkage.

The rule shown in above figure is one of a set of Shrinkage Rules as made by our publishers. They are *about* 2 feet long (which is a much more useful size than 12 inches, as adopted by some makers), 1½ inches wide and ⅛ inch thick, of polished boxwood with brass ends, and being engine divided their accuracy may be fully relied upon.

These rules are made $24^3/_{10}$, $24\frac{1}{4}$, $24\frac{3}{8}$, $24\frac{1}{2}$, 25, $25\frac{1}{2}$, 26 and $26\frac{3}{4}$ inches long, thus giving shrinkage allowances of $^1/_{10}$th, $\frac{1}{8}$th, $^3/_{16}$ths, $\frac{1}{4}$, $\frac{1}{2}$, $\frac{3}{4}$, 1 and $1\frac{3}{8}$ths inches per foot, from which the pattern maker can select those most suitable for his class of work. Each rule has four divided edges, the graduations being tenths and sixteenths on one side, (as shown in the figure) and eighths and twelfths on the other side, so that they may be directly used for all classes of measurements.

The longer rules will be found useful in those cases in which "double shrinkage" has to be taken into account, also for patterns of objects intended to be cast in terra cotta, etc., in which the shrinkage is much greater than in metals.

The special advantages claimed for these rules are accuracy and simplicity, errors made by adding the shrinkage allowance to any given measurement being impossible.

LIGHT: ITS REFLECTION AND REFRACTION. XIV.

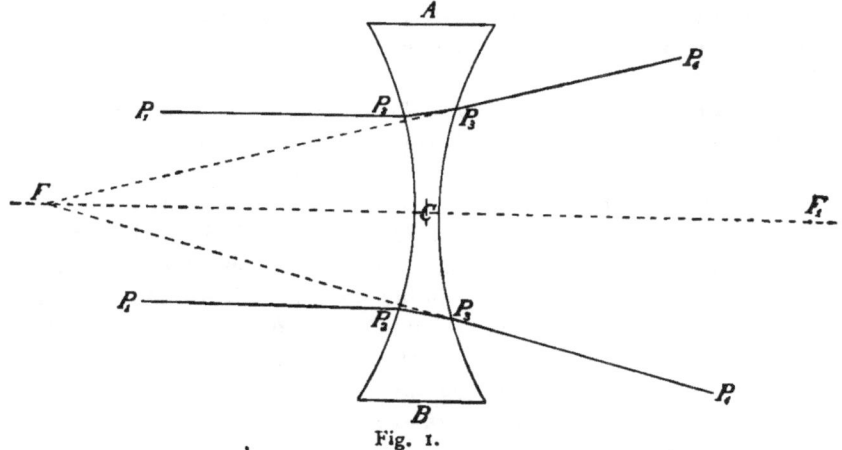

Fig. 1.

If, instead of a double convex lens, we now take a double concave one, the same laws of refraction will apply, but it will be seen that their effects are very different from those described.

Let in above figure P_1 P_2 be parallel rays of light falling upon the concave lens A B. Their path through the lens from P_2 to P_3 may be traced exactly as in the case of a double convex lens, by drawing through P_2 a tangent to the surface of the lens, and erecting upon this a perpendicular or normal, or, if the radius of curvature is known, drawing a radius through the point P_2 which will be the normal. The angle formed by the normal and the incident parallel ray being measured to be, say 15°, we have, supposing the index of refraction to be 1.5,

$$\text{Sine Angle of Refraction} = \frac{\text{Sine } 15° \times 1}{1.5}$$

$$= 0.1725 = \text{Sine of } 9° \, 56'.$$

The course of the ray through the lens from P_2 to P_3 will, therefore, be at an angle of 9° 56' with the normal. Arrived at P_3 its path beyond the lens will be found to be the converse of the former, as it passes from a denser medium to a rarer one. The angle of incidence at P_3 will, therefore be 9° 56', while the angle of refraction is 15°, thus directing the ray from P_3 to P_4, seemingly as if it proceeded from the point F on the axis of the lens. The distance of the lower parallel ray P_1 P_2 from the axis of the lens being the same as that of the upper ray, it would also be refracted to a point P_4, as if it also proceeded from the same point F.

If we follow in the same manner other parallel rays, they would be found to be refracted to different points on the off side of the lens as if they also emanated from the same point F. This point F, from which parallel rays *appear* to diverge, is the principal focus of the lens, or as it is generally termed in the case of convex lenses, the *virtual focus*, and the distance F C of the focus from the optical centre of the lens is its *focal distance*.

If, instead of parallel rays, we take converging ones, they will after refraction be found to diverge relatively to the direction of the incident rays, although not always in regard to the axis of the lens. Thus, converging rays, which if unobstructed would proceed to a point beyond F_1 (the distance C F_1 being equal to the focal distance C F) would after refraction diverge, thus becoming more and more distant from the axis of the lens, and appearing to proceed in diverging directions from a point in front of the lens, and beyond the principal focus F. The two points beyond F and F_1, from which the diverging or refracted rays appear to come, and to which the converging or incident rays would, if unobstructed, proceed, are called the *conjugate foci*, their several positions varying relatively to each other.

If, however, the rate of convergence is such that the rays would, if unobstructed meet in F_1, then they would on emerging from the lens continue their course in parallel lines, whilst if their rate of convergence were such that the unobstructed rays met in a point nearer to the lens than the principal focus F_1, then the emerging rays would be refracted to a point on the axis of the lens beyond F_1.

Diverging rays will also continue after refraction to diverge, but in a still greater degree, their *apparent point* of emanation on the axis of the lens, which is the focus of such rays, being nearer to the lens than the real point from which they emanate. The nearer to the lens is the real point from which the rays proceed, the nearer is also the apparent point of emanation, or the focus, and vice versa, the one varying with the other.

The formulæ for obtaining the position of the principal focus, etc., of double concave lenses are the same as those already given on page 105,* relating to double convex lenses, except that they have the minus sign prefixed, showing that the principal focus is on the *near side* of the lens; thus, the formula for the focal distance of parallel rays is

$$CF = - \frac{R\,r}{(\mu - 1)(R + r)} \quad \dots\dots\dots\dots (4)$$

the minus sign showing that the point F is on the near side, as shown in Fig. 1.

We add a few formulæ relating to some other kinds of lenses more or less used.

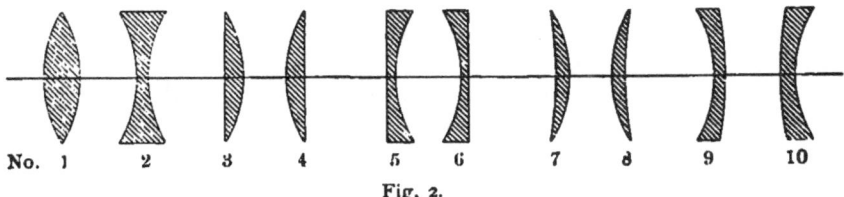

No. 1   2   3   4   5   6   7   8   9   10
Fig. 2.

In a plano-convex or a convexo-plane lens, shown in Fig. 2. Nos. 3 and 4, the optical centre C is in the axis of the lens, on the convex surface, and the focal distance is

$$CF = + \frac{r \text{ or } R}{\mu - 1} \quad \dots\dots\dots\dots\dots\dots (5)$$

the focus F being on the off side.

---

* We regret to note that formula (2) was erroneously given by the printer. It should be

$$\text{Distance } CE = \frac{R \times r}{R + r} \quad \dots\dots\dots\dots\dots\dots (2)$$

In the same way the corresponding example given lower down on the same page should be

$$\text{Distance } CE = \frac{2.31 \times 0.25}{2.31 + 2.31}\; 0.125 \text{ inches.}$$

In a plano-concave or a concavo-plane lens, Nos. 5 and 6, Fig. 2, the optical centre C is in the axis of the lens on the concave surface, the formula for the focal distance being

$$CF = -\frac{r \text{ or } R}{\mu - 1} \qquad \ldots \ldots \ldots \ldots \ldots \ldots \ldots \ldots (6)$$

the minus sign showing that the principal focus is on the *near* side, that is, on the side from which the rays of light proceed.

The optical centre C of a concave or convex meniscus, Nos. 7 and 8, or of concavo-convex and convexo-concave lenses, Nos. 9 and 10, is not on either of the surfaces of the lens but at some distance from it, its position being obtained by means of the following formula,

$$\left.\begin{array}{l}\text{Distance of optical centre}\\ \text{from } \textit{near} \text{ surface of lens}\end{array}\right\} = \frac{R\,r}{r - R} \ldots \ldots \ldots \ldots (7)$$

C being on the near side of the lens when the distance is plus ($+$), and on the off side when it is minus ($-$).

The position of the optical centre may also be obtained graphically,

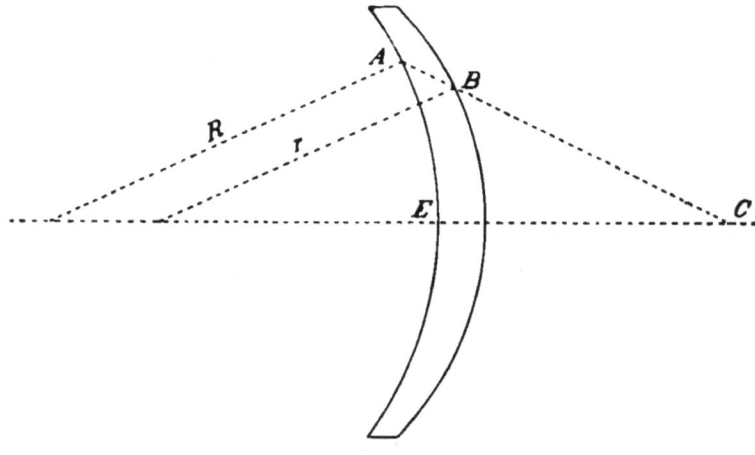

Fig. 3.

as shown in Fig. 3, where R is the radius of the near surface of the lens, and r the radius of the off surface, the lines R and r being drawn parallel to each other. A straight line is then drawn through the points A and B on the surfaces of the lens and extended to C on its axis. The point C, so found, is the optical centre of the lens, and the distance CE is its distance from the near surface of the lens as found by formula (7).

The principal focus or focus of parallel rays of a concave or convex meniscus lens like No. 7 or 8 is obtained by the following formula.

$$CF = + \frac{Rr}{(\mu - 1)(R - r)} \quad \ldots \ldots \ldots \ldots \ldots \quad (8)$$

where CF is the distance of the focus from the optical centre C of the lens, and being plus ($+$) is measured on the off side.

Formula (8) applies equally to concavo-convex and convexo-concave lenses, Nos. 9 and 10, only in these the position of the focus is reversed, so that we have

$$CF = - \frac{Rr}{(\mu - 1)(R - r)} \quad \ldots \ldots \ldots \ldots \quad (9)$$

the distance CF of the focus from the optical centre C of the lens being measured on the near side in accordance with the sign ($-$).

The following points in connection with these formulæ (1) to (9) must be distinctly noted and borne in mind, reference being in all cases to parallel rays of light.

1. THE FOCUS F of a convex lens is plus ($+$), that is, on the off side.
2. THE FOCUS F of a concave lens is minus ($-$), that is, on the near side.
3. THE OPTICAL CENTRE C is measured from the near surface of the lens, and is on the near or off side, as the algebraic sign of its distance CE is plus or minus.
4. THE FOCAL LENGTH CF, or the distance of the principal focus is measured from the optical centre C of the lens.
5. BY PARALLEL RAYS is to be understood rays of light parallel to each other and also to the axis of the lens.

PARTITION OF LAND.

BY T. W. DAVENPORT, C.E., SILVERSTON, ORE.

AS EVERY PRACTICAL surveyor can testify, there is one question or problem with which he has frequently to deal, namely, the laying out upon land of trapezoidal forms containing a given area.

More than forty years ago it was perplexing to me, as at that time I was unacquainted with any short and easily remembered formula for solving such problems. I do not remember having seen any work upon surveying giving such a formula, and I know of no surveyor who uses any other method than the old "cut and try" one. Possibly you may know of some recent publication containing the requisite proposition, but I do not, and as the one I discovered and use fulfills all the requirements of the profession I herein give it to you for the benefit of such as need it.

The usual form of the problem is about as follows:—

Given the line A and the bearings of the lines drawn from its extremities, to find the fourth side x of the trapezoid which shall contain a given required area M.

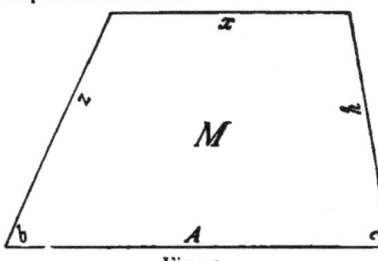

Fig. 1.

In figure 1, let b and c be the known angles, and let a be the sum of these angles subtracted from $180°$. We then have for the length of the fourth side

$$x = \left(A^2 - M \frac{2 \sin a}{\sin b \cdot \sin c} \right)^{\frac{1}{2}}$$

Logarithms of the nat. sines of the angles are used in the solution of the formula. After obtaining x, the sides y and z are easily found as follows:

$$\sin a : \sin b :: A - x : y,$$
$$\text{and } \sin a : \sin c :: A - x : z,$$

and this completes the work.

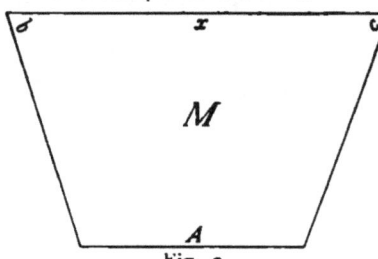

Fig. 2.

When x is greater than A as in Fig. 2, the formula is the same except that the sign after A^2 is plus ($+$) instead of minus ($-$), thus,

$$x = \left(A^2 + M \frac{2 \sin a}{\sin b \cdot \sin c} \right)^{\frac{1}{2}}$$

the angles b and c being on the inside of x, whilst a is found as before.

The following is the method by which I obtained the formula. In Fig. 3.

$$\sin a : \sin b :: A : B$$
$$\text{and } \sin a : \sin c :: A : C$$

Multiplying these proportions we have

$$\sin^2 a : \sin b \cdot \sin c :: A^2 : B \cdot C$$

Equating we have

$$\sin^2 a \times B.C = A^2 \times \sin b \cdot \sin c$$

The first member of the equation is double the area of the greater triangle after dividing both members by $\sin a$, therefore

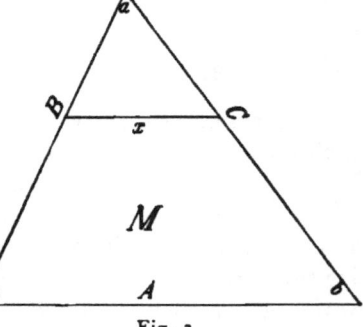

Fig. 3.

$$\frac{\sin a \times B.C}{2} = A^2 \frac{\sin b \cdot \sin c}{2 \sin a}$$

Reserving the second member and taking the proportion

$$A^2 \frac{\sin b . \sin c}{2 \sin a} : A^2 \frac{\sin b . \sin c}{2 \sin a} - M : : A^2 : x^2$$

then dividing the first couplet by the antecedent we have

$$1 : 1 - \frac{M}{A^2 \frac{\sin b . \sin c}{2 \sin a}} : : A^2 : x^2$$

Equating

$$x^2 = A^2 - \frac{A^2 . M}{A^2 \frac{\sin b . \sin c}{2 \sin a}}$$

Reducing

$$x^2 = A^2 - M \frac{2 \sin a}{\sin b . \sin c}$$

whence

$$x = \left(A^2 - M \frac{2 \sin a}{\sin b . \sin c} \right)^{\frac{1}{2}}$$

(Although this problem with the same solution of x appears in Gillespie's *Treatise on Surveying*, and was, we are informed, included in the first edition printed in 1851 and published in 1855, we are pleased to find space for Mr. Davenport's communication, as the problem and method of solving it may be of interest to some of our readers. It furnishes another instance of different minds seeking independently the solution of a mathematical problem, the result being a plurality of "original" discoveries.—ED.)

THE HELIOGRAPH.—A SUGGESTION.

THE ORDINARY SERVICE pattern of Heliograph is not very often made use of by Engineers in charge of Railway Surveys; and yet a pair of these instruments would be found to be a very useful addition to the usual survey equipment. They can be worked satisfactorily after two or three days' practice by the ordinary twenty-five or thirty rupee railway signaller and were so used for over a year on the East Coast Railway for the transmission of the usual lot of railway service messages across the Godavari River, at Rajahmandri, a distance of a couple of miles. They are slower than the ordinary telegraphic signalling, but still quite fast enough for all that will ordinarily be required of them, transmitting perhaps about half the usual number of words per minute that can be sent by telegraph. The instruments, as issued by the Mathematical Instrument Department, Calcutta, are extremely handy, about as much so as a pair of common prismatic compasses with light tripods. The signallers require a few days' preliminary practice to make them accustomed to reading by the eye instead of the ear. To all practical Railway Engineer Surveyors, many occasions will suggest themselves in which much time and misunderstanding may be saved through their being able to speak direct with their assistants across a few miles of country, especially in rough ground.—*Indian Engineering.*

(Our friends have frequently informed us that the Heliograph is extensively used on the prairies of the Argentine Republic, where telephonic or telegraphic communication is out of the question, not only on account of the frequently altered positions of the stations, but also on account of the sudden tornadoes which sweep everything before them. One great advantage of this method of communication is that when the sun is invisible, artificial lights may be very effectively used. We illustrated and described in a former number (June 1893) of THE COMPASS the Heliograph as made by Keuffel & Esser Co. They have supplied to the U. S. Government a number of screens, composed of two plates hinged at the top and bottom and opening simultaneously by turning the key. This screen was designed by Captain Kilbourne, Signal Corps, U. S. A., and is considered the most satisfactory pattern yet invented.—ED.)

THE SOLAR TRANSIT. VII.

WE HAVE SHOWN that if the telescope of a transit is elevated to the co-latitude of a place of observation, and if another or a solar telescope, revolving upon an axis perpendicular to the transit telescope which represents the plane of the equator, is elevated or depressed to the sun's declination, (according as it is North or South) this declination being set off for the noon hour of the day when the observation is being made, (care being taken to see that the two telescopes are in the same vertical plane) —then, when at noon the solar telescope is directed towards the sun (the transit telescope being moved simultaneously with it), the transit telescope will point due south. If in this position the vernier zero is made to coincide with zero of the horizontal limb of the transit, the direction of the compass needle will indicate the amount of its declination.

If the sun's declination were constant throughout the day, the solar telescope could be revolved upon its axis and thus follow its motion from morning to evening, provided of course that the transit telescope remained the whole time in the same position pointing to the south. If it is, however, revolved upon its vertical axis, the polar axis or vertical axis of the solar telescope will no longer point to the north, and consequently the correct declination set off by the solar telescope will be disturbed, just the same as, if at noon the transit telescope were not pointed due south, the solar telescope would not set off the sun's correct meridian altitude, that is, the co-latitude $+$ the declination.

If we now set off the sun's declination for say 10 A.M., and point the transit telescope to the south, then on revolving the solar telescope upon its axis, it would at 10 o'clock strike the sun. If the transit telescope were not directed due south, the solar telescope would not strike the sun, but would be above or below it according to the direction in which the transit telescope was horizontally revolved.

It will be, therefore, evident that if the transit telescope has been set to the co-latitude of the place and the solar telescope to the declination (in regard to the equatorial plane of the transit telescope) for a given predetermined hour of the day, the sun will at that hour come into the field of view only *when the transit telescope is on the meridian.* By *mutually* revolving, therefore, the two telescopes upon their respective vertical axes *until* the sun's image is seen in the solar telescope, (and that at the given hour for which the declination was previously set off) the transit telescope is and must be brought into the meridian, while the angle formed by the vertical planes passing through the two telescopes is the sun's azimuth.

We obtain from what precedes the following simple

DIRECTIONS FOR USING THE SOLAR ATTACHMENT TO DETERMINE THE MERIDIAN.

1. Having seen that the transit and the solar attachment are in adjustment, take from the Nautical Almanac, or from the monthly Solar Ephemeris published in each current number of THE COMPASS, the declination for the day and hour at which the observation is to be made, and correct such declination for refraction. Incline the transit telescope until this angle is indicated by the vertical limb or arc, depressing the telescope if the sun's declination is north, and elevating it if it is south.

2. Bring the solar telescope into the vertical plane of the transit telescope, (without disturbing the position of the latter) and also to a horizontal position by means of its level. The two telescopes will now enclose an angle equal to the amount of the declination.

3. Without disturbing the relative positions of the two telescopes, elevate the transit telescope (and with it the solar) until the amount of the co-latitude is indicated by the vernier of the vertical limb.

4. Revolve the two telescopes mutually upon their respective vertical axes until the image of the sun is brought into the field of the solar telescope; when this is accurately bisected the transit telescope will be in the meridian and the compass needle will indicate the amount of its declination at the place of observation. It will of course considerably facilitate this last operation if, before commencing to revolve the two telescopes, the transit one is approximately pointed toward the south by means of the transit compass needle.

It will be noted from these directions that two data only are required before making an observation, one being the latitude and the other the sun's declination. The former is generally known, although it may also be obtained with the Solar Attachment, as will be hereafter explained. The declination must, however, be previously ascertained for the day and hour of observation, and corrected for refraction, the following being the simplest manner of effecting this.

PREPARATION OF THE DECLINATION SETTINGS FOR A DAY'S OBSERVATIONS.

Example. Let a table of declinations be required for March 10, 1894, the place of observation being 40° North Latitude and 75° West Longitude.

From the Nautical Almanac, or from the Ephemeris now being published monthly in THE COMPASS, we see that the sun's declination at Greenwich at noon is 3° 59' 25" S, with an hourly difference of $+$ 58."8, the affix S showing that the sun is below the celestial equator, and the plus ($+$) prefix showing that the sun is going North, and that the South declination is consequently hourly decreasing.

The longitude of the place of observation being West, and 15 degrees of longitude being equal to one hour of time, it is clear that Greenwich noon is equivalent to $12^h - (\frac{75}{15}) = 7$ A.M. at the place of observation. [If the longitude were 75° East, then the difference of time would be $0^h + (\frac{75}{15}) = 5$ P.M.] The declination given in the almanac is, therefore, the apparent and true declination* at the place of observation at 7^h A.M. We, therefore, by successive *algebraic* additions of the hourly difference of 59" obtain the following results:—

Time	7 A.M.	8 A.M.	9 A.M.	10 A.M.	11 A.M.
Declination	3° 59' 25"	3° 58' 26"	3° 57' 27"	3° 56' 28"	3° 55' 29"
Time	1 P.M.	2 P.M.	3 P.M.	4 P.M.	5 P.M.
Declination	3° 53' 31"	3° 52' 52"	3° 51' 33"	3° 50' 34"	3° 49' 35"

These quantities must now be corrected for refraction as follows. We showed on page 84, note 2, that when the *true* altitude of an object is known (as in the case of the declinations given in the Nautical Almanac,) and its *apparent* altitude is sought, (as when by calculation a telescope is to be directed upon it,) then the correction for refraction must be *added*

---

* *Apparent*, because it is the position in which the sun would appear to an observer on the surface of the earth, and *true*, because it would thus appear if refraction did not change the direction of the rays of light proceeding from it and bend them downwards making the object appear higher than it really is.

to the calculated quantity. From the Ephemeris we find that the amounts of refraction to be added for latitude 40° are

For 1 hour before and 1 hour after noon.......... 0' 55"
" 2   "   "   2 "   " 1 02
" 3   "   "   3 "   " 1 15
" 4   "   ".   4 "   " 1 47
" 5   "   "   5 "   " 3 34

With these data we therefore make out a table of corrected declinations for the different hours of the day selected for observation, thus

Declination Settings for March 10, 1894, Lat. 40° N., Long. 75° W.

Hour	Declination.	Refraction Correction	Setting.	Hour	Declination.	Refraction Correction	Setting.
A. M.	South.		South.	P. M.	South.		South.
7	3° 59' 25"	+ 3' 34"	4° 2' 59"	1	3° 53' 31"	+ 0' 55"	3° 54' 26"
8	3 58 26	+ 1 47	4 0 13	2	3 52 32	+ 1 02	3 53 34
9	3 57 27	+ 1 15	3 58 42	3	3 51 33	+ 1 15	3 52 48
10	3 56 28	+ 1 02	3 57 30	4	3 50 34	+ 1 47	3 52 21
11	3 55 29	+ 0 55	3 56 24	5	3 49 35	+ 3 34	3 53 09

If the latitude had been 38° the Refraction Corrections would have had to be multiplied by 0.92, and if the latitude had been 42° the multiplier or coefficient would be 1.08 and similarly in other cases, according to the table of coefficients on page 110. We do not give a declination setting for noon as no solar work should be undertaken between 11 A.M. and 1 P. M., if anything like accuracy is desired, the best results being generally secured between 7 and 10 in the morning and 2 and 5 in the afternoon, although the uncertainty as to the real amout of the refraction coefficient at sunrise and sunset may lead to considerable error, refraction having then its greatest value.

Particular attention should be paid when making out a table of declination settings to the signs, thus

Period.	Declination.	Hourly Change.
March 20 to June 20,	Positive or *N*.	Positive or +
June 20 to Sept. 20	"	Negative or —
Sept. 20 to Dec. 20	Negative or *S*.	Negative or —
Dec. 20 to March 20	"	Positive or +

thus showing that the Hourly Change must always be *algebraically added* to the declination. The Refraction Correction is always positive or + .

NON-USE OF METRIC WEIGHTS AND MEASURES A HINDRANCE TO FOREIGN TRADE.

MR. FRED. BROOKS, of Boston, sends us a communication received from Acting Secretary Johnson of the New Decimal Association, London, to which it is desirable to give publicity in view of the fact that the trade of the United States with metric countries in America south of us has been increasing, and that it is the general desire that it should be much further increased.

Secretary Johnson writes:—

In the last published Foreign Office Report (No. 1300) on the trade, etc., of Bulgaria, it is stated that would-be sellers in England do sometimes go so far as to send out catalogues in French or some other foreign language, but that even then they "persist in retaining the intricate English Standards of weights and measures." It is added: The metric system is the one now employed throughout Bulgaria, and it is useless for English manufacturers,—especially of machinery, and hardware—to expect that their potential foreign customers will give themselves the trouble of learning our avoirdupois and dimension tables, in order to be able to puzzle out quarters, pounds and ounces, yards and inches, gallons, pints, etc., into their metric equivalents.

Regarding Peru a correspondent writes complaining of the inconvenience he suffers when consigning machinery. The shipping specifications have to be sent out in metric weights and measures, and if there are any errors his customers are liable to a fine. This means that he has to make out the specifications twice over, first in English and then in metric weights and measures. He therefore urges, and not unreasonably, that the metric system should be adopted officially in England. This would doubtless lead to its being adopted by all shipowners and carriers, and one more step in the direction of an international system of weights would be taken. Great Britain is almost the only civilized country of first rank which is blind to the interests at stake in this question, and it is high time that a public inquiry should be instituted.

IN THE NEXT number of THE COMPASS we shall have an interesting article relating to the New Telemeter Target, described in previous issues. Mr. Claudio Urrutia, the patentee, has sent us a few interesting particulars of some of his investigations which will, we are sure, interest many of our readers. It may meanwhile be stated that one of the valuable features of this instrument lies in the fact that HORIZONTAL DISTANCES are always obtained directly, thus rendering any correction when the direct distance to the target is not horizontal, unnecessary, as was erroneously stated to be the case in our former articles. We have received a good many letters and expressions of opinion on this point, some maintaining one and others the contrary side of the question. Space does not allow of our reproducing them, but the consensus of opinion, with which we fall in line, clearly points to the solution above stated. We therefore resume, for the sake of clearness and easy reference, the different formulæ applicable to measurements taken with this valuable instrument.

Let m = total angle of all the measurements in minutes;
n = number of measurements taken;

(*A*.) TARGETS SPACED AT 1 METRE:—

Horizontal Distance in metres $= 3437.74 \times \frac{n}{m}$ .... (1)

" " " feet $= 11278.56 \times \frac{n}{m}$ .... (2)

(*B*.) TARGETS SPACED AT 2.9089 FEET.

Horizontal Distance in feet $= 10000 \frac{n}{m}$ .... (3)

(*C*.) TARGETS SPACED AT 1.1635 METRES.

Horizontal Distance in Metres $= 4000 \frac{n}{m}$ .... (4)

In all cases we have

Vertical Height = Horizontal Distance $\times \tan a$ .... (5)

where a = the vertical angle taken on the vertical limb or arc of the transit, and

Direct Distance = Horizontal Distance $\times \sec a$ .... (6)

or

$= \dfrac{\text{Horizontal Distance}}{\cos a}$ .... (7)

THE UNITED STATES GEOLOGICAL SURVEY has issued a number of topographical maps of sections of New York State, Massachusetts and Connecticut. These maps are on separate sheets, 20x16½ inches in size, and show in detail the location of villages, highways, railroads, streams and boundary lines, besides indicating the density of settlement, and showing very plainly the contour of the country. The sheets thus far issued comprise the following sections: In New York—Coxsackie, Poughkeepsie, Troy, Albany, Schenectady, Durham and Cohoes; in Connecticut—Stamford, Carmel and Clove, and Pittsfield Sheet in Massachusetts.—*The Iron Age.*

GLOSSARY AND DEFINITIONS OF TERMS EMPLOYED IN SURVEYING, ASTRONOMY, ETC. VIII.

Graphometer. Gr. *graphein*, to write, and *metron*, measure. An instrument used for measuring angles, based on the law of the double reflection of light. (For full description: see Vol. II., p. 33.)

Graphoscope. Gr. *graphein*, to write, and *skopein*, to view. An optical instrument provided with a double convex lens and a pair of stereoscopic lenses, for viewing photographs, engravings, drawings, etc.

Heliograph. Gr. *helios*, the sun, and *graphein*, to write. An instrument by which the sun's rays are intermittently reflected from a mirror to a distant observer, thus serving as a means of communication by varying the duration of the flashes of light and combining them in accordance with a predetermined code. Sometimes also called a heliotrope, from *helios* and *tropein*, to turn.

Heliostat. Gr. *helios*, and *statos*, placed or standing. An instrument similar in many respects to a heliograph, but only capable of producing continuous reflected rays instead of intermittent ones.

Heterogeneous. *heteros*, other, and *genos*, race or kind. Unlike in kind, having different characteristics. Employed in reference to the particles which make up the mass of a body.

Homogeneous. Gr. *homos*, the same, and *genos*, race or kind. Of the same kind or having the same characteristics. The converse of heterogeneous, and employed in a like manner.

Horizon. Gr. *horizon*, the bounding line. In general terms, the circle which limits on all sides an observer's view of the earth from any given point. In astronomy, we distinguish three horizons:—the VISIBLE or APPARENT, which is the one just stated; the SENSIBLE, which is a boundless imaginary plane, perpendicular in all directions to the radius of the earth on which the observer is standing and passing through his eye, ($=N_2 A\, S_2$, Plate I); and the TRUE or CELESTIAL, which is a plane parallel to the sensible horizon, but passing through the centre of the earth ($=N\, O\, S_1$). The DIP of the horizon is the vertical angle formed by the visible and the sensible horizons, and is approximately equal to 57.4 $\sqrt{H}$, where $H =$ the height of the observer's eye in feet, the dip thus obtained being in seconds of a degree.

Hyaloid. Gr. *hualos*, glass, and *eidos*, appearance:—thus glassy, transparent. The vitreous humor which fills that part of the eye between the crystalline lens and the retina, is not in immediate contact with the retina, but is enclosed in a fine, transparent membrane, called the hyaloid. (*Nugent*).

SOLAR EPHEMERIS, MARCH 1894.
For Greenwich Apparent Noon.

Day of Week	Day of Month	The Sun's Apparent Declination			Difference for 1 Hour	Equation of Time *to be added* to Apparent Time		Day of Month	Refraction * Correction Latitude 40°		
			°	′	″	″	m	s				
Thurs.	1	S	7	28	25.7	+ 57.06	12	28.15				
Frid.	2		7	5	33.0	57.32	12	15.95		1 h.	0′	59″
Sat.	3		6	42	34.1	57.57	12	3.28	5	2	1	06
Sun.	4		6	19	29.6	57.80	11	50.16	to	3	1	21
Mon.	5		5	56	19.6	58.02	11	36.59	9	4	1	56
										5	4	04
Tues.	6		5	33	4.8	+ 58.22	11	22.61				
Wed.	7		5	9	45.5	58.40	11	8.21		1 h.	0′	55″
Thurs.	8		4	46	22.2	58.55	10	53.43	10	2	1	02
Frid.	9		4	22	55.2	58.69	10	38.27	to	3	1	15
Sat.	10		3	59	24.9	58.82	10	22.75	14	4	1	47
										5	3	34
Sun.	11		3	35	51.8	+ 58.93	10	6.89				
Mon.	12		3	12	16.3	59.02	9	50.70		1 h.	0′	52″
Tues.	13		2	48	38.7	59.10	9	34.22	15	2	0	58
Wed.	14		2	24	59.4	59.16	9	17.44	to	3	1	10
Thurs.	15		2	1	18.9	59.21	9	0.40	19	4	1	39
										5	3	08
Frid.	16		1	37	37.4	+ 59.24	8	43.12				
Sat.	17		1	13	55.5	59.25	8	25.61		1 h.	0′	48″
Sun.	18		0	50	13.2	59.26	8	7.90	20	2	0	54
Mon.	19		0	26	31.2	59.24	7	50.01	to	3	1	05
Tues.	20	S	0	2	49.6	59.22	7	31.97	24	4	1	32
										5	2	51
Wed.	21	N	0	20	51.2	+ 59.18	7	13.80				
Thurs.	22		0	44	30.8	59.12	6	55.52		1 h.	0′	45″
Frid.	23		1	8	9.0	59.05	6	37.16	25	2	0	50
Sat.	24		1	31	45.4	58.97	6	18.74	to	3	1	01
Sun.	25		1	55	19.7	58.88	6	0.28	29	4	1	25
										5	2	34
Mon.	26		2	18	51.5	+ 58.77	5	41.82				
Tues.	27		2	42	20.6	58.65	5	23.36		1 h.	0′	42″
Wed.	28		3	5	46.5	58.51	5	4.93	30	2	0	47
Thurs.	29		3	29	8.9	58.35	4	46.56	to	3	0	57
Frid.	30		3	52	27.6	58.18	4	28.26	Apl. 3	4	1	19
										5	2	18
Sat.	31		4	15	42.1	58.00	4	10.04				

* By permission from "The Theory and Practice of Surveying", by Prof. J. B. Johnson, C. E.

In this column the hours are counted each way from noon; thus, 9 A. M. and 3 P. M. would each correspond to the 3d hour in the table. The hourly corrections are exact for the middle day of the five-day period corresponding to any given set of hourly corrections. For other days interpolations can be made where extreme accuracy is required.

"COPYRIGHT, 1892, BY WILLIAM COX, NEW YORK."

A Monthly Journal for Engineers, Surveyors, Architects, Draughtsmen and Students.

Vol. III.   APRIL 1, 1894.   No. 9.

THE SOLAR TRANSIT. VIII.

WHEN WORKING with the Solar Attachment it is necessary that both the Transit and the Attachment be in perfect adjustment, otherwise errors more or less serious will inevitably creep in. The most important points in connection with the transit requiring attention are the levels on the telescope and the plate, as well as the vertical circle; all of which must be accurately adjusted, (or the index error of the latter at least carefully ascertained and noted) otherwise the correct latitude and declination cannot be set off; the cross axis of the telescope must be perfectly horizontal, so that the plane of revolution of the telescope may pass through the earth's radius upon which the observer is situated, whatever may be the position of the transit telescope.

The adjustments of the attachment are as follows:

1. *The polar axis must be perpendicular to the plane passing through the line of collimation and the horizontal axis of the transit telescope.*— Level the transit and bring its telescope bubble to the middle of its run. In this position its line of sight and its horizontal axis should be in one and the same horizontal plane, whence consequently the polar axis of the solar should be perfectly vertical. To test this, level and revolve the solar tele-

scope about its polar axis, when, if the bubble of the level which surmounts the solar telescope maintains its position in the centre of its run during a whole revolution of the telescope, the polar axis is perpendicular to the telescopic plane, as stated. If the bubble does not remain stationary, half the error must be corrected by means of the small adjusting screws by which the two lower or base plates of the solar are attached to each other, the other half of the error being corrected by again leveling the solar telescope. This adjustment is similar to the one described in Vol. II., page 155, where we showed that the apparent error is double the real error, and that by correcting half the apparent error we in fact rectify the whole of the real error. Bringing the bubble again to the centre of its run by revolving the telescope on its horizontal axis is but a means whereby we test the accuracy of the adjustment of the plates just effected.

2. *The line of sight of the solar telescope must be parallel to the axis of its bubble.*—Level both telescopes, as in the last adjustment, by bringing their respective bubbles to the centre of their runs. Sight with each telescope upon a rod placed at a suitable distance and note exactly the two readings; if their difference is the same as the vertical distance between the horizontal axes of the two telescopes, then this adjustment is in order. If not, adjust the cross hairs of the solar telescope so that there shall be the required agreement.

These adjustments should be frequently examined, and if in perfect order the meridian may be determined by the method we have described to the nearest minute of azimuth, if the observations be made in the limit of the hours stated in our last as being the best, and provided that these are not within one hour of sunrise or sunset.

DIRECTIONS FOR USING THE SOLAR ATTACHMENT TO ASCERTAIN THE LATITUDE.

Level the transit carefully, and having directed its telescope towards the south, incline it an amount equal to the sun's meridian declination, uncorrected for refraction, depressing the telescope if the declination is north and elevating it if it is south. Now bring the solar telescope into the vertical plane of the transit telescope and to a perfectly horizontal position by means of its level, then clamp it. A few minutes before noon (the moment of the sun's culmination) bring the sun's image between the two horizontal wires of the solar telescope by moving the *transit telescope* only in altitude and azimuth. By means of the tangent screws of the transit keep the sun, as it continues to rise and travel southwards, in this position relatively to the cross hairs of the solar telescope. When it has ceased to rise, take the reading of the vertical arc of the transit, deduct from it the refraction due to this altitude as given in the table, page 85, and the remainder is the co-latitude, which deducted from 90° gives the latitude. This position of the two telescopes is identical with that shown in Fig. 4, page 109.

Observation for Time.

Having brought the two telescopes into their final positions for determining the meridian, that is the transit one in the meridian and the solar telescope bisecting the sun (par : 4, page 122) revolve them both upon their *horizontal* axes, without disturbing their vertical, until they are both perfectly level. The angle formed by their respective lines of sight, which can be determined by sighting with the two telescopes upon any clearly defined distant object, and taking the difference of the respective readings of the transit horizontal limb, is the hour angle $S P Z$ of the astronomical triangle, or the arc $H D$, Plate I. This is then reduced to time before or after apparent noon as explained page 52, where it is shown that 1 degree of arc = 4 minutes of time and 1 minute of arc = 4 seconds of time. Time obtained by such an observation is reliable to a few seconds.

A NEW TELEMETER TARGET. I.
By Mr. Claudio Urrutia, C. E., Guatamala.

NOTWITHSTANDING that the idea of employing a horizontal bar with or without discs or targets placed in front of an observer provided with a transit, for ascertaining the distance between the target and the transit by means of the angle subtended by the bar or the discs, is probably, like the Italian Stadia, about a century old,—it yet seems to me that it has not received the attention which it deserves. This may be due to the supposed inconvenience resulting from the acuteness of the triangle formed by such a short base as the bar, causing any error in the measurement of the apex angle to produce serious error in the resulting measurement. The method of determining angles with greater accuracy, or at least approximately, by repetition must, however, naturally have occurred to many, but it has the disadvantage that the calculation of the triangle necessitates the use of a table of trigonometrical tangents reading seconds or even fractions of a second, and besides being a laborious operation, the results do not at first sight inspire confidence. It is possible that the idea so prevalent of depreciating the method of making observations *by repetition*, and exalting that *by reiteration** in spite of the many proofs in favor of the former, may have largely influenced the rejection of the method of repeating the angle subtended by the extremities of the bar. Be this as it may, my system is based upon a theory, purely and simply geometrical, not concerned with the triangle formed by the bar and the two lines of sight, but only considering the polygon formed by the first and last lines of sight after repeated observations of the bar,—a polygon which does not sensibly differ in form from that of a circular sector when the distance between the targets (or the length of the bar) is *very small*.

The repetition of the angle is in fact altogether equal (not taking into account small errors which will be treated of later) to the measurement of what would form the extremities of a large target in the shape of a line divided into a number of equal sections, and placed in such a manner that its several parts or sections would be equally distant from the point occupied by the transit, and composed of as many sections as there may have been made repetitions of the angle. It is clear that such a sector could be easily resolved from the known magnitude of each section of the target thus divided, the number of the sections, and the total angle formed by the lines of sight directed upon the extremities of this multiple target. The formula to be used is as follows:—

$$\text{Distance} = \frac{3437.7468 \times \text{number of repetitions}}{\text{Number of minutes of the total angle.}}$$

It must, of course, be understood that if the distance between the target and the transit is a sloping one, no notice must be taken of the difference of level of the two stations, seeing that the distance obtained by the formula is, when using a transit like the modern ones, which reduce the measured angle to the horizontal plane, always the horizontal distance.

The Probable Error in the Measurement of Distances with the Telemeter Target.

Leaving out of question the errors caused by unskillful use of the

---

* By *reiteration*, we presume Mr. Urrutia means the system known here as *by series*.

transit, those due to any obliquity of the bar in regard to the direction of the line to be measured, and those which would result from assuming that the bar is equivalent to the arc of the circle whose radius is the distance to be measured:—seeing that the first are not subject to calculation, and the others are of but little importance, because the obliquity of the bar could scarcely in any case be more than two or three degrees, which would not cause an error greater than 0.1%, while the last cause of error is so insignificant that at a distance of 8 metres it would only be $1^c/_m$ or 0.125%, and at a distance of 57 metres not more than 0.003%;—therefore, ignoring these sources of error, which are not only easily avoided but may be easily accounted for, we pass on to the consideration of certain inevitable errors such as those due to the limit of appreciation of the transit and to the absence of precision in the coincidence of the lines of sight with the extremities of the bar, due to the imperfections of our visual sense.

I. *The acuteness of vision*, that is, the angle subtended by a distant object at which it begins to be distinctly perceptible, has been found to be according to the experiments of Mager, Th. Weber, Helmholt and Bergman, 92, 90.6, 93 and 75 seconds. The mean of these values is 87.6 seconds for the angle in question. We will assume that it is 90 seconds, that is 0.00044 per unit of distance. Calling the magnifying power of a telescope a and the distance of an object sighted with it D, this object will be distinctly perceptible when it has a magnitude greater than $\frac{0.00044\ D}{a}$, so that with the "Telemeter Target" an error of coincidence of the vertical thread of the cross hairs with the centre of one of the discs smaller than that quantity cannot be estimated.

Two coincidences are necessary every time we use the Target, and taking v to be the number of observations or repetitions of the angle formed by the centres of the two discs, the number of the coincidences of the vertical thread with the discs will clearly be $2v$; hence, those which tend to increase the magnitude of the bar will produce a positive error of $+\frac{0.00044\ D}{a}$, while those tending to decrease the length of the bar will produce a negative error of $-\frac{0.00044\ D}{a}$. These errors are compensated by the extraction of the square root of the number of coincidences, or $\sqrt{2v}$, therefore, the value of the final error formed by the lines of sight is

$$\pm \sqrt{2v}\,\frac{0.00044\ D}{a}$$

while the value of the Target multiple will be

$$v \pm \sqrt{2v}\,\frac{0.00044\ D}{a}.$$

CORRECTIONS FOR PARALLAX AND REFRACTION IN SOLAR WORK.

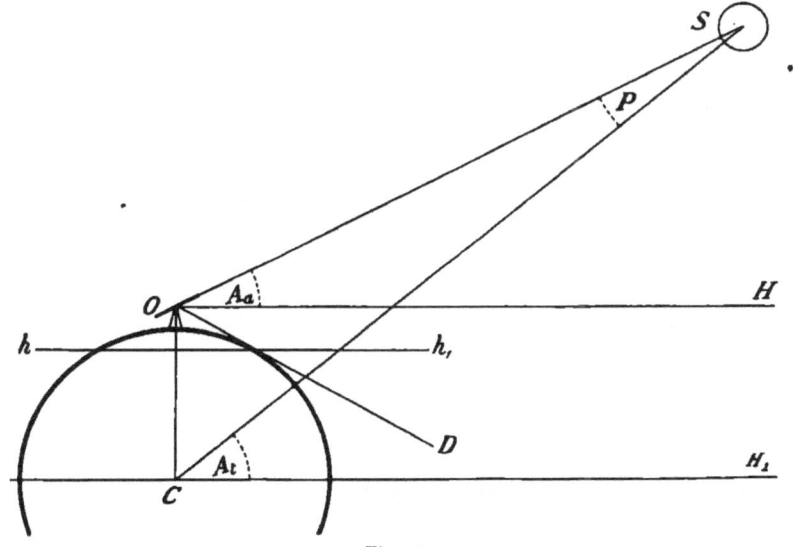

Fig. 1.

THE ACCOMPANYING DIAGRAMS will enable the nature of the different corrections required in Solar work to be clearly understood. The following points should be carefully noted.

1. The position of the sun or other celestial body in the heavens as determined by its angle of elevation is, as *we* see it from the surface of the earth, its APPARENT or OBSERVED ALTITUDE.

2. The position of the sun, as it would be seen by an observer situated at the centre of the earth, is called its TRUE ALTITUDE, and the angle, formed by the line of sight from the observer on the surface of the earth and the line from the centre of the earth to the sun, is the sun's parallax. The angle of true altitude is, therefore, greater than that of apparent altitude.

3. The DIP of the horizon is the angle of depression formed by the sensible horizon and the plane reaching from the observer to the bounding line of the visible horizon of the sea. Altitudes measured at sea with a sextant (or from an eminence looking toward the sea) are, therefore, too great by the amount of the dip of the horizon, while altitudes measured with a transit give the angle of elevation from the sensible horizon. The *dip* and the *visible horizon* enter but rarely into the surveyor's calculations.

4. REFRACTION, or the bending of the course of a ray of light as it passes from a celestial object through the atmosphere to an observer,

makes that object appear higher than it really is. When the object is in the zenith, there is neither parallax nor refraction, but both have their greatest value when the object is on the horizon. A ray of light from the sun at S (Fig. 2) would not, therefore, follow the direct line SO to the observer, but the bent one SrO, so that the light would appear to come to the observer from S_1 in the straight line S_1O.

In the figures let

$CH_1 = $ The *true* horizon.
$OH = $ The *sensible* horizon parallel to CH_1.
$hh_1 = $ The *visible* or *apparent* horizon; then we have in Fig. 1,
$SOH = $ Apparent or observed Altitude of S, if with transit $= A_a$.
$SOD = $ Observed Altitude of S if with sextant $= A_o$.
$SCH_1 = $ True Altitude of $S = A_t$.
$CSO = $ Parallax $= P$.
$HOD = $ Dip of the horizon $= D$,

whence

True Altitude = Apparent Altitude + Parallax.
Apparent Altitude = True Altitude — Parallax,
or $A_t = A_a + P$, and
$A_a = A_t - P$.

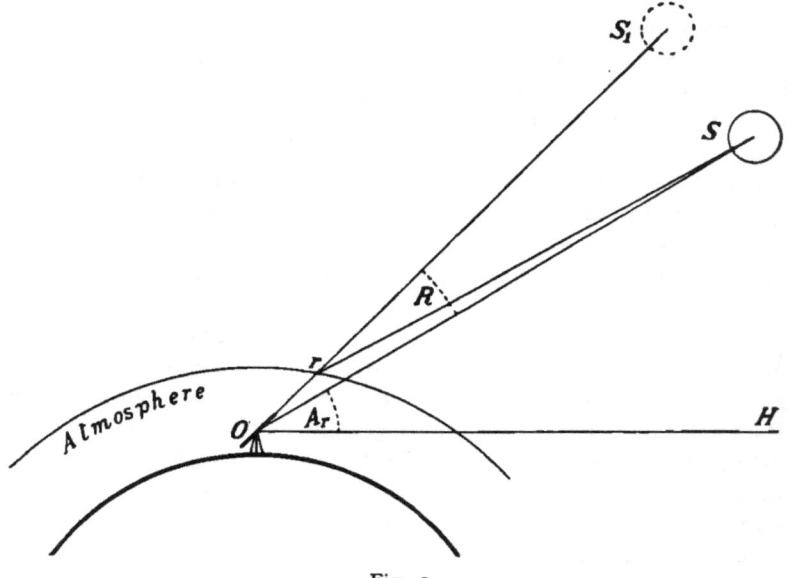

Fig. 2.

Also

Apparent Altitude = $\begin{cases}\text{Observed Altitude} \\ \text{(with Sextant.)}\end{cases}$ — Dip

    or $A_a = A_o - D$, and

    $A_t = A_o - D + P.$

We also have in Fig. 2,

    $S_1\ O\ H$ = Apparent Altitude of $S = A_a$

    $S\ O\ S_1$ = Angle of Refraction = R

    $S\ O\ H$ = Corrected Altitude of $S = A_r$,

whence

Corrected Altitude = Apparent Altitude — Refraction.

Apparent Altitude = Corrected Altitude + Refraction,

    or $A_r = A_a - R$, and

    $A_a = A_r + R.$

We are induced to explain these points thus minutely because we sometimes find a certain degree of confusion existing as to whether Parallax and Refraction are to be added or subtracted. We deduce, therefore, from what precedes the two following rules :—

1. GIVEN :—the *observed* or *apparent* altitude of the sun :—to FIND the *true* altitude,

    ADD *Parallax*, and

    SUBTRACT *Refraction*.

2. GIVEN : —the *true* altitude of the sun, to FIND the *apparent* altitude,

    SUBTRACT *Parallax*, and

    ADD *Refraction*.

Rule 2 serves to correct the sun's Declination as taken from the Nautical Almanac, when used with the Solar Attachment, while Rule 1 is used when the sun's Azimuth is computed by means of the astronomical triangle, as shown on page 82.

DRAWING INSTRUMENTS. III.

THE FINISH of drawing instruments is a very important point, not only of itself but also as indicative to a considerable extent of the quality of the material and workmanship, and thus indirectly of the value of the instrument. Finish cannot, however, be always properly appreciated, because to some the bright glossy appearance of an inferior article will be evidence of good workmanship and quality, while the fine "mathematical instrument finish" which brings into prominence the defects (if any) as well as the superior workmanship are looked upon as an indication of inferiority.

As so often happens in other circumstances, a certain special education is necessary to a true appreciation of what we may term the "refined" in drawing instruments, as contrasted with what is coarse and vulgar. This finest and best degree of finish is indefinable; it bears, however, on its face clear evidence of faithful, painstaking *hand labor*, which is always costly and cannot, therefore, be expended upon cheap instruments. It sets off in clear outline the grace of form and correspondence of the different parts, any faults and flaws being evident so that the importance to be attached to them can be easily estimated. The finish of cheap instruments is, however, of a totally different nature. It is obtained by mechanical means, and, therefore, is cheap and in harmony with the quality of the materials and workmanship to which it is applied. The buffing wheel gives a high polish to the surfaces of the metal, but it not only frequently destroys the regularity of outline, effacing the clearly defined edges and angles, but it also hides defects of material and construction, which alas make themselves too evident after the instrument has been a short time in use.

Besides material, workmanship and finish, the fitting together of the component parts of an instrument, as well as of the interchangeable pieces, is a very important point which should be carefully examined when purchasing. Bad joints, ill-fitting interchangeable points are a source of annoyance frequently causing bad work.

Our advice to the intending purchaser is to examine as carefully as he can all the various points named, and rather than let himself be seduced into buying a "case" of third-rate instruments, (apparently cheap) purchase from time to time those separate instruments which he really needs, of the very best quality procurable, and when his collection is complete have a case made to suit his assortment. We have known draughtsmen who, after using such instruments continually for twenty years and more, could not be persuaded to exchange them for any new ones offered to them. Long use seems to have made the instrument a part of its owner, to which he is persistently attached, knowing as he does its exact capabilities, while the feeling of its touch in his fingers gives him confidence in his work. On the other hand a possessor of poor instruments has frequently to do his work several times over on account of errors arising during its execution from the causes named, resulting in his being disheartened and oftentimes tracing the cause of annoyance to a wrong source,—to himself instead of to the bad policy which led him to be "penny wise and pound foolish."

THE HELIOGRAPH.

WE GAVE IN our last an extract from *Indian Engineering* on the subject of the use made of the Heliograph by Engineers in Railway Surveys, and referred our readers to a previous number of THE COMPASS, (June, 1893) in which this useful instrument is fully described. We now reproduce the illustration then given, but with substitution of the new screen designed by Captain Kilbourne, Signal Corps, U. S. A. The use of two plates opening and closing together allows of the intermittent flashes of light being made more spontaneously, thus facilitating the receiver's work, as the difference between dots and dashes is rendered more pronounced.

SEVERAL OF OUR subscribers have called our attention to the fact that in consequence of the monthly tables of the Ephemeris not being published in advance, they are unable to make use of them in the earlier part of the month. We have given in this issue the tables for April and May, and shall continue to publish them one month ahead, so that subscribers may rely in the future upon their being to hand to enable them to prepare for solar work they may wish to undertake at any time.

MEASUREMENT OF HEIGHTS WITH THE ANEROID BAROMETER.

IN A FORMER number of THE COMPASS (October 1892, Vol. II., page 45) we described the methods of using the Aneroid Barometer for ascertaining the difference of elevation of two stations, stating that the different formulæ generally adopted required a table of altitudes corresponding to the scale of barometric pressures. We now submit a condensed table based on Prof. Airy's, to enable our readers to compute differences of elevation without the scale of feet found on most barometers. Table I. gives the barometer readings in inches and tenths of an inch, but to facilitate computations for smaller divisions of an inch, we have added two columns of *differences* for $1/100$th of an inch. The first column is to be used for any required hundredths between 0.0 and 0.5 inch, and the second column between 0.5 and the next succeeding whole inch. Thus, if the reading is 27."33, the value of 0."03 will be taken from the first column of differences, namely $3 \times 10 = 30$ feet, whereas for the reading 27."83, the value of 0."03 should be taken from the second column, namely $3 \times 9.82 = 29.46$ feet.

The formula to be used in connection with this table is the following one:

$$\text{Difference of Elevation} = (H - h) \times \left(\frac{900 + T + t}{1000} \right),$$

where H and h are the heights taken from the table corresponding to the pressures at the two stations, while T and t are the respective temperatures in degrees Fahrenheit at the lower and upper stations.

Example:—Needle at lower station = 30.29 inches,
" " upper " = 27.06 "
Thermometer at lower " = 75°.5 F,
" " upper " = 60°.2 F.
27.06 inches = 3765 — (6 × 9.82) = 3706 feet
30.29 " = 712 — (9 × 9) = 631 "
$H - h$ = 3075 feet.

With the correction for temperature we have

$$\text{Difference of elevation} = 3075 \times \frac{900 + 75°.5 + 60°.2}{1000}$$

$$= 3075 \times 1.035 = 3182.6 \text{ feet.}$$

The differences in feet given in the table for 0.01 inch will be found to be very nearly correct. Somewhat greater accuracy may be had by finding the difference between any two consecutive tenths of an inch, and the n taking its proportional part for the required number of hundredths of an inch. The above example worked in this way would give $H - h$ = 3074 instead of 3075 feet.

As the Aneroid is often divided in accordance with the metric system, we give in Table II the heights in metres corresponding to barometer readings in millimetres, to which is also added a column for differences of readings of $0.1^m/_m$. The formula to be used in the case of metric computations is

$$\text{Difference of altitude of two stations in Metres} = (H - h) \times \left(1 + \frac{2(T + t)}{1000}\right)$$

where H and h are altitudes in metres corresponding to the barometer readings in millimetres, and T and t are the temperatures in degrees Centigrade.

Example:—The following observations were made by Humboldt in the case of the City of Guanajuato, Mexico;

	Barometer.	Thermometer.
Lower Station	$763.15^m/_m$	$25°.3$ Cent.
Upper "	600.95 "	$21°.3$ "

from which we have

$$600.95^m/_m = 1908.7 - (9\tfrac{1}{2} \times 1.32) = 1896.16 \text{ Metres}$$

$$763.15 \text{ " } = -\left(10.5 + (1\tfrac{1}{2} \times 1.04)\right) = -12.06 \text{ "}$$

$$H - h = 1908.22 \text{ Metres.}$$

To correct for temperature we have

$$\text{Difference of elevation} = 1908.22 \times \left(1 + \frac{2(25°.3 + 21°.3)}{1000}\right)$$

$$= 1908.22 \times 1.093 = 2086 \text{ Metres}$$

which is 3.6 metres more than the measured altitude obtained by Poisson. —(*Mécanique, II.,* 631.)

The refinements of barometric measurements of heights require some other corrections, but the Surveyor or Civil Engineer will not find them necessary in ordinary cases, as, where comparatively absolute exactitude is required, he will naturally resort to other methods.

We trust that the compactness of these tables will commend them to those who use this valuable instrument, whether professionally or to add to the interest afforded by travel. For fuller information on the subject of Barometric Measurements of Heights, we recommend the study of "How to use the Aneroid Barometer:" by Edward Whymper, or "The Aneroid Barometer, its construction and use," by Prof. Plympton, either of which we can supply post-paid at the publisher's prices, namely 75 and 50 cents each. We have followed the tables given in the latter in compiling our own condensed ones.

TABLE I. FOR ESTIMATING HEIGHTS BY THE ANEROID.

BAROMETER READINGS IN INCHES. CORRESPONDING HEIGHTS IN FEET.

Inches	0.0	0.1	0.2	0.3	0.4	0.5	0.6	0.7	0.8	0.9	Differences for 0.01 inch 0.0 to 0.5	0.5 to 0.0
	Feet	Feet	Feet	Feet	Feet	Feet	Feet	Feet	Feet	Feet	Feet	Feet
20	11945	11808	11673	11536	11404	11270	11136	11006	10876	10746	13.50	13.14
21	10613	10484	10355	10228	10101	9974	9848	9722	9597	9472	12.78	12.52
22	9348	9224	9100	8977	8855	8733	8615	8495	8374	8254	12.30	11.98
23	8134	8015	7900	7782	7667	7550	7433	7316	7203	7090	11.68	11.48
24	6976	6862	6750	6637	6525	6412	6302	6192	6082	5972	11.28	10.98
25	5863	5754	5646	5537	5429	5323	5216	5110	5004	4899	10.80	10.58
26	4794	4690	4585	4482	4378	4274	4173	4070	3968	3866	10.40	10.18
27	3765	3665	3564	3464	3365	3265	3166	3068	2969	2873	10.00	9.82
28	2774	2677	2580	2483	2387	2297	2196	2100	2001	1913	9.66	9.46
29	1818	1725	1630	1537	1445	1352	1260	1169	1076	985	9.32	9.18
30	893	803	712	622	533	443	354	265	177	88	9.00	8.86

TABLE II. FOR ESTIMATING HEIGHTS BY THE ANEROID.

BAROMETRIC READINGS IN MILLIMETRES. CORRESPONDING ALTITUDES IN METRES.

Milli-metres	0	1	2	3	4	5	6	7	8	9	Differences for 0.1 m/m.
	Metres	Metres	Metres	Metres	Metres	Metres	Metres	Metres	Metres	Metres	Metres
530	2899.8	2884.7	2869.7	2854.7	2839.7	2824.7	2809.8	2794.9	2780.0	2765.2	1.50
540	2750.4	2735.6	2720.9	2706.1	2691.4	2676.8	2662.1	2647.5	2632.9	2618.3	1.47
550	2603.8	2589.3	2574.8	2560.3	2545.9	2531.5	2517.1	2502.7	2488.4	2474.1	1.44
560	2459.8	2445.6	2431.4	2417.2	2403.0	2388.8	2374.7	2360.6	2346.5	2332.5	1.41
570	2318.4	2304.4	2290.4	2276.5	2262.6	2248.7	2234.8	2220.9	2207.1	2193.3	1.39
580	2179.5	2165.7	2152.0	2138.3	2124.6	2110.9	2097.3	2083.7	2070.1	2056.5	1.37
590	2042.9	2029.4	2015.9	2002.4	1989.0	1975.5	1962.1	1948.7	1935.4	1922.0	1.34
600	1908.7	1895.4	1882.1	1868.8	1855.6	1842.4	1829.2	1816.0	1802.9	1789.8	1.32
610	1776.7	1763.6	1750.5	1737.5	1724.4	1711.4	1698.5	1685.5	1672.6	1659.7	1.30
620	1646.8	1633.9	1621.0	1608.2	1595.4	1582.6	1569.8	1557.1	1544.4	1531.7	1.28
630	1519.0	1506.3	1493.7	1481.0	1468.4	1455.8	1443.3	1430.7	1418.2	1405.7	1.26
640	1393.2	1380.7	1368.3	1355.8	1343.4	1331.0	1318.7	1306.3	1294.0	1281.7	1.24
650	1269.4	1257.1	1244.8	1232.6	1220.4	1208.2	1196.0	1183.8	1171.7	1159.5	1.22
660	1147.4	1135.3	1123.3	1111.3	1099.2	1087.2	1075.2	1063.2	1051.2	1039.3	1.20
670	1027.3	1015.4	1003.5	991.7	979.8	968.0	956.1	944.3	932.6	920.8	1.18
680	909.0	897.3	885.6	873.9	862.2	850.5	838.9	827.3	815.6	804.0	1.17
690	792.5	780.9	769.3	757.8	746.3	734.8	723.3	711.9	700.4	689.0	1.15
700	677.6	666.2	654.8	643.4	632.1	620.7	609.4	598.1	586.8	575.6	1.13
710	564.3	553.1	541.8	530.6	519.5	508.3	497.1	486.0	474.8	463.7	1.12
720	452.6	441.6	430.5	419.4	408.4	397.4	386.4	375.4	364.4	353.5	1.10
730	342.5	331.6	320.7	309.8	298.9	288.0	277.2	266.3	255.5	244.7	1.09
740	233.9	223.1	212.3	201.6	190.8	180.1	169.4	158.7	148.1	137.4	1.07
750	126.7	116.1	105.5	94.9	84.3	73.7	63.1	52.6	42.0	31.5	1.06
760	21.0	10.5	0.0	−10.5	−20.9	−31.4	−41.8	−52.2	−62.6	−73.0	1.04
770	−83.4	−93.7	−104.1	−114.4	−124.7	−135.0	−145.3	−155.6	−165.9	−176.1	1.03

SOLAR EPHEMERIS, APRIL 1894.
For Greenwich Apparent Noon.

Day of Week	Day of Month	The Sun's Apparent Declination	Difference for 1 Hour	Equation of Time to be *added to* substructed *from Apparent Time*	Day of Month	Refraction* Correction Latitude 40°
		° ′ ″	″	m s		
Sun.	1	N 4 38 52.0	+ 57.81	3 51.94		1 h. 0′ 39″
Mon.	2	5 1 57.1	57.60	3 33.96	4	2 0 44
Tues.	3	5 24 56.9	57.37	3 16 13	to	3 0 54
Wed.	4	5 47 51.1	57 13	2 58 46	8	4 1 14
Thurs.	5	6 10 39.3	56.87	2 40 96		5 2 08
Frid.	6	6 33 21.1	+ 56.59	2 23.65		1 h. 0′ 36″
Sat.	7	6 55 56.1	56.30	2 6 54	9	2 0 41
Sun.	8	7 18 24.0	56.00	1 49.65	to	3 0 51
Mon.	9	7 40 44.4	55 69	1 32.99	13	4 1 10
Tues.	10	8 2 57.0	55.35	1 16.58		5 1 58
Wed.	11	8 25 1.4	+ 55.00	1 0.43		1 h. 0′ 34″
Thurs.	12	8 46 57.3	54.64	0 44.56	14	2 0 38
Frid.	13	9 8 44.2	54 26	0 28.98	to	3 0 48
Sat.	14	9 30 21.9	53 87	0 13.71	18	4 1 06
Sun.	15	9 51 50.1	53 47	0 1.23		5 1 49
Mon.	16	10 13 8.4	+ 53.05	0 15.83		1 h. 0′ 32″
Tues.	17	10 34 16.5	52.62	0 30.08	19	2 0 36
Wed.	18	10 55 14.1	52.17	0 43.94	to	3 0 45
Thurs.	19	11 16 0.9	51.71	0 57.42	23	4 1 02
Frid.	20	11 36 36.7	51.24	1 10.48		5 1 42
Sat.	21	11 57 1.0	+ 50.77	1 23.12		1 h. 0′ 30″
Sun.	22	12 17 13.6	50.28	1 35.31	24	2 0 34
Mon.	23	12 37 14.2	49.77	1 47.04	to	3 0 42
Tues.	24	12 57 2.5	49.25	1 58.30	28	4 0 58
Wed.	25	13 16 38.2	48.71	2 9.06		5 1 36
Thurs.	26	13 36 0.9	+ 48.16	2 19.33		1 h. 0′ 28″
Frid.	27	13 55 10.4	47.61	2 29.08	29	2 0 32
Sat.	28	14 14 6.2	47.04	2 38.31	to	3 0 39
Sun.	29	14 32 48.2	46 46	2 47.00	May 3	4 0 55
Mon.	30	N 14 51 15.9	45.86	2 55.15		5 1 30

* By permission from "The Theory and Practice of Surveying", by Prof. J. B. Johnson, C. E.

In this column the hours are counted each way from noon; thus, 9 A. M. and 3 P. M. would each correspond to the 3d hour in the table. The hourly corrections are exact for the middle day of the five day period corresponding to any given set of hourly corrections. For other days interpolations can be made where extreme accuracy is required.

For Table of Latitude Coefficients, see Vol. III., page 110.

SOLAR EPHEMERIS, MAY 1894.
For Greenwich Apparent Noon.

Day of Week	Day of Month	The Sun's Apparent Declination			Difference for 1 Hour	Equation of Time to be substracted from Apparent Time		Day of Month	Refraction * Correction Latitude 40°		
		°	′	″	″	m	s				
Tues.	1	N15	9	29.0	+ 45.24	3	2.75				
Wed.	2	15	27	27.2	44.61	3	9.80		1 h.	0′	26″
Thurs.	3	15	45	10.1	43.97	3	16 30	4	2	0	30
Frid.	4	16	2	37.4	43 31	3	22.23	to	3	0	37
Sat.	5	16	19	48.8	42.65	3	27.60	8	4	0	53
									5	1	26
Sun.	6	16	36	44.0	+ 41.96	3	32.41				
Mon.	7	16	53	22.5	41.26	3	36.65		1 h.	0′	25″
Tues.	8	17	9	44.1	40.55	3	40.33	9	2	0	29
Wed.	9	17	25	48.5	39.82	3	43.46	to	3	0	36
Thurs.	10	17	41	35.3	39.08	3	46.02	13	4	0	51
									5	1	22
Frid.	11	17	57	4.3	+ 38.33	3	48.02				
Sat.	12	18	12	15.1	37.57	3	49.47		1 h.	0′	23″
Sun.	13	18	27	7.6	36.79	3	50.36	14	2	0	27
Mon.	14	18	41	41.3	36.00	3	50.70	to	3	0	34
Tues.	15	18	55	56.1	35.21	3	50.48	18	4	0	49
									5	1	18
Wed.	16	19	9	51.6	+ 34.41	3	49.71				
Thurs.	17	19	23	27.7	33.59	3	48.38		1 h.	0′	22″
Frid.	18	19	36	44.1	32.76	3	46.51	19	2	0	26
Sat.	19	19	49	40.6	31.93	3	44.08	to	3	0	33
Sun.	20	20	2	16.8	31.08	3	41.12	23	4	0	47
									5	1	15
Mon.	21	20	14	32.6	+ 30.22	3	37.60				
Tues.	22	20	26	27.7	29.35	3	33.55		1 h.	0′	21″
Wed.	23	20	38	1.9	28.48	3	28.96	24	2	0	25
Thurs.	24	20	49	15.0	27.60	3	23.84	to	3	0	32
Frid.	25	21	0	6.7	26.70	3	18.20	28	4	0	46
									5	1	13
Sat.	26	21	10	36.8	+ 25.79	3	12.04				
Sun.	27	21	20	45.1	24.88	3	5.38	29	1 h.	0′	20″
Mon.	28	21	30	31.3	23.96	2	58.24	to	2	0	24
Tues.	29	21	39	55.3	23 03	2	50.61	June	3	0	31
Wed.	30	21	48	56.7	22.09	2	42.51	2	4	0	44
									5	1	11
Thurs.	31	21	57	35.5	+ 21.14	2	33.98				

* By permission from "The Theory and Practice of Surveying", by Prof. J. B. Johnson, C. E.

In this column the hours are counted each way from noon; thus, 9 A. M. and 3 P. M. would each correspond to the 3d hour in the table. The hourly corrections are exact for the middle day of the five-day period corresponding to any given set of hourly corrections. For other days interpolations can be made where extreme accuracy is required.

For Table of Latitude Coefficients, see Vol. III., page 110.

A Monthly Journal for Engineers, Surveyors, Architects, Draughtsmen and Students.

Vol. III.   MAY 1, 1894.   No. 10.

THE SOLAR TRANSIT. IX.

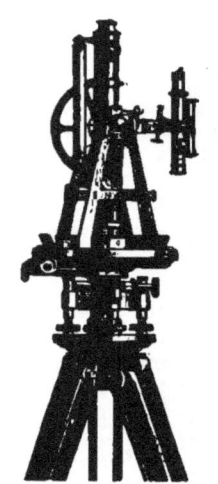

THE QUESTION WILL now naturally present itself, "What degree of accuracy is possible with the Solar Attachment we have been describing?" The following extracts from a paper read by Professor J. B. Johnson, of Washington University, St. Louis, Mo., before the Engineers' Club of St. Louis, on November 18, 1885, which we are enabled to lay before our readers by the author's kind permission, will have more weight than any assurances we might give on our own behalf.

"I spent two days in making observations on a line whose azimuth had been determined by observations on two nights on Polaris at elongation, the instrument being reversed to eliminate errors of adjustment. Forty-five observations were made with the solar attachment on Oct. 24, 1885, from 9 to 10 A. M., and from 1.30 to 4 P. M., and on Nov. 7, forty-two observations between the same hours.

"On the first day's work the latitude used was that obtained by an observation on the sun at its meridian passage, being 38° 39', and the mean azimuth was 20 seconds in error. On the second day, the instrument having been more carefully adjusted, the latitude used was 38° 37', which was supposed to be about the true latitude of the point of observation, which was the corner of Park and Jefferson avenues in this city. It was afterwards found this latitude was 38° 37' 15", as referred to Washington University Observatory, so that when the mean azimuth of the line was corrected for this 15" error in latitude it agreed exactly with the stellar azimuth of the line, which might have been 10" or 15" in error. On the first day all the readings were taken without a reading glass, there being four circle readings to each result. On the second day a glass was used.

"On the first day the maximum error was 4 minutes, the average error was 0.8 minute, and the 'probable error of a single observation' was also 0.8 minute. On the second day the maximum error was 2.7 minutes, the average error was 1 minute, and the 'probable error of a single observation' was 0.86 minute. The time required for a single observation is from 3 to five minutes.

"I believe this accuracy is attainable in actual practice, as no greater care was taken in the adjustment or handling of the instrument than should be exercised in the field.

"The transit has come to be the universal instrument for the engineer, and should be for the surveyor, so it is more desirable to have the solar apparatus attached to the transit than to have a separate instrument. The principal advantages of this attachment are:

"1. Its simplicity.

"2. Its accuracy of pointing, being furnished with a telescope which is accurately set on the sun's disk.

"3. In its providing that all angles be set off on the vertical and horizontal limbs of the transit, thus eliminating the eccentricity and other inaccuracies usually found in attachment circles or arcs.

"4. Its small cost.

"It is also readily removed and replaced without affecting its adjustments, and is out of the way in handling and reversing the telescope. It may be attached to any transit."

The following table and remarks, from the same paper, will also be found of considerable value in solar work:—

"This table is valuable in indicating the errors to which the work is liable at different hours of the day and for different latitudes, as well as serving to correct the observed bearings of lines when it afterwards appears that a wrong latitude or declination has been used. Thus on the first day's observations I used a latitude in the forenoon of 38° 37', but when I came to make the meridian observation for latitude I found the instrument gave 38° 39'. This was the latitude that should have been used, so I corrected the mornings observations for two minutes error in latitude by this table.

ERRORS IN AZIMUTH (BY SOLAR COMPASS) FOR 1 MIN. ERROR IN DECLINATION OR LATITUDE.

Hour.	For 1 Min. Error in Declination.			For 1 Min. Error in Latitude.		
	Lat. 30°.	Lat. 40°.	Lat. 50°.	Lat. 30°.	Lat. 40°.	Lat. 50°.
	Min.	Min.	Min.	Min.	Min.	Min.
11 30 A. M. 12.30 P. M.	8.85	10.00	12.90	8.77	9.92	11.80
11 A. M. 1 P. M.	4.46	5.05	6.01	4.33	4.87	5.80
10 A. M. 2 P. M.	2.31	2.61	3.11	2.00	2.26	2.70
9 A. M. 3 P. M.	1.63	1.85	2.20	1.15	1.30	1.56
8 A M. 4 P. M.	1.34	1.51	1.80	0.67	0.75	0.90
7 A M. 5 P M.	1.20	1.35	1.61	0.31	0.35	0.37
6 A. M. 6 P. M.	1.15	1.30	1.56	0.00	0.00	0.00

NOTE.—Azimuths observed with erroneous declination or co-latitude may be corrected by means of this table by observing that for the line of collimation set *too high* the azimuth from any line *from the south point* in the direction S. W. N. E. is found *too small* in the *forenoon* and *too large* in the *afternoon* by the tabular amounts for each minute of error in the altitude of the line of sight. The reverse is true for the line set too low.

" It is evident, that if the instrument is out of adjustment the latitude found by a meridian observation will be in error; but *if this observed latitude be used* in setting off the co-latitude the instrumental error is eliminated. Therefore always use for the co-latitude that given by the instrument itself in a meridian observation.

"It must not be forgotten that a *meridian* observation is not usually a *noon* observation, as the sun is always either 'slow' or 'fast' of *mean* solar time. Thus on Nov. 7 the sun was over sixteen minutes fast, so that the observation had to be taken about 11 hours 44 minutes."

As we described in a former number of THE COMPASS, (Volume I., No. 7, February 1892) the use of this attachement for vertical sighting, as is often required in mining work, we do not further refer to this advantage obtained by reason of its special form of construction. Sufficient has been said, we trust, to make its principle, use and manipulation clearly understood, and its simplicity appreciated. No surveyor should be without one; its moderate price, and the fact of its being attachable to any transit, cannot be said to place it beyond the reach of any.

SPIDERS' WEBS AS SCIENTIFIC INSTRUMEMTS.

The astronomers of the Naval Observatory at Washington have sought all over the world for spiders' webs. Such gossamer filaments spun by industrious arachnids are utilised in telescopes for cross lines extended at right angles with each other across the field of view, so as to divide the latter into mathematical spaces. Threads of cobwebs are employed for the purpose because they are wonderfully strong for their exceeding fineness, and also for the reason that they are not affected by moisture or temperature, neither expanding nor contracting under any conditions. Specimens were obtained from China by the Directors of the Observatory, because it was imagined that the large spider of that country would perhaps produce a particularly excellent quality of web. However it was found that the best web is spun by spiders of the United States, such as are found in the neighborhood of Washington. Accordingly, expeditions are made early in June each year to get from the fences and barns thereabout the cocoons of the big "turtle back" spiders. Each cocoon is composed of a single silken filament wound round and round, though there are apt to be some breaks in it where Mistress Spider left off work for a time. Attempts have been made to use the cocoons of spiders like those of silkworms, and exquisite fabrics have been manufactured from them. Unfortunately, it was found impossible to make the industry a commercial success owing to the combative inclination of these creatures. When kept together they will always gobble each other up in a short time, the final result being a single very large and fat spider and one cocoon.—*The Optician.*

LIGHT: ITS REFLECTION AND REFRACTION. XV.

WE HAVE SHOWN that in the case of a double convex lens the point, towards which rays of light converge when they emanate from a point at a distance from the lens, varies according to that distance. This gives us three cases as follows:

1. When the rays proceed from a point so distant that they may be considered as parallel rays, they are refracted and converge to a point in the axis of the lens called the *focus*, or the *principal focus*, at a certain distance from the lens called the *focal length* of the lens, this distance depending upon the radii of curvature of the surfaces of the lens.

2. When the rays proceed from a point nearer the lens, in divergent directions, they converge after passing through the lens to a point further away from the lens than the principal focus, the distance from the lens to this point varying with the distance of the source of the rays, being greater as that source is nearer to the lens, and vice versa.

3. When diverging rays of light proceed from a point whose distance from the lens is the same as its principal focus, the rays emerge from the lens in parallel lines.

If a double convex lens be held between a star and a sheet of white paper,—the distance between the centre of the lens and the paper being equal to the focal length of the lens,—a distinct image of the star will be formed on the paper.

In the same manner, in Fig. 1, let AB be an object held up at a

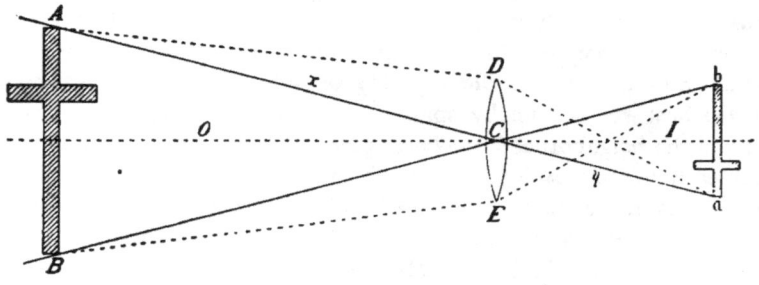

Fig. 1.

given distance from a double convex lens DE. Rays of light from the points A and B of the object will pass through the centre of the lens, intersect each other and produce similar and distinct, but inverted images at the points a and b, at a distance from the lens dependent upon the distance of AB from the centre of the lens C, and upon its principal focus. Rays of light from all other portions of AB will in the same way pass through the lens and complete the image ab. In fact, rays will proceed from every portion of the object and strike every portion of the lens. The direction of any one of these might be traced by the methods we have stated, when its corresponding inverted position in the image would be found.

The relationship which exists between the distance from the object to the centre of the lens, the distance of the image from the centre of the lens, and the focal length of the lens, is expressed by the fundamental equation

$$\frac{1}{x} + \frac{1}{y} = \frac{1}{f}$$

where $x =$ the distance of the rays $A\ C$ and $B\ C$ from the object to the centre of the lens ;

$y =$ the distance of the rays $a\ c$ and $b\ c$ from the image to the centre of the lens ;

$f =$ the focal length of the lens, measured from its centre C.

From the above we have

$$\text{Focal length } f = \frac{x \cdot y}{x + y} \quad \dots \dots \dots \dots \dots \dots \dots \dots (1)$$

$$\text{Distance of object } x = \frac{y \cdot f}{y - f} \quad \dots \dots \dots \dots \dots \dots \dots \dots (2)$$

$$\text{Distance of image } y = \frac{x \cdot f}{x - f} \quad \dots \dots \dots \dots \dots \dots \dots \dots (3)$$

We also obtain from Fig. 1 another relationship, that of the size of the object to the size of the image, which is expressed by

$$A\ B : a\ b : : O : I \dots \dots \dots \dots \dots \dots \dots \dots \dots \dots \dots (4)$$

where $O =$ distance of the object from the centre of the lens ;

$I =$ distance of the image from the centre of the lens.

From these formulæ we can now prove the correctness of the three cases stated at the commencement of this chapter, thus:—

1. Let x be infinite $= \infty$, then

$$y = \frac{x \cdot f}{x - f} \quad \frac{\infty \cdot f}{\infty - f} = f;$$

that is, parallel rays proceeding from a very distant object form an image at the principal focus of the lens; or, the distance y from the image to the centre of the lens is equal to the focal length of the lens, whence $y = f$.

2. Let the focal length of a double convex lens be 6 inches, and let an object $A\ B$ be 24 inches distant from the centre of the lens, then the image will be more than 6 inches (the focal length) from the lens, thus $f = 6$, $x = 24$, whence

$$y = \frac{24 \times 6}{24 - 6} = \frac{144}{18} = 8 \text{ inches.}$$

If the object be still further distant, say 10 feet, we have

$$y = \frac{120 \times 6}{120 - 6} = \frac{720}{114} = 6\ 316 \text{ inches,}$$

so that the distance of the image and the distance of the object vary inversely, the one becoming greater as the other becomes smaller.

3. When the distance of the object from the centre of the lens is the same as its focal length, that is $x = f$, we have

$$y = \frac{x \cdot f}{x - f} = \frac{f \cdot f}{f - f} = \frac{f^2}{0} = \infty$$

that is, the distance of the image is infinite, showing that the emerging rays are parallel, which is exactly the converse of the first case.

We can in the same way calculate the principal focus of a lens, thus: —An object, say a candle placed 2 feet in front of the centre of a lens produces a distinct image 8 inches behind the lens, then

$$\text{focal length } f = \frac{24 \times 8}{24 + 8} = \frac{192}{32} = 6 \text{ inches.}$$

The following method of practically finding the focal length of a convex lens is given by Heather. "Place a lighted candle at one extremity of a scale of inches and parts, with which the lens has been connected in such a manner as to slide along, and always have its axis parallel to the scale. A flat piece of card is also to be made to slide along, so as to be always in a line with the light and the lens, the lens being between the light and the card. The lens and card are then to be moved along, backwards and forwards, till the least distance between the card and light is discovered, at which a clear image of the light is formed upon the card; and this distance is four times the focal length."

The correctness of this method can be easily ascertained by means of formula (1) if we make $x = y$, for we then have

$$f = \frac{x \cdot y}{x + y} = \frac{x \cdot x}{x + x} = \frac{x^2}{2 x}$$

from which

$$f = \frac{x + y}{4},$$

or the distance of the object to the image is equal to four times the focal length of the lens.

STADIA MEASUREMENTS. I.

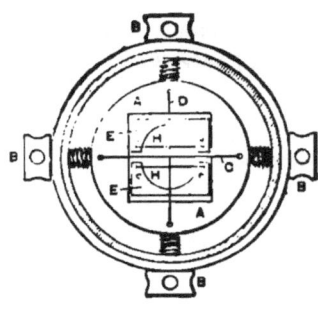
Fig. 1

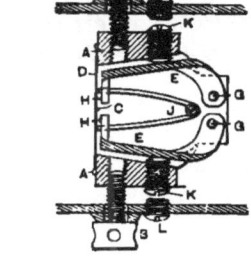
Fig. 2.

THE SURVEYOR'S WORK comprises three general classes of operations,

The measurement of distances.

The measurement of angles and consequent determination of directions, and

The determining of horizontal lines.

The MEASUREMENT OF DISTANCES may be performed in various ways, according to the instruments and methods employed. We thus have

1. *Direct Measurements*, for which any of the following instruments may be used, the choice being dictated by the special circumstances of the case and the preferences of the surveyor;—

Chains, Tapes, Rods, Steel Bars, etc.

Passometer, Odometer, Perambulator, etc.

2. *Indirect Measurements.* The methods and instruments at disposal are both numerous and various, and may be classified according to the principles which govern them, all, however, requiring a *base line*, whose exact length is known or can be easily ascertained. We thus have

a. Base of fixed or variable length at the *point of observation*, measurement of one or more angles, and subsequent computation of the distance. The instruments which are generally used are Angle Mirrors, Prisms, the Sextant, Graphometers, Range Finders, etc., many of which have already been described in these pages. The construction of some of these is such that the distance is at once given without computation.

b. Base of fixed length at the distant point, measurement of the subtended angle and computation of the distance. Two instruments and methods embodying these features have been described in THE COMPASS, the Gradienter and the Telemeter Target, the principles in each being almost analagous.

Another and very important method of ascertaining the distance of a remote point remains to be described, namely, the method of Stadia Measurements, in which a variable base is placed at the distant point, while a small fixed base, determined by two horizontal hairs is inserted in the telescope. The principle involved is the geometrical theorem that *two triangles, which are mutually equiangular, have their homologous sides proportional and are similar.*

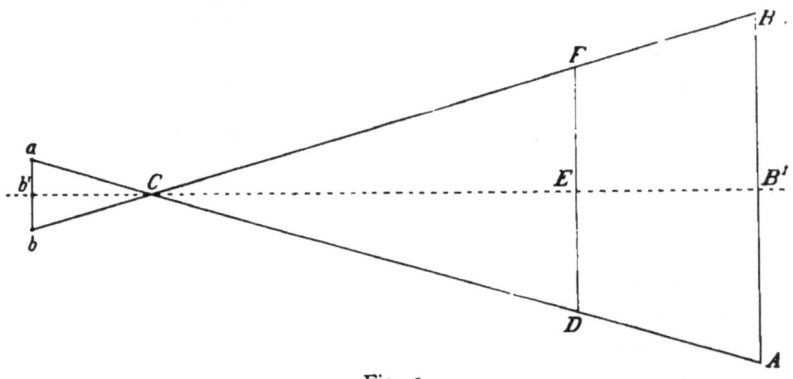

Fig. 3.

This general principle is represented in the above figure where $a\,b$ is a fixed base of small dimensions, while the common apex C of the two triangles $a\,C\,b$ and $A\,C\,B$ is generally at such a distance from b^1 that $\dfrac{b^1\,C}{a\,b} = 100$. The angle $A\,C\,B$ being equal to the angle $a\,C\,b$, and $a\,b$ and $A\,B$ being parallel to each other, the two triangles $A\,B\,C$ and $a\,b\,C$ are similar, and their homologous sides are proportional, whence, whatever may be the length of $C\,B^1$, $\dfrac{B^1\,C}{A B}$ is also equal to 100. If $A\,B$ is measured in feet, then $B^1\,C$ is equal to the same number of feet multiplied by 100, and similarly, $C\,E = D\,F \times 100$.

In applying this principle to Stadia measurements, the line $a\,b$ represents a small fixed base in the diaphragm of the telescope, determined by two horizontal hairs a and b, called the stadia hairs, placed at equal distances above and below the horizontal cross hair,* represented by the point b^1. The line $A\,B$ is a variable base composed of any distance on a rod held vertically over the point whose distance is to be ascertained, the points A, B and B^1 on the rod appearing to be covered by the three horizontal hairs, a, b and b^1, when looking through the telescope at the rod.

---

* In figures 1 and 2 representing the stadia case or diaphragm, H, H are the stadia hairs, and C and D the horizontal and vertical cross-hairs, all fully described in Vol. I, page 86. (January 1892.)

C is the common apex of the two similar triangles formed by the lines proceeding from the stadia hairs to the points on the rod intercepted by these hairs, and the bases $a\,b$ and $A\,B$, from which we obtain the proportion

$$a\,b : b^1\,c :: A\,B : B^1\,C$$

whence

$$\text{Distance } B^1\,C = \frac{A\,B \times b^1 c}{a\,b}$$

If the ratio $a\,b : b^1\,c$ be made a fixed one then we should have, calling this ratio k,

Distance $B^1\,C = A\,B \times k$, and similarly

Distance $C\,E = D\,F \times k$.

It now remains for us to determine the position of the common apex C of the two triangles, so that we may know from what exact point the distance $B_1\,C$ to the rod $A\,B$ has been thus ascertained. Several suppositionary opinions have been advanced on the subject, each of the following having had its advocates:—the centre of the instrument; the stadia hairs; and the front face of the objective; none of these are, however, really exact. In our next we will endeavor to elucidate this point.

THE LATEST DETERMINATION OF THE SUN'S DISTANCE.

An extensive series of observations was made in 1889 upon the planet Victoria (asteroid No. 12) for the purpose of ascertaining the distance of the sun, and incidentally also the mass of the moon—quantities which to the 'uninitiated would seem to bear no obvious relation to the motions of the little asteroid, though in fact the connection is close and positive.

The work was very thoroughgoing, involving the co-operation of no less than twenty-one different observatories in determining with their meridian circles the places of the stars which were used as reference points along the planet's track. Then all through the summer the position of the planet itself, with reference to these stars, was assiduously observed by Gill and Amvers at the Cape of Good Hope, by Elkin and Hall at New Haven, and in Germany at Gottingen and by Schur at Bamberg. The instruments employed in their observations were heliometers of the most perfect construction, and the measurements made with them rank among the most accurate and refined known in astronomy, Altogether, between June 15 and August 27, while the planet was near its opposition and for a time at a distance from the earth less than four-fifths the distance of the sun, over eight hundred complete sets of measures were secured, and only six nights were wholly missed. The reduction of this mass of material has occupied nearly three years, and the result has only just been published. Dr. Gill, who originated the campaign and has reduced the observations, finds for the parallax of the sun 8.809″, corresponding to a distance of 92,800,000 miles; and he further finds that the hitherto accepted mass of the moon must be reduced somewhat more than one per cent. to satisfy the observations; in other words, the earth's monthly swing, due to her motion around the common centre of gravity of earth and moon, was found to be about one per cent. less than had been assumed. It is interesting to note that this newest value of the solar parallax agrees to the very last decimal with that deducted two years ago by Professor Harkness in his elaborate "least square" discussion of all the then available data relating to the constants of the solar system. The still outstanding error in our knowledge of the astronomical unit can hardly be as great as one part in a thousand.—*Prof. C. A. Young in the Cosmopolitan.*

A NEW TELEMETER TARGET. II.

By Mr. Claudio Urrutia, C.E., Guatemala.

II. The formula to determine the distance is

$$D = \frac{v \times F}{m}$$

where D = distance;

v = number of repetitions of the angle subtended by the extremities of the target; *

F = a constant factor which for centessimal graduations is 6366.19772;

m = number of minutes in the total angle after v repetitions.

Without any inconvenience we can suppose that the repetition of the angle subtended by the target is equal to the angle which would be subtended by a target of the magnitude of

$$v + \sqrt{2v} \, \frac{0.00044 \, D}{a} \quad \text{or} \quad v - \sqrt{2v} \, \frac{0.00044 \, D}{a}.$$

In the reiteration of this angle the positive and negative errors are compensated by the extraction of the square root of their number: if we call the number of reiterations n, the total Target or multiplied reiterations will have a value of

---

* The word "target" is here used to indicate the space between the central vertical lines of the two discs.

$$n v \pm \sqrt{n}\sqrt{2v}\frac{0.00044\,D}{a}$$

which divided by n to obtain the mean will give as the value of the total Target the quantity

$$\frac{v \pm \sqrt{n}\sqrt{2v}\dfrac{0.00044\,D}{a}}{n}$$

$$= v \pm \sqrt{\frac{1}{n}}\sqrt{2v}\frac{0.00044\,D}{a} = v \pm \sqrt{\frac{2v}{n}}\frac{0.00044\,D}{a}$$

and the magnitude of the simple Target would be equal to

$$\frac{v \pm \sqrt{\dfrac{2v}{n}}\dfrac{0.00044\,D}{a}}{v} = 1 \pm \sqrt{\frac{2}{vn}}\frac{0.00044\,D}{a}.$$

III. On the other hand the following error occurs in the reiteration:

Let x be the angular error of coincidence in observing each one of the extremities of the total Target, and n, as stated, the number of reiterations. The compensations will not be effected by the square root of the number of coincidences, which is $2n$, because each angle is observed twice. The total angular error will be $\pm \sqrt{2nx}$, and the simple angle

$$\pm \frac{\sqrt{2nx^2}}{n} = \pm \frac{\sqrt{2x^2}}{n}.$$

The formula for the distance will consequently be

$$\frac{D = vF\left(1 \pm \sqrt{\dfrac{2}{vn}}\dfrac{0.00044\,D}{a}\right)}{m \pm \sqrt{\dfrac{2x^2}{n}}} = \frac{vF \pm vF\sqrt{\dfrac{2}{vn}}\dfrac{0.00044\,D}{a}}{m \pm \sqrt{\dfrac{2x^2}{n}}}$$

As the maximum error would occur when one of the terms of the fraction is positive and the other negative, if we suppose that the numerator carries the minus sign and the denominator the plus sign, the preceding formula could be simplified in the following manner:

$$D = \frac{vF}{m + \sqrt{\dfrac{2x^2}{n}}} - \frac{vF\sqrt{\dfrac{2}{vn}}\dfrac{0.00044\,D}{a}}{m + \sqrt{\dfrac{2x^2}{n}}}D;$$

$$\frac{D\left(1 + vF\sqrt{\dfrac{2}{vn}}\dfrac{0.00044\,D}{a}\right)}{m + \sqrt{\dfrac{2x^2}{n}}} = \frac{vF}{m + \sqrt{\dfrac{2x^2}{n}}}$$

and withdrawing D, we successively obtain:

$$D = \dfrac{vF}{m + \sqrt{\dfrac{2x^2}{n}} + vF\sqrt{\dfrac{2}{vn}}\dfrac{0.00044\,D}{a}}$$

$$= \dfrac{vF}{m + \sqrt{\dfrac{2x^2}{n}} + F\sqrt{\dfrac{v\,0.0000003872}{v\,n\,a^2}}}$$

$$= \dfrac{vF}{m + \sqrt{\dfrac{2x^2}{n}} + F\sqrt{\dfrac{v.0.0000003872}{n\,a^2}}}$$

$$= \dfrac{vF}{m + x\sqrt{\dfrac{2}{n}} + \dfrac{F}{a}\sqrt{\dfrac{v.0\,0000003872}{n}}}$$

$$= \dfrac{vF}{m + x\sqrt{2}\sqrt{\dfrac{1}{n}} + \dfrac{F}{a}\sqrt{v.0000003872}\sqrt{\dfrac{1}{n}}}$$

$$= \dfrac{vF}{m + (x\sqrt{2} + \dfrac{F}{a}\sqrt{v}\sqrt{v.0.0000003872})\sqrt{\dfrac{1}{n}}};$$

$$D = \dfrac{vF}{m + (1.4742\,x + 0.0006222\,\dfrac{F}{a}\sqrt{v})\sqrt{\dfrac{1}{n}}}$$

According to the formula the real value would only be obtained when the second term of the denominator disappears, which will never be attained because all its terms are positive. If, therefore, we increase x or v, the error increases, if we increase m, a or n, it diminishes, but as for such an instrument x will never vary nor a, the only diminution of error which can be obtained is to increase v to such an extent that in equal proportion m will be increased, notwithstanding that with the first comes the increasing of the second member of the denominator, but with the favorable circumstance of being affected by the radical. In consequence of this it is found convenient to use a large Target to obtain an increased value of m without increasing v, but being compelled by necessity to use a small Target, it will be convenient to increase v to the same extent that we should increase m, and it will also be found convenient to increase n, that is the reiterations.

Let us give an illustration in which the distance is one thousand times greater than the length of the Target, let us suppose the reiteration to be unnecessary, and that the Goniometer is a Troughton & Simm's or other Tacheometer in which $a = 30$ and $x = 0.5$ minutes, the formula will then be

$$D = \frac{v F}{m + (0.707 + 0.132 \sqrt{v})}$$

If we take $v = 100$ and $m = 700$, the distance will be found to be 906.83; leaving out of consideration the errors, the exact distance will be 909.46, the resulting error being but 0.28 %.

It is, therefore, demonstrated that the theoretical error is tolerable in ordinary cases of topographical work.

And in practice? This question would naturally suggest itself, and to it I would reply that in practice we commit less errors, and also that the preceding theory is probably exaggerated as to its basis. It would be very easy to test the system and become convinced of the truth of my assertions. I am sorry that I have not with me at the present moment the data and proofs of the results I have obtained, but I can guarantee that even in the measurement of distances of more than two kilometres, the results obtained with my Target have been found perfectly satisfactory.

There is no question that with a larger Target than the one I use which is one metre, and sometimes only $50°/_m$, the possibility of errors would be greatly lessened, but my Target is fully sufficient for ordinary cases in which the distance to be measured does not exceed one kilometre.

To measure greater distances I would suggest in place of a Target, two separate discs mounted on independent tripods, placed at a convenient distance apart, the distance between them being carefully measured with a tape or rod.

WATER-MARKS IN PAPER.

WE GAVE IN our "correspondence" column last month a brief reply to a query which had been submitted to us respecting Water-Marks in Paper, and as the subject is one of general interest to surveyors and others, we now lay before our readers a further contribution on the same subject, kinkly sent us by Mr. Harold M. Duncan, Managing Editor of *Paper and Press* and other of "Patton's Popular Publications." Mr. Duncan writes us:—

"In determining the age and place of manufacture of papers used in documents of any kind, and where absence of date or suspicion of non-genuiness combine to render further knowledge needful, the water-mark has a questionable value, save in a few indisputable cases, where the paper is of home manufacture and modern make. In most cases, where old land paper or kindred documents are concerned, the stock is of foreign manufacture, generally English hand made paper.

"Mr. Briquet, a well-known French scientist, is now working upon a 'History of Paper and Water Marks,' with the avowed intention of facilitating historical research by helping to fix the situation of paper mills employing these marks, and of thus determining approximately the date of paper bearing similar water-marks. His task is a gigantic one ; the life of a mould is a short one, its average length being about two years, when it is replaced by another which is never absolutely identical with the preceding original. It differs from it in the horizontal wire marks, in the distance between them, in the contours and dimensions of the water mark, or by the position occupied by this on the mould. Mr. Briquet himself acknowledges that in order to communicate precisely the date of manufacture of a sheet of paper, it is not sufficient that it bears a water mark analogous to that of a sheet of known date, but that the two water-marks must be identical, placed on the same spot on the mould, and the size of paper and wire marks must correspond. Successive moulds used at the same mill vary gradually, in most instances.

From the foregoing, Mr. Briquet proposes to adopt a plan which will enable him to make known to those interested the geographical distribution of water-marks, on the one hand, and on the other, the space of time during which the especial kinds of papers bearing them were produced. His efforts are the first in this much desired direction, but I very much question whether such a collection would not be too considerable for any publisher to dream of publishing. He has already traced 8407 water-marks, of which 7420 were absolutely different, and noted the repetition of the groups 11,106 times. He distributed the varieties into 1226 groups, or well differentiated types. And so on.

"Remembering that Mr. Briquet is dealing with ancient marks, and with those of foreign usage, we are brought face to face with the same problem for this country, and I conclude that his plan would be inestimably valuable if adapted and rendered complete. To be adequate, this collection should cover the variations in mark of the identical type, and their date of gradual differentiation. So much for the water-mark.

"Beyond this, it is needless to go. It is not at all difficult to ascertain the age of a paper, provided you consult an expert, one who is not only familiar with the analysis of stock entering into its manufacture and able to differentiate its country, but is also able to follow out his conclusions, inductively—a process which, manifestly, the surveyor is precluded from practising, if he be not expert in his acquaintance. I regret that I should be unable to satisfy your readers, for I feel the insufficiency of my communication, nevertheless, the sum of our exact knowledge in this field is not large, and the field itself is comparatively unexplored."

SOLAR EPHEMERIS, JUNE 1894.
For Greenwich Apparent Noon.

Day of Week	Day of Month	The Sun's Apparent Declination	Difference for 1 Hour	Equation of Time to be *substracted from* / *added to Apparent Time*	Day of Month	Refraction * Correction Latitude 40°
		° ′ ″	″	m s		
Frid.	1	N22 5 51.4	+ 20.18	2 25.02		1 h. 0′ 19″
Sat.	2	22 13 44.1	19.21	2 15.64		2 0 23
Sun.	3	22 21 13.6	18.24	2 5.89	3	3 0 30
Mon.	4	22 28 19.6	17.26	1 55.77	to	4 0 43
Tues.	5	22 35 2.0	16.27	1 45.30	7	5 1 10
Wed.	6	22 41 20.6	+ 15.28	1 34.51		1 h. 0′ 18″
Thurs.	7	22 47 15.3	14.28	1 23.43		2 0 22
Frid.	8	22 52 46.0	13.28	1 12.08	8	3 0 29
Sat.	9	22 57 52.5	12.27	1 0.47	to	4 0 43
Sun.	10	23 2 34.7	11.25	0 48.64	12	5 1 09
Mon.	11	23 6 52.6	+ 10.23	0 36.61		1 h. 0′ 18″
Tues.	12	23 10 46.0	9.21	0 24.39		2 0 22
Wed.	13	23 14 14.9	8.19	0 12.00	13	3 0 29
Thurs.	14	23 17 19.3	7.17	0 0.52	to	4 0 42
Frid.	15	23 19 59.0	6.14	0 13.16	17	5 1 08
Sat.	16	23 22 14.1	+ 5.11	0 25.90		1 h. 0′ 18″
Sun.	17	23 24 4.4	4.08	0 38.73		2 0 22
Mon.	18	23 25 30.1	3.05	0 51.62	18	3 0 29
Tues.	19	23 26 31.0	2.02	1 4.55	to	4 0 42
Wed.	20	23 27 7.1	+ 0.99	1 17.50	22	5 1 08
Thurs.	21	23 27 18.5	— 0.04	1 30.46		1 h. 0′ 18″
Frid.	22	23 27 5.1	1.08	1 43.40		2 0 22
Sat.	23	23 26 26.9	2.11	1 56.30	23	3 0 29
Sun.	24	23 25 23.9	3.15	2 9.15	to	4 0 42
Mon.	25	23 23 56.2	4.18	2 21.92	27	5 1 08
Tues.	26	23 22 3.8	— 5.20	2 34.58		1 h. 0′ 18″
Wed.	27	23 19 46.8	6.23	2 47.12	28	2 0 22
Thurs.	28	23 17 5.1	7.25	2 59.50	to	3 0 29
Frid.	29	23 13 58.8	8.27	3 11.72	July	4 0 43
Sat.	30	23 10 28.1	9.29	3 23.73	2	5 1 09

* By permission from "The Theory and Practice of Surveying", by Prof. J. B. Johnson, C. E.

In this column the hours are counted each way from noon; thus, 9 A. M. and 3 P. M. would each correspond to the 3d hour in the table. The hourly corrections are exact for the middle day of the five-day period corresponding to any given set of hourly corrections. For other days interpolations can be made where extreme accuracy is required.

For Table of Latitude Coefficients, see Vol. III., page 110.

"COPYRIGHT, 1892, BY WILLIAM COX, NEW YORK."

A Monthly Journal for Engineers, Surveyors, Architects, Draughtsmen and Students.

| Vol. III. | JULY 1, 1894. | No. 12. |

ABBREVIATIONS AND SIGNS USED IN SURVEYING, ETC.

Sta.	Station.
B. M.	Bench mark.
B. T.	Bearing-tree; (or other mark).
B. S.	Back-sight.
F. S.	Fore-sight.
I. S.	Intermediate sight.
H. I.	Height of instrument.
S. E.	Surface elevation.
T. P.	Turning point.
C. P.	Contour point.
I. C.	Index correction.
D. M. D.	Double meridian distance.
E. I S.	Elevation of instrumental station.
E. S. S.	Elevation of staff station.
D.	Distance.
H. C.	Horizontal component.

V. C.	Vertical component.
O. A.	Elevation of optical axis.
T.	Tangent.
B. C.	Beginning of Curve; (same as *P. C.*)
E. C.	End of Curve; (same as *P. T*)
P. C.	Point of Curve; (same as Beginning of Curve.)
P. T.	Point of Tangent; (same as End of Curve.)
C. R.	Curve Right.
C. L.	Curve Left.
P. C. C.	Point of Compound Curve.
P. R. C.	Point of Reverse Curve.
P. I.	Point of Intersection of Tangents.
⌶	Stadia Station.
△	Triangulation Station.
不	Bench Mark.
θ	Total Tangential Angle.
Δ	Total Deflection Angle or Angle of Total Curvature, $= 2\,\theta$.

BOOKS RECEIVED.

A DIRECTORY OF WATER-MARKS, TRADE-MARKS AND SPECIAL BRANDS IN USE IN THE PAPER TRADE, is the title of the small volume just published by the Clark W. Bryan Co., Springfield, Mass., to which we referred in our April "Correspondence," in reply to an enquiry from Mr. A. A. Hamlet, Surveyor, Jupiter, N. C. These American Trade-Marks, numbering 1668, are arranged alphabetically, and have been obtained by careful canvas and extensive correspondence, every known one that could be authenticated having its place in the list. It is intended to issue the Directory as a yearly publication with the additions and changes that may take place in the trade from year to year. The price of the book is One Dollar.

WE HAVE BEFORE us the first number of the Second Volume of THE CANADIAN ENGINEER. It is a bright, well got-up paper which deserves the success and reputation it has won, as proved by its having been already twice found necessary to enlarge it, the last time by the addition of 12 pages upon entering the second year of its career. It treats of civil, mechanical, mining, electrical, marine, locomotive, stationary and sanitary Engineering etc., and devotes considerable space to industrial and personal items bearing upon the resources and industries of the Dominion.

STADIA MEASUREMENTS. III.

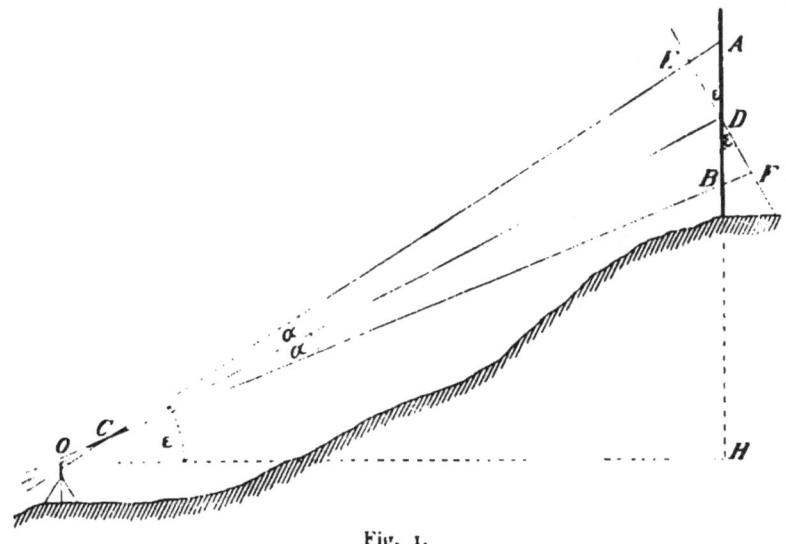

Fig. 1.

As stated in our last, the general formula (5) for ascertaining distances by means of the stadia applies only to measures made on horizontal ground. For measurements on sloping ground, there are, as with the gradienter, two methods followed, the one being to hold the rod plumb, and the other to hold it perpendicular to the line of sight of the telescope. The former is the method usually preferred in this country.

In Fig. 1, let OD be the line of sight of the telescope, D being the point on the rod covered by the horizontal cross hair, then DOH is the angle of elevation of the telescope, as read on the vertical limb of the transit, and AB is the space intercepted on the rod by the two stadia hairs.

If the rod were held perpendicular to the line of sight, the intercept would be EF, and the inclined distance from the centre of the instrument $= OD$ would be found by equation (5) of our last thus:

Inclined Distance, $CD + f + C$ } $OD = k.\ EF + (f + C)\ldots\ldots\ldots (9)$

What is required however is to ascertain the horizontal distance OH by means of the rod reading AB and not by the intercept EF.

The first point therefore is to find an expression for EF in terms of AB, from which we can obtain the inclined distance OD, and then from this value of OD find the expression giving the value of the horizontal distance OH.

Let the angles formed by the line of sight and the points on the rod covered by the stadia hairs, that is, angles ACD and $BCD = \alpha$, and the angle of elevation of the telescope $DOH = \varepsilon$, also equal to angles ADE and BDF, then

$$\text{Angle } DEA = 90° + \alpha \text{ and}$$
$$\text{Angle } DFB = 90° - \alpha.$$

As CA and CB are very nearly parallel to CD,* and consequently very nearly perpendicular to EF, we may assume that the triangles ADE and BDF are right-angled ones, so that we have

$$ED = AD \cos \varepsilon$$

and
$$DF = BD \cos \varepsilon$$

whence by addition
$$EF = AB \cos \varepsilon,$$

or, calling $AB = A$ as before

$$EF = A \cos \varepsilon \ \ldots\ldots\ldots\ \ldots\ldots \quad (10)$$

Inserting now this value of EF in equation (9), we have

$$\left.\begin{array}{l}\text{Inclined Distance}\\\text{from centre of Inst.}\end{array}\right\} = OD = k.\,A \cos \varepsilon + (f + C)\ldots. \quad (11)$$

Now DOH being a right-angled triangle,

$$OH = OD \cos \varepsilon$$

and taking the value of OD in equation (11), we obtain

$$\left.\begin{array}{l}\text{Horizontal Distance}\\\text{from centre of Inst.}\end{array}\right\} = OH = k.\,A \cos^2 \varepsilon + (f + C) \cos \varepsilon \ \ldots (12)$$

and, when $k = 100$, as is generally the case

$$\text{Horizontal Distance} = 100A \cos^2 \varepsilon + (f + C) \cos \varepsilon \ldots. \quad (13)$$

which is the formula generally used for reducing stadia readings with inclined lines of sight to their horizontal distances from the centre of the instrument.

The stadia is also used in such cases for obtaining the difference of

---

*The divergence being 1 foot in 100 feet, which is equal to an angle of about 34½ minutes.

elevation of the instrument and the rod $= HD$. The formula employed is obtained as follows:—

$$\text{Difference of Elevation } DH = OD \sin \varepsilon,$$

but by equation (11)

$$OD = k.A \cos \varepsilon + (f + C)$$

therefore

$$DH = \Big(k.A \cos \varepsilon + (f + C)\Big) \sin \varepsilon$$

$$= k.A \cos \varepsilon \sin \varepsilon + (f + C) \sin \varepsilon.$$

But from the expression for the sine and cosine of "twice an angle," we have

$$\sin 2\varepsilon = 2 \sin \varepsilon \cos \varepsilon$$

whence

$$\sin \varepsilon \cos \varepsilon = \frac{\sin 2\varepsilon}{2}$$

so that our final equation becomes

$$\text{Difference of Elevation } DH = k.A \frac{\sin 2\varepsilon}{2} + (f + C) \sin \varepsilon \ldots \ldots (14)$$

and when $k = 100$ as before

$$\text{Difference of Elevation} = 100 A \frac{\sin 2\varepsilon}{2} + (f + C) \sin \varepsilon \ldots \ldots (15)$$

The difference of elevation thus obtained is the difference in height between the centre of the horizontal axis of the telescope, and the point on the rod covered by the horizontal cross hair.

As the calculation of $\cos^2 \varepsilon$ in equation (12) and $\frac{\sin 2\varepsilon}{2}$ in equation (14) would be very tedious when a great number of measurements have been taken, various tables have been calculated to facilitate this work. We append a Stadia Table computed by Mr. Arthur Winslow of the State Geological Survey of Pennsylvania, which will be found both simple and expeditious, the only computation necessary for obtaining the final results being one multiplication and one addition.

The table gives in parallel columns the values of $100 \cos^2 \varepsilon$, and $100 \frac{\sin 2\varepsilon}{2}$, for angles of elevation from 0 to 31 degrees, advancing by 2 minutes. It also gives at the foot of each column the value of $(f + C) \cos \varepsilon$ and $(f + C) \sin \varepsilon$ for three different values (0.75, 1.0 and 1.25 foot) of $f + C$, for each degree. The following example will clearly explain the method of using the table.

Let:—Stadia Reading $A = 4.37$ feet,

Angle of Elevation $\varepsilon = 5°26'$, and

Constant $f + C = 1$ foot, then

1.—$100 \cos^2 \varepsilon \times 4.37 = 99.10 \times 4.37 = 433.07$ feet.

$(f + C) \cos \varepsilon \ldots\ldots\ldots = .99$ "

Horizontal Distance $\ldots\ldots = 434.06$ feet.

2.—$100 \dfrac{\sin 2\varepsilon}{2} \times 4.37 = 9.43 \times 4.37 = 41.21$ feet.

$(f + C) \sin \varepsilon \ldots\ldots\ldots = .09$

Difference of Elevation $\ldots = 41.30$ feet.

The STADIA SLIDE RULE, described in Vol. I, page 92, is another very simple means for calculating the horizontal distance and the difference of elevation; it gives at sight the values of $100\,A\,\cos^2 \varepsilon$ and $100\,A\,\dfrac{\sin 2\varepsilon}{2}$, and that with a considerable degree of accuracy.

Sometimes reduction diagrams are used for the same purpose, but they are much less handy for outside work.

Notwithstanding that the method of stadia measurements is admitted to be theoretically correct, a good deal of difference of opinion exists amongst surveyors as to its merits and advantages. Objections to it are however mostly of a personal nature, dictated by the kind of work engaged on, other methods being considered more suitable, although not necessarily more accurate. For topography and preliminary survey it is undoubtedly most useful, and its efficiency is well recognized. To obtain reliable results, great care must be exercised to secure accurate rod readings, also to see that the rod is held perfectly vertical. This is especially important in the case of inclined sights; thus, if the angle of elevation be 30°, the horizontal distance 400 feet, and the rod inclined 5° forward from the vertical, the stadia reading will be 0.22 foot too little, that is 3.78 instead of 4 feet. This is the strongest argument that can be advanced in favor of the rod being held perpendicular to the line of sight, as divergences from the correct position produce very much smaller errors when the rod is so held.

The stadia method was largely used on the U. S. Lake Survey, and as an instance of its reliability it is stated that in the case of 141 lines of about 8000 feet each, with average sights of 800 to 1000 feet, the average error was one in 650. In the topographical survey of the city of St. Louis, Mo., the stadia was largely employed as being the best and most rapid method of locating points and obtaining their elevation. The error of closure, after making the known corrections for inclination and graduation of rods, was about 1 in 800. Elevations were carried by means of distance and vertical angles. The average error of elevations was less than 0.2 of a foot per mile. [a.]

Mr. J. F. Brown, in discussing a paper read by Mr. James Ritchie, before the Civil Engineers' Club of Cleveland, stated in regard to the accuracy of the stadia method that he had made some use of the stadia in the past two or three years in running random lines in rough country, for locating a line; that is, in measuring a random from point to point over the knolls or hills. He ran one random 3800 feet long, and measured the distance with the stadia rod, and summed up the total; and after checking over the true lines by actual measurement there was only a difference of 0.13 ft.

He had also measured some dock lines where it was difficult to span the distance, and those distances had been carefully computed by the city engineer, and found on distances of 500 to 600 ft., the stadia would read down to within 0.03 ft. or 0.04 ft. of actual distance. He was satisfied that the stadia is more correct than the actual measurement for that kind of work. Running random lines 3500 ft. long with the stadia saved half the work. [b.]

The stadia will also be found very useful in connection with the plane table. It has been so used by the officers of the United States Coast Survey, and from their experience it has been "satisfactorily ascertained that the rapidity with which the details of a survey can be determined and sketched, the smaller number of men necessary to be employed, and that whatever errors may occur rest with the observer only, and the facility in using it in places where the use of the chain is impracticable, or at least difficult, render the telemeter (stadia) a very important acquisition." [c.]

(a.) From a paper by Oliver W. Connet, in "The Technograph," No. 5, 1890-91. pages 12 and 13.

(b.) From "Engineering News," Oct. 12, 1893.

(c.) "The Plane-Table and its use in Topographical Surveying," from the Papers of the United States Coast Survey.

HORIZONTAL DISTANCES AND DIFFERENCES OF ELEVATION.

Minutes.	0°		1°		2°		3°	
	Hor. Dist.	Diff. Elev	Hor. Dist.	Diff. Elev.	Hor. Dist.	Diff. Elev.	Hor. Dist.	Diff. Elev.
0	100.00	0.00	99.97	1.74	99.88	3.49	99.73	5.23
2	"	0.06	"	1.80	99.87	3.55	99.72	5.28
4	"	0.12	"	1.86	"	3.60	99.71	5.34
6	"	0.17	99.96	1.92	"	3.66	"	5.40
8	"	0.23	"	1.98	99.86	3.72	99.70	5.46
10	"	0.29	"	2.04	"	3.78	99.69	5.52
12	"	0.35	"	2.09	99.85	3.84	"	5.57
14	"	0.41	99.95	2.15	"	3.90	99.68	5.63
16	"	0.47	"	2.21	99.84	3.95	"	5.69
18	"	0.52	"	2.27	"	4.01	99.67	5.75
20	"	0.58	"	2.33	99.83	4.07	99.66	5.80
22	"	0.64	99.94	2.38	"	4.13	"	5.86
24	"	0.70	"	2.44	99.82	4.18	99.65	5.92
26	99.99	0.76	"	2.50	"	4.24	99.64	5.98
28	"	0.81	99.93	2.56	99.81	4.30	99.63	6.04
30	"	0.87	"	2.62	"	4.36	"	6.09
32	"	0.93	"	2.67	99.80	4.42	99.62	6.15
34	"	0.99	"	2.73	"	4.48	"	6.21
36	"	1.05	99.92	2.79	99.79	4.53	99.61	6.27
38	"	1.11	"	2.85	"	4.59	99.60	6.33
40	"	1.16	"	2.91	99.78	4.65	99.59	6.38
42	"	1.22	99.91	2.97	"	4.71	"	6.44
44	99.98	1.28	"	3.02	99.77	4.76	99.58	6.50
46	"	1.34	99.90	3.08	"	4.82	99.57	6.56
48	"	1.40	"	3.14	99.76	4.88	99.56	6.61
50	"	1.45	"	3.20	"	4.94	"	6.67
52	"	1.51	99.89	3.26	99.75	4.99	99.55	6.73
54	"	1.57	"	3.31	99.74	5.05	99.54	6.78
56	99.97	1.63	"	3.37	"	5.11	99.53	6.84
58	"	1.69	99.88	3.43	99.73	5.17	99.52	6.90
60	"	1.74	"	3.49	"	5.23	99.51	6.96
C=0.75	0.75	0.01	0.75	0.02	0.75	0.03	0.75	0.05
C=1.00	1.00	0.01	1.00	0.03	1.00	0.04	1.00	0.06
C=1.25	1.25	0.02	1.25	0.03	1.25	0.05	1.25	0.08

HORIZONTAL DISTANCES AND DIFFERENCES OF ELEVATION.

Minutes.	4°		5°		6°		7°	
	Hor. Dist.	Diff. Elev.	Hor. Dist.	Diff. Elev.	Hor. Dist.	Diff. Elev.	Hor. Dist.	Diff. Elev.
0	99.51	6.96	99.24	8.68	98.91	10.40	98.51	12.10
2	"	7.02	99.23	8.74	98.90	10.45	98.50	12.15
4	99.50	7.07	99.22	8.80	98.88	10.51	98.48	12.21
6	99.49	7.13	99.21	8.85	98.87	10.57	98.47	12.26
8	99.48	7.19	99.20	8.91	98.86	10.62	98.46	12.32
10	99.47	7.25	99.19	8.97	98.85	10.68	98.44	12.38
12	99.46	7.30	99.18	9.03	98.83	10.74	98.43	12.43
14	"	7.36	99.17	9.08	98.82	10.79	98.41	12.49
16	99.45	7.42	99.16	9.14	98.81	10.85	98.40	12.55
18	99.44	7.48	99.15	9.20	98.80	10.91	98.39	12.60
20	99.43	7.53	99.14	9.25	98.78	10.96	98.37	12.66
22	99.42	7.59	99.13	9.31	98.77	11.02	98.36	12.72
24	99.41	7.65	99.11	9.37	98.76	11.08	98.34	12.77
26	99.40	7.71	99.10	9.43	98.74	11.13	98.33	12.83
28	99.39	7.76	99.09	9.48	98.73	11.19	98.31	12.88
30	99.38	7.82	99.08	9.54	98.72	11.25	98.29	12.94
32	99.38	7.88	99.07	9.60	98.71	11.30	98.28	13.00
34	99.37	7.94	99.06	9.65	98.69	11.36	98.27	13.05
36	99.36	7.99	99.05	9.71	98.68	11.42	98.25	13.11
38	99.35	8.05	99.04	9.77	98.67	11.47	98.24	13.17
40	99.34	8.11	99.03	9.83	98.65	11.53	98.22	13.22
42	99.33	8.17	99.01	9.88	98.64	11.59	98.20	13.28
44	99.32	8.22	99.00	9.94	98.63	11.64	98.19	13.33
46	99.31	8.28	98.99	10.00	98.61	11.70	98.17	13.39
48	99.30	8.34	98.98	10.05	98.60	11.76	98.16	13.45
50	99.29	8.40	98.97	10.11	98.58	11.81	98.14	13.50
52	99.28	8.45	98.96	10.17	98.57	11.87	98.13	13.56
54	99.27	8.51	98.94	10.22	98.56	11.93	98.11	13.61
56	99.26	8.57	98.93	10.28	98.54	11.98	98.10	13.67
58	99.25	8.63	98.92	10.34	98.53	12.04	98.08	13.73
60	99.24	8.68	98.91	10.40	98.51	12.10	98.06	13.78
C=0.75	0.75	0.06	0.75	0.07	0.75	0.08	0.74	0.10
C=1.00	1.00	0.08	0.99	0.09	0.99	0.11	0.99	0.13
C=1.25	1.25	0.10	1.24	0.11	1.24	0.14	1.24	0.16

HORIZONTAL DISTANCES AND DIFFERENCES OF ELEVATION.

Minutes.	8°		9°		10°		11°	
	Hor. Dist.	Diff. Elev.	Hor. Dist.	Diff. Elev.	Hor. Dist.	Diff. Elev.	Hor. Dist.	Diff. Elev.
0	98.06	13.78	97.55	15.45	96.98	17.10	96.36	18.73
2	98.05	13.84	97.53	15.51	96.96	17.16	96.34	18.78
4	98.03	13.89	97.52	15.56	96.94	17.21	96.32	18.84
6	98.01	13.95	97.50	15.62	96.92	17.26	96.29	18.89
8	98.00	14.01	97.48	15.67	96.90	17.32	96.27	18.95
10	97.98	14.06	97.46	15.73	96.88	17.37	96.25	19.00
12	97.97	14.12	97.44	15.78	96.86	17.43	96.23	19.05
14	97.95	14.17	97.43	15.84	96.84	17.48	96.21	19.11
16	97.93	14.23	97.41	15.89	96.82	17.54	96.18	19.16
18	97.92	14.28	97.39	15.95	96.80	17.59	96.16	19.21
20	97.90	14.34	97.37	16.00	96.78	17.65	96.14	19.27
22	97.88	14.40	97.35	16.06	96.76	17.70	96.12	19.32
24	97.87	14.45	97.33	16.11	96.74	17.76	96.09	19.38
26	97.85	14.51	97.31	16.17	96.72	17.81	96.07	19.43
28	97.83	14.56	97.29	16.22	96.70	17.86	96.05	19.48
30	97.82	14.62	97.28	16.28	96.68	17.92	96.03	19.54
32	97.80	14.67	97.26	16.33	96.66	17.97	96.00	19.59
34	97.78	14.73	97.24	16.39	96.64	18.03	95.98	19.64
36	97.76	14.79	97.22	16.44	96.62	18.08	95.96	19.70
38	97.75	14.84	97.20	16.50	96.60	18.14	95.93	19.75
40	97.73	14.90	97.18	16.55	96.57	18.19	95.91	19.80
42	97.71	14.95	97.16	16.61	96.55	18.24	95.89	19.86
44	97.69	15.01	97.14	16.66	96.53	18.30	95.86	19.91
46	97.68	15.06	97.12	16.72	96.51	18.35	95.84	19.96
48	97.66	15.12	97.10	16.77	96.49	18.41	95.82	20.02
50	97.64	15.17	97.08	16.83	96.47	18.46	95.79	20.07
52	97.62	15.23	97.06	16.88	96.45	18.51	95.77	20.12
54	97.61	15.28	97.04	16.94	96.42	18.57	95.75	20.18
56	97.59	15.34	97.02	16.99	96.40	18.62	95.72	20.23
58	97.57	15.40	97.00	17.05	96.38	18.68	95.70	20.28
60	97.55	15.45	96.98	17.10	96.36	18.73	95.68	20.34
C=0.75	0.74	0.11	0.74	0.12	0.74	0.14	0.73	0.15
C=1.00	0.99	0.15	0.99	0.16	0.98	0.18	0.98	0.20
C=1.25	1.23	0.18	1.23	0.21	1.23	0.23	1.22	0.25

HORIZONTAL DISTANCES AND DIFFERENCES OF ELEVATION.

Minutes.	12°		13°		14°		15°	
	Hor. Dist.	Diff. Elev.	Hor. Dist.	Diff. Elev.	Hor. Dist.	Diff. Elev.	Hor. Dist.	Diff. Elev.
0	95.68	20.34	94.94	21.92	94.15	23.47	93.30	25.00
2	95.65	20.39	94.91	21.97	94.12	23.52	93.27	25.05
4	95.63	20.44	94.89	22.02	94.09	23.58	93.24	25.10
6	95.61	20.50	94.86	22.08	94.07	23.63	93.21	25.15
8	95.58	20.55	94.84	22.13	94.04	23.68	93.18	25.20
10	95.56	20.60	94.81	22.18	94.01	23.73	93.16	25.25
12	95.53	20.66	94.79	22.23	93.98	23.78	93.13	25.30
14	95.51	20.71	94.76	22.28	93.95	23.83	93.10	25.35
16	95.49	20.76	94.73	22.34	93.93	23.88	93.07	25.40
18	95.46	20.81	94.71	22.39	93.90	23.93	93.04	25.45
20	95.44	20.87	94.68	22.44	93.87	23.99	93.01	25.50
22	95.41	20.92	94.66	22.49	93.84	24.04	92.98	25.55
24	95.39	20.97	94.63	22.54	93.81	24.09	92.95	25.60
26	95.36	21.03	94.60	22.60	93.79	24.14	92.92	25.65
28	95.34	21.08	94.58	22.65	93.76	24.19	92.89	25.70
30	95.32	21.13	94.55	22.70	93.73	24.24	92.86	25.75
32	95.29	21.18	94.52	22.75	93.70	24.29	92.83	25.80
34	95.27	21.24	94.50	22.80	93.67	24.34	92.80	25.85
36	95.24	21.29	94.47	22.85	93.65	24.39	92.77	25.90
38	95.22	21.34	94.44	22.91	93.62	24.44	92.74	25.95
40	95.19	21.39	94.42	22.96	93.59	24.49	92.71	26.00
42	95.17	21.45	94.39	23.01	93.56	24.55	92.68	26.05
44	95.14	21.50	94.36	23.06	93.53	24.60	92.65	26.10
46	95.12	21.55	94.34	23.11	93.50	24.65	92.62	26.15
48	95.09	21.60	94.31	23.16	93.47	24.70	92.59	26.20
50	95.07	21.66	94.28	23.22	93.45	24.75	92.56	26.25
52	95.04	21.71	94.26	23.27	93.42	24.80	92.53	26.30
54	95.02	21.76	94.23	23.32	93.39	24.85	92.49	26.35
56	94.99	21.81	94.20	23.37	93.36	24.90	92.46	26.40
58	94.97	21.87	94.17	23.42	93.33	24.95	92.43	26.45
60	94.94	21.92	94.15	23.47	93.30	25.00	92.40	26.50
C=0.75	0.73	0.16	0.73	0.17	0.73	0.19	0.72	0.20
C=1.00	0.98	0.22	0.97	0.23	0.97	0.25	0.96	0.27
C=1.25	1.22	0.27	1.21	0.29	1.21	0.31	1.20	0.34

HORIZONTAL DISTANCES AND DIFFERENCES OF ELEVATION.

Minutes.	16°		17°		18°		19°	
	Hor. Dist.	Diff. Elev.	Hor. Dist.	Diff. Elev.	Hor. Dist.	Diff. Elev.	Hor. Dist.	Diff. Elev.
0	92.40	26.50	91.45	27.96	90.45	29.39	89.40	30.78
2	92.37	26.55	91.42	28.01	90.42	29.44	89.36	30.83
4	92.34	26.59	91.39	28.06	90.38	29.48	89.33	30.87
6	92.31	26.64	91.35	28.10	90.35	29.53	89.29	30.92
8	92.28	26.69	91.32	28.15	90.31	29.58	89.26	30.97
10	92.25	26.74	91.29	28.20	90.28	29.62	89.22	31.01
12	92.22	26.79	91.26	28.25	90.24	29.67	89.18	31.06
14	92.19	26.84	91.22	28.30	90.21	29.72	89.15	31.10
16	92.15	26.89	91.19	28.34	90.18	29.76	89.11	31.15
18	92.12	26.94	91.16	28.39	90.14	29.81	89.08	31.19
20	92.09	26.99	91.12	28.44	90.11	29.86	89.04	31.24
22	92.06	27.04	91.09	28.49	90.07	29.90	89.00	31.28
24	92.03	27.09	91.06	28.54	90.04	29.95	88.96	31.33
26	92.00	27.13	91.02	28.58	90.00	30.00	88.93	31.38
28	91.97	27.18	90.99	28.63	89.97	30.04	88.89	31.42
30	91.93	27.23	90.96	28.68	89.93	30.09	88.86	31.47
32	91.90	27.28	90.92	28.73	89.90	30.14	88.82	31.51
34	91.87	27.33	90.89	28.77	89.86	30.19	88.78	31.56
36	91.84	27.38	90.86	28.82	89.83	30.23	88.75	31.60
38	91.81	27.43	90.82	28.87	89.79	30.28	88.71	31.65
40	91.77	27.48	90.79	28.92	89.76	30.32	88.67	31.69
42	91.74	27.52	90.76	28.96	89.72	30.37	88.64	31.74
44	91.71	27.57	90.72	29.01	89.69	30.41	88.60	31.78
46	91.68	27.62	90.69	29.06	89.65	30.46	88.56	31.83
48	91.65	27.67	90.66	29.11	89.61	30.51	88.53	31.87
50	91.61	27.72	90.62	29.15	89.58	30.55	88.49	31.92
52	91.58	27.77	90.59	29.20	89.54	30.60	88.45	31.96
54	91.55	27.81	90.55	29.25	89.51	30.65	88.41	32.01
56	91.52	27.86	90.52	29.30	89.47	30.69	88.38	32.05
58	91.48	27.91	90.48	29.34	89.44	30.74	88.34	32.09
60	91.45	27.96	90.45	29.39	89.40	30.78	88.30	32.14
C=0.75	0.72	0.21	0.72	0.23	0.71	0.24	0.71	0.25
C=1.00	0.96	0.28	0.95	0.30	0.95	0.32	0.94	0.33
C=1.25	1.20	0.35	1.19	0.38	1.19	0.40	1.18	0.42

HORIZONTAL DISTANCES AND DIFFERENCES OF ELEVATION.

Minutes.	20°		21°		22°		23°	
	Hor. Dist.	Diff. Elev.	Hor. Dist.	Diff. Elev.	Hor. Dist.	Diff. Elev.	Hor. Dist.	Diff. Elev.
0	88.30	32.14	87.16	33.46	85.97	34.73	84.73	35.97
2	88.26	32.18	87.12	33.50	85.93	34.77	84.69	36.01
4	88.23	32.23	87.08	33.54	85.89	34.82	84.65	36.05
6	88.19	32.27	87.04	33.59	85.85	34.86	84.61	36.09
8	88.15	32.32	87.00	33.63	85.80	34.90	84.57	36.13
10	88.11	32.36	86.96	33.67	85.76	34.94	84.52	36.17
12	88.08	32.41	86.92	33.72	85.72	34.98	84.48	36.21
14	88.04	32.45	86.88	33.76	85.68	35.02	84.44	36.25
16	88.00	32.49	86.84	33.80	85.64	35.07	84.40	36.29
18	87.96	32.54	86.80	33.84	85.60	35.11	84.35	36.33
20	87.93	32.58	86.77	33.89	85.56	35.15	84.31	36.37
22	87.89	32.63	86.73	33.93	85.52	35.19	84.27	36.41
24	87.85	32.67	86.69	33.97	85.48	35.23	84.23	36.45
26	87.81	32.72	86.65	34.01	85.44	35.27	84.18	36.49
28	87.77	32.76	86.61	34.06	85.40	35.31	84.14	36.53
30	87.74	32.80	86.57	34.10	85.36	35.36	84.10	36.57
32	87.70	32.85	86.53	34.14	85.31	35.40	84.06	36.61
34	87.66	32.89	86.49	34.18	85.27	35.44	84.01	36.65
36	87.62	32.93	86.45	34.23	85.23	35.48	83.97	36.69
38	87.58	32.98	86.41	34.27	85.19	35.52	83.93	36.73
40	87.54	33.02	86.37	34.31	85.15	35.56	83.89	36.77
42	87.51	33.07	86.33	34.35	85.11	35.60	83.84	36.80
44	87.47	33.11	86.29	34.40	85.07	35.64	83.80	36.84
46	87.43	33.15	86.25	34.44	85.02	35.68	83.76	36.88
48	87.39	33.20	86.21	34.48	84.98	35.72	83.72	36.92
50	87.35	33.24	86.17	34.52	84.94	35.76	83.67	36.96
52	87.31	33.28	86.13	34.57	84.90	35.80	83.63	37.00
54	87.27	33.33	86.09	34.61	84.86	35.85	83.59	37.04
56	87.24	33.37	86.05	34.65	84.82	35.89	83.54	37.08
58	87.20	33.41	86.01	34.69	84.77	35.93	83.50	37.12
60	87.16	33.46	85.97	34.73	84.73	35.97	83.46	37.16
C=0.75	0.70	0.26	0.70	0.27	0.69	0.29	0.69	0.30
C=1.00	0.94	0.35	0.93	0.37	0.92	0.38	0.92	0.40
C=1.25	1.17	0.44	1.16	0.46	1.15	0.48	1.15	0.50

HORIZONTAL DISTANCES AND DIFFERENCES OF ELEVATION.

Minutes.	24°		25°		26°		27°	
	Hor. Dist.	Diff. Elev.	Hor. Dist.	Diff. Elev.	Hor. Dist.	Diff. Elev.	Hor. Dist.	Diff. Elev.
0	83.46	37.16	82.14	38.30	80.78	39.40	79.39	40.45
2	83.41	37.20	82.09	38.34	80.74	39.44	79.34	40.49
4	83.37	37.23	82.05	38.38	80.69	39.47	79.30	40.52
6	83.33	37.27	82.01	38.41	80.65	39.51	79.25	40.55
8	83.28	37.31	81.96	38.45	80.60	39.54	79.20	40.59
10	83.24	37.35	81.92	38.49	80.55	39.58	79.15	40.62
12	83.20	37.39	81.87	38.53	80.51	39.61	79.11	40.66
14	83.15	37.43	81.83	38.56	80.46	39.65	79.06	40.69
16	83.11	37.47	81.78	38.60	80.41	39.69	79.01	40.72
18	83.07	37.51	81.74	38.64	80.37	39.72	78.96	40.76
20	83.02	37.54	81.69	38.67	80.32	39.76	78.92	40.79
22	82.98	37.58	81.65	38.71	80.28	39.79	78.87	40.82
24	82.93	37.62	81.60	38.75	80.23	39.83	78.82	40.86
26	82.89	37.66	81.56	38.78	80.18	39.86	78.77	40.89
28	82.85	37.70	81.51	38.82	80.14	39.90	78.73	40.92
30	82.80	37.74	81.47	38.86	80.09	39.93	78.68	40.96
32	82.76	37.77	81.42	38.89	80.04	39.97	78.63	40.99
34	82.72	37.81	81.38	38.93	80.00	40.00	78.58	41.02
36	82.67	37.85	81.33	38.97	79.95	40.04	78.54	41.06
38	82.63	37.89	81.28	39.00	79.90	40.07	78.49	41.09
40	82.58	37.93	81.24	39.04	79.86	40.11	78.44	41.12
42	82.54	37.96	81.19	39.08	79.81	40.14	78.39	41.16
44	82.49	38.00	81.15	39.11	79.76	40.18	78.34	41.19
46	82.45	38.04	81.10	39.15	79.72	40.21	78.30	41.22
48	82.41	38.08	81.06	39.18	79.67	40.24	78.25	41.26
50	82.36	38.11	81.01	39.22	79.62	40.28	78.20	41.29
52	82.32	38.15	80.97	39.26	79.58	40.31	78.15	41.32
54	82.27	38.19	80.92	39.29	79.53	40.35	78.10	41.35
56	82.23	38.23	80.87	39.33	79.48	40.38	78.06	41.39
58	82.18	38.26	80.83	39.36	79.44	40.42	78.01	41.42
60	82.14	38.30	80.78	39.40	79.39	40.45	77.96	41.45
C=0.75	0.68	0.31	0.68	0.32	0.67	0.33	0.66	0.35
C=1.00	0.91	0.41	0.90	0.43	0.89	0.45	0.89	0.46
C=1.25	1.14	0.52	1.13	0.54	1.12	0.56	1.11	0.58

HORIZONTAL DISTANCES AND DIFFERENCES OF ELEVATION.

Minutes.	28°		29°		30°	
	Hor. Dist.	Diff. Elev.	Hor. Dist.	Diff. Elev.	Hor. Dist.	Diff. Elev
0	77.96	41.45	76.50	42.40	75.00	43.30
2	77.91	41.48	76.45	42.43	74.95	43.33
4	77.86	41.52	76.40	42.46	74.90	43.36
6	77.81	41.55	76.35	42.49	74.85	43.39
8	77.77	41.58	76.30	42.53	74.80	43 42
10	77.72	41.61	76.25	42.56	74.75	43.45
12	77.67	41.65	76.20	42.59	74.70	43.47
14	77.62	41.68	76.15	42.62	74.65	43 50
16	77.57	41.71	76.10	42.65	74.60	43.53
18	77.52	41.74	76.05	42.68	74.55	43.56
20	77.48	41.77	76.00	42 71	74.49	43.59
22	77.42	41.81	75.95	42.74	74.44	43.62
24	77.38	41.84	75.90	42.77	74.39	43.65
26	77.33	41.87	75.85	42 80	74.34	43.67
28	77.28	41.90	75.80	42.83	74.29	43.70
30	77.23	41.93	75.75	42.86	74.24	43.73
32	77.18	41.97	75.70	42.89	74.19	43.76
34	77.13	42.00	75.65	42.92	74.14	43.79
36	77.09	42.03	75.60	42.95	74.09	43.82
38	77.04	42.06	75.55	42.98	74.04	43.84
40	76.99	42.09	75.50	43.01	73.99	43.87
42	76.94	42.12	75.45	43.04	73.93	43.90
44	76.89	42.15	75.40	43 07	73.88	43.93
46	76.84	42.19	75.35	43.10	73.83	43.95
48	76.79	42 22	75.30	43 13	73.78	43.98
50	76.74	42.25	75.25	43.16	73.73	44.01
52	76.69	42.28	75.20	43.18	73.68	44.04
54	76.64	42.31	75.15	43.21	73.63	44 07
56	76.59	42.34	75.10	43.24	73.58	44.09
58	76.55	42.37	75.05	43.27	73.52	44 12
60	76.50	42.40	75.00	43.30	73.47	44.15
C=0.75	0.66	0.36	0.65	0.37	0.65	0.38
C=1.00	0.88	0 48	0.87	0.49	0.86	0.51
C=1.25	1.10	0.60	1.09	0 62	1.08	0.64

SOLAR EPHEMERIS, AUGUST 1894.
For Greenwich Apparent Noon.

Day of Week	Day of Month	The Sun's Apparent Declination	Difference for 1 Hour	Equation of Time to be *added to* / *subtracted from Apparent Time*	Day of Month	Refraction * Correction Latitude 40°
		° ′ ″	″	m s		
Wed.	1	N 17 58 22.4	— 37.96	6 6 87		
Thurs.	2	17 43 2.4	38 69	6 3 01		1 h. 0′ 26″
Frid.	3	17 27 25.0	39.41	5 58 55	2	2 0 30
Sat.	4	17 11 30.7	40.12	5 53.47	to	3 0 37
Sun.	5	16 55 19 7	40.81	5 47.78	6	4 0 53
						5 1 26
Mon.	6	16 38 52.3	— 41.48	5 41.49		
Tues.	7	16 22 8.8	42.14	5 34.58		1 h. 0′ 28″
Wed.	8	16 5 9.6	42.79	5 27.07	7	2 0 32
Thurs.	9	15 47 55.0	43.43	5 18.96	to	3 0 39
Frid.	10	15 30 25.3	44.05	5 10.25	11	4 0 55
						5 1 30
Sat.	11	15 12 40.8	— 44 66	5 0.96		
Sun.	12	14 54 41.8	45.26	4 51.08		1 h. 0′ 30″
Mon.	13	14 36 28.7	45.84	4 40.64	12	2 0 34
Tues.	14	14 18 1.6	46.41	4 29.64	to	3 0 42
Wed.	15	13 59 21.0	46.96	4 18.10	16	4 0 58
						5 1 36
Thurs.	16	13 40 27.0	— 47.51	4 6.03		
Frid.	17	13 21 20.1	48.05	3 53.44		1 h. 0′ 32″
Sat.	18	13 2 0.5	48.58	3 40.35	17	2 0 36
Sun.	19	12 42 28.4	49.09	3 26.76	to	3 0 45
Mon.	20	12 22 44.2	49.59	3 12.71	21	4 1 02
						5 1 42
Tues.	21	12 2 48.2	— 50.08	2 58.20		
Wed.	22	11 42 40.6	50.55	2 43.24		1 h. 0′ 34″
Thurs.	23	11 22 21.7	51.01	2 27.86	22	2 0 38
Frid.	24	11 1 52 0	51.46	2 12.06	to	3 0 48
Sat.	25	10 41 11.5	51.90	1 55.86	26	4 1 06
						5 1 49
Sun.	26	10 20 20.8	— 52.32	1 39.28		
Mon.	27	9 59 20.2	52 73	1 22.31		1 h. 0′ 36″
Tues.	28	9 38 9.9	53.12	1 4.98	27	2 0 41
Wed.	29	9 16 50.3	53.49	0 47.30	to	3 0 51
Thurs.	30	8 55 21.7	53.85	0 29.29	31	4 1 10
						5 1 58
Frid.	31	8 33 44.5	— 54.21	0 10.96		

* By permission from "The Theory and Practice of Surveying", by Prof. J. B. Johnson, C. E.

In this column the hours are counted each way from noon; thus, 9 A. M. and 3 P. M. would each correspond to the 3d hour in the table. The hourly corrections are exact for the middle day of the five-day period corresponding to any given set of hourly corrections. For other days interpolations can be made where extreme accuracy is required.

For Table of Latitude Coefficients, see Vol. III., page 110.

www.ingramcontent.com/pod-product-compliance
Lightning Source LLC
Chambersburg PA
CBHW031440160426
43195CB00010BB/803